TH
DISCIPLE'S HANDBOOK

Third Edition

Resources for Growing Christians

ILLUMINATION PUBLISHERS

www.ipibooks.com

ISBN: 978-1-958723-35-7

Printed in the United States of America

Illumination Publishers
6010 Pinecreek Ridge Court
Spring, Texas 77379
www.ipibooks.com

Third Edition Editor: Toney Mulhollan
Editors: Thomas/Sheila Jones

Cover design: Toney C. Mulhollan

Illumination Publishers titles may be purchased in bulk for classroom instruction, business, fund-raising, or sales promotional use. For information, please email paul.ipibooks@me.com.

Illumination Publishers cares deeply about using renewable resources and uses recycled paper whenever possible.

ILLUMINATION PUBLISHERS

Contents

Contents

Part Three: Ideas and Admonitions

Part Four: Planning and Evaluation

Part One

Bible Studies

Deep Convictions

A thirteen-week study guide especially designed for the new disciple who seeks to build a powerful life in Jesus Christ and for the older disciple seeking to revitalize his walk with God. (Available as a separate booklet from Illumination Publishers [www.ipibooks.com].)

Edited by
Thomas Jones
Nashville, Tennessee

For the entire book by Tom Jones go to www.ipibooks.com.

Contents

Introduction

Most likely, this study guide is being given to you on the day of your baptism into Christ. If so, this day is, without question, the most important day in your life. This is the day for which you were born! The decision you have made to die with Christ in your baptism, accept his grace and put on his new life will affect every area of your life. As God's word says in Colossians 3:3: "you died, and your life is now hidden with Christ in God."

The study you are about to begin is designed to help you develop deep convictions from God's word each day for the next 13 weeks. It can also be used by those who have been disciples for a while to find "renewed life" through a return to the basics. As you begin this study to learn God's word, you need to understand how important this is for you. If you build a strong foundation now, it will serve you well for years to come.

Knowing the Scriptures is vital. They equip you for every good work (2 Timothy 3:1–7). Jesus was deeply committed to the Scriptures, using them powerfully in crucial moments in the spiritual battle (Matthew 4:1–11 and Luke 4:1–13). With his example, Jesus shows us that we too need to love the Scriptures and use them daily. Jesus said, "Man does not live on bread alone, but on every word that comes from the mouth of God" (Matthew 4:4). Make up your mind that you will not let anything get in the way of your daily study of God's word. Your life depends on it.

For the Greatest Growth

1. *Buy a notebook and keep the notes that you will make as you go through this material.* Writing down your answers and thoughts will be very helpful to you. The better you learn these things now, the more effective you will be in sharing what you know with others.

2. *Have a regular time and place to do your study.* Pick both so that you will be as free as possible from interruptions and distractions. For those with normal schedules, early morning times are usually the very best.

3. *Read and underline, mark or somehow identify every scriptural reference in your study.* This will help you in remembering where passages are located and will give you one more way of being effective as Jesus' disciple.

4. *Have a great relationship with a more mature Christian who can check your progress as you move through the study.* Take advantage of all the help you can get. Be eager to receive instruction and correction. The crucial issues you will study out will serve you powerfully the rest of your life. You want to give this your very best.

5. *As you work on each lesson, write the current date in the space provided.* This will kelp you keep track of the consistency of your own pattern of study.

6. *Keep these notes and review these convictions.* Your own notes can become a valuable resource when you need encouragement in these areas and when you are sharing with others.

May God bless you with great times in his word and may those times always draw you personally closer to him, enabling you to bring others to Christ.

Week One
MISSION

Therefore go and make disciples of all nations...

Matthew 28:19

You have just made the greatest decision a person can ever make. In your very first week as a disciple, you will study how God plans to use you to bring others to the new life you have found in Jesus Christ. The other studies that will follow will help prepare you for this mission, but it is good at the beginning to understand what your exciting and fulfilling mission is as a disciple of Jesus.

Day 1—Crucial Last Words

1. If you have not read the introduction on the previous page, please do so before you begin.

2. Before you actually begin this plan for Bible study, please take a few minutes to write in your notebook what your baptism into Jesus Christ meant to you. Why did you do it? What has changed because of your decision? Keep this statement in a safe place and refer to it often. Even as the years pass it will serve as a powerful reminder to you of the significance of your decision and of what you want to share with others.

3. The last words a person speaks usually tell us a lot about the major things on that person's heart. Turn to Matthew 28:18–20 and read again the final commission of Jesus Christ before he left this world.

4. What does it mean that Jesus has all authority over you? How do you feel about that? Where is he telling you that he wants you to "go"? What does he want you to do with the life he has given you? Who in your life heard Jesus say "go" and went to you? How do you feel about them because of it?

5. Jesus is sending you into your world to bring others to him. Write down the names of some of the people in your world right now that you want to be "going" to with his good news. Pray every day this week for them to be open to the gospel.

Day 2—Talking Babies

1. Begin by reading 1 Peter 2:2–3. Who are some of the people receiving this letter? In what way are you a "newborn baby"?

2. Now read 3:13–17 (especially looking at vv15 and 16). Does it seem that Peter thought the newborn babies should wait a while before sharing their faith? As a "newborn" what do you have to share with others?

3. Write down what you think is involved in each of these statements and why each is so important in making disciples.

a.) "In your hearts acknowledge Christ as the Holy Lord."
b.) "Always be prepared to give an answer."
c.) "With gentleness and respect."
d.) "Keeping a clear conscience."

4. Decide which friends on your prayer list that you will talk to about God and when you will do it. Pray for them specifically.

Day 3—The Committed

1. Begin today by reading the following passages from the Book of Acts:

a.) Acts 4:16–20

b.) Acts 5:40–42
c.) Acts 8:1–4

2. Write down what you see in these early Christians that impresses and convicts you.

3. Why do you suppose they were so committed to sharing the gospel with other people?

4. Opposition will always come to those who work to make disciples. You see it here in Acts. Read also Jesus warnings in Matthew 10:21–25. Why would you expect negative reactions from some people as you share the message of Jesus? How will you respond?

5. Write down at least three different places where you will go today, and then pray about taking God's message into those places.

Day 4—Sharing Your Life

1. Read 1 Thessalonians 2:7–9 as Paul talks about the relationship he had with some that he had led to Christ.

2. What do we need to learn from Paul's example about how to reach out to other people?

3. What would be involved in "sharing not only the gospel with someone, but our lives as well"?

4. Someone once said: "People don't care how much you know, until they know how much you care." How can you show some of the non-Christians around you that you really care for them?

5. Read Matthew 25:31–36. How are other Christians around you seeking to fulfill this passage in their lives? Who can you talk with this week about this passage and how to live it out in your life?

6. Decide which friend you most want to reach out to and ask another disciple to help you develop a plan.

Day 5—The Love of Christ Compels

1. Read 2 Corinthians 5:11–21.

2. Write down at least five things this passage teaches about evangelism (sharing your faith).

3. Go back to 2 Corinthians 4:7–12. What we need to learn from Paul's experiences in sharing the Word with people?

4. Read 2 Corinthians 4:1 and commit it to memory.

5. Why could there be no greater purpose in life than bringing others to Christ?

6. What great feelings do you have when you share your faith? What does it do for your convictions?

Day 6—Pray, Then Proclaim

1. Begin today by reading Colossians 4:2–6.

2. List all the things you find here in regard to sharing your faith with someone.

3. What do you think Paul meant by "making the most of every opportunity"?

4. List some opportunities you could have used recently if you had been more alert and ready to speak.

5. Have you heard the term "lifestyle evan-

gelism"? It refers to the fact that we should not reserve one night of the week for evangelism or even two or three, but that we should be living lives that are always evangelistic. What are some things that we need to be saying to ourselves at the beginning of every day in order to live an evangelistic lifestyle?

6. How will your lifestyle be evangelistic today?

Day 7—We Plant; God Makes It Grow

1. Read carefully Jesus' words in Mark 4:26–29.

2. Now turn and read Paul's words in 1 Corinthians 3:5–9.

3. What is our role in making disciples?

4. What is God's role?

5. Why can we never be prideful about the fact that we have been used to lead someone else to Christ?

6. If God is really the one who brings change to people's hearts and lives, why would he want us to share in the work?

7. Look back over the people and opportunities you have written about this week. Pray about these and commit yourself to be used for the rest of your life to bring other people to Jesus Christ. If reaching out is a big difficulty for you, admit that to someone and let them help you to overcome it. But believe that it can happen in your life! Look forward to being used in a great way.

8. Decide who you will reach out to next week and how.

Week Two
AUTHORITY

All scripture is God-breathed...
2 Timothy 3:16

In your second week you will be studying passages that show the importance of living by God's Word and no other authority. This is a deep conviction that you need to have in your heart and one that you need to pass on to others.

Day 8—The Final Authority

1. As you begin to live your life for God, it is important that you begin studying God's word with the right type of respect and eagerness. Read 2 Timothy 2:15. How can you be obedient to this scripture?

2. Read again Matthew 28:18. Write down what the authority of Christ now means in your life.

3. Turn to John 12:47–50. What happens to the one who does not accept the words of Jesus? What does God want for us? How do we find that?

4. It is important to remember that God's word is our authority. His word is our standard for living. It doesn't matter what people have taught you before or what "you" think; but rather, what is final is what God says. Write down a specific example of how this needs to work in your life.

5. Look back at the names of those you want to share with that you wrote down last week. What have you shared with them? Are you praying for them daily?

Day 9—Ungodly Religion

1. Begin today by reading 2 Timothy 3:1–5.

2. What is the problem with the kind of religion or "ungodliness" described here?

3. Come down to 2 Timothy 4:1–4 and read another description of powerless religion.

4. Why would people ever substitute men's teachings for God's teaching on a given subject? How do you think this tendency might creep into your life?

5. Why would carefully following God's message lead to powerful religion as opposed to powerless religion?

Day 10—Skill Needed

1. Begin your study today by reading 2 Timothy 2:15. Take a few minutes and memorize this.

2. What do you believe God is communicating to you here?

3. Write a brief explanation of each of these statements:

   a. To handle God's word correctly we must have great respect for it.
   b. To handle God's word correctly we must spend time studying it.
   c. To handle God's word correctly we must share it with a godly attitude. (See 2 Timothy 2:24–26.) List both godly and ungodly ways in which we can share our faith.

4. In some translations this passage speaks of "rightly dividing the word of truth." This was once interpreted to mean we need to know the difference between the Old Testament Scriptures and the New Testament Scriptures. The verse certainly refers to more than this, but no one can handle the Word correctly without understanding the difference. What is the difference in the Old Testament and the New Testament? (Have a mature Christian check your answer.)

Day 11—Sound Doctrine

1. Read Romans 1:16–17. Before you start today's study, ask yourself: "Is anything hindering me from sharing the word of God with my friends?" If there is something, then it needs to be put to death. Remember that it is God's word that has the power to save. Turn to 1 Corinthians 2:1–5 for reinforcement.

2. Turn to 1 Timothy 4:16 and write down what two things are necessary to save yourself and your hearers.

3. There is no power in the things we tell people if we are not living the life we proclaim. Let God's word convict people and let your life convince them that his word is truth.

4. Read Titus 2:1. What is sound doctrine and how might you learn it? What is the attitude of so many "religious" people toward sound doctrine? Why is it important to learn exactly what God has commanded?

5. Read Titus 1:9. What will we be able to do by holding to sound doctrine?

6. Turn to 1 Timothy 6:3–5 and write down what this verse means to you. What is the connection between false teaching and a bad heart or a bad attitude? Why is keeping a pure heart so important in understanding God's word?

Day 12—The Powerful Word

1. Read 2 Timothy 3:16–17 and Hebrews 4:12–13. Make a list of all the things that God's word can do for you.

2. Not only is it important to know what God's word is, but it is equally important to do what it says. Turn to James 1:22–25.

3. What happens to the man who does what he has learned? God cannot use us if we do not do what he tells us.

4. The person who doesn't put God's word into practice will forget what he or she looks like. Write down some things that you know are right and that you intend to put into practice today.

5. Turn in the Old Testament to Ezekiel 33:30–33. You will not be able to understand the true meaning of God's word until you do what it says.

Day 13—'Seems Right' or 'Is Right'?

1. Very often in the practice of religion people make a decision to do something because what they "think" seems more right to them than what God's word actually says. What warning do you hear for your life in Proverbs 14:12?

2. For an excellent example of this problem, turn to and read 1 Samuel 15:1–23.

3. Why were Saul's actions judged to be wrong? What was his justification for what he had done? Why was God not "won over" by his argument?

4. Write down some examples of how Saul's problem might be found in someone's life today.

5. In view of Saul's problem, what attitude do you want to have toward God's word?

Day 14—Building on a Rock

1. You have now been a Christian for two weeks. Write down some things you have learned and are wanting to do your third week as a Christian. Share these things with a brother or sister and let them help you and encourage you.

2. Turn to Matthew 7:21–27. Read this passage several times and write down what it means to you. Who are the people who will be turned away?

3. Now turn to Luke 6:46–49. What does Luke say about the one who builds his house on the rock?

4. The right attitude toward God's Word is a crucial foundation for future growth. Read and memorize Psalm 1:1–3. It is so important to stay planted by the stream. Carry this Psalm in your heart, meditate on it often, respond to its challenge, and you will grow!

Week Three
GRACE

For it is by grace you have been saved.

Ephesians 2:8

"Amazing Grace" is not just a great song. It is one of the great themes of the Bible. We are saved by God's amazing grace. We are useful to God because of his amazing grace. We are to receive his grace with thanksgiving and with eagerness to let it change our lives.

Day 15—Lavished on Us

1. The grace of God makes our salvation possible. The grace of God also makes our growth and development possible. His grace is the source of everything that is good in us. Turn and read Ephesians 1:1–10. Mark each reference to the word "grace."

2. Grace is "giving to someone who deserves nothing as though he or she deserves everything," and that's what happens to us in Jesus Christ. We deserve nothing, but in him we are given everything. In spite of our sin, we are treated as if we were like Christ himself. This means we are judged not on the basis of our performance, but on the basis of grace. Incredible!

3. The NIV translation in 1:8 speaks of the grace God has lavished on us. What does the word "lavished" mean to you? What picture does that give you of God? How does this differ from some views of God that you may be familiar with?

4. What is Paul's response, described in 1:3, to such incredible grace? How should your understanding of God's grace change your attitude and outlook on life?

5. Spend some time just trying to comprehend how blessed you are to have been taught about the grace of God. Give praise to God with all your heart.

Day 16—Standing in Grace

1. Turn to Romans 5:1–11. Why is it so amazing that God has shown his grace to us?

2. In view of the teaching of this passage why is it so foolish for us to ever be proud, arrogant or boastful in any situation or relationship?

3. In v2 he says it is in "this grace which we now stand." Grace is a state in which you now stand and in which you will continue to stand as you continue in your faith. How does it give you security to know that you are standing (living) in a state of grace?

4. Suppose you fail in some way tomorrow and feel defeated. What difference will it make that in Christ you "stand in grace"?

Day 17—United with Christ

1. Read Acts 2:36–38 and then Romans 5:20–6:7.

2. Does baptism look like something that merits you salvation, or is it the way God tells us to say "yes" to his grace which we could never merit?

3. Write down what Romans 6 is saying happened to you in your baptism by the grace of God?

4. How does what happened (what God did) need to affect your attitude toward sin?

5. What is wrong with saying "let's continue in sin so grace can abound"?

Day 18 —Saved for Good Works

1. Read Ephesians 2:1–10.

2. Write a short explanation of each verse in this text.

3. Look carefully at v10. What is the whole purpose of grace? If a person does little or nothing as a disciple because "I am saved by grace anyway," what are they missing?

4. What good works do you see that God's grace has equipped you to do? What specif-

ically are you wanting to do today out of appreciation for being saved?

5. If God has treated you with grace, how are you going to treat other people who sin and make mistakes? Read Ephesians 4:32.

Day 19—Grace that Teaches

1. Read Titus 2:11–14.

2. This passage could be translated "the grace of God gives us an education." What is the whole purpose of God giving us his grace?

3. List some things that the grace of God educates you to do.

4. Why must a "yes" to God's grace be followed by "no" to worldly passions and ungodliness?

5. Is there anything still in your life that God's grace is teaching you to say "no" to?

6. Using your answer in question 5, now write out the following: "God's grace is sufficient to enable me to say 'no' to ________________________________."

Day 20—When We Sin

1. By today you have probably realized that you are not doing all for Jesus Christ that you determined to do almost three weeks ago. You want to love him with all your heart, soul, mind and strength. But you have failed in some specific areas. What you will study today will be very important in dealing with this for the rest of your life.

2. Turn to 1 John 1:5–10. Read it carefully.

3. Think of the difference in light and darkness. Think of the difference between a bright open room with lots of windows and a totally dark basement area. In one, things are out in the open. You can see them as they really are. In the other, things are hidden and covered by the darkness. With this in mind, what does he mean when he calls us to "walk in the light"? Do you see how this fits with v9 and the call to confess our sins?

4. We all—from the oldest to the youngest in Christ—sin. If we claim that we don't, we lie (v10). How, then, are we to handle all of this? Do we cover and hide our sins? Or do we bring them out into the open through confession?

5. Write down the two results of walking out in the light as described in v7. Why is this passage comforting? What does it teach you about relationships in Christ?

6. Remember this: Satan's only ground is darkness. When we confess our sins and bring them out into the light, we take away from him his only base of operation, and we enjoy the power of God's grace and the blood of Christ continually cleanses us from all sin.

7. Have you been open about your sins? Has God forgiven you?

Day 21—Not Without Effect

1. Read 1 Corinthians 15:9–11.

2. In what sense can you say something similar to what Paul says in v9?

3. What do you think he means when he says "and his grace to me was not without effect"?

4. How can you respond so that God's grace will not be without effect?

5. Why do you think Paul adds that last comment in v10 "Yet not I. but the grace of God that was with me"?

6. End this week of study with time to thank God and praise him for his marvelous grace. Look at your lostness without him and his great mercy that you in no way deserved. Make sure there is no self-righteousness or arrogance in your heart but that you truly believe "by the grace of God I am what I am." Remember and write down where you were headed and what would have happened if you had not become a disciple. Share this with someone you want to be saved. Be a grateful Christian.

Week Four
DYING TO SELF

But if it dies, it bears much fruit...
John 12:24 RSV

This week you will be studying passages in the Scriptures that show so clearly what the real problem in life is. The problem is the "old self" that lives for itself. Jesus Christ calls for the old self to be crucified, and he promises to raise up a new and very different "self." It is in dying that we find life.

Day 22—The Power of Dying

1. Turn to Luke 9:18–26. Read this passage through at least twice, underlining or making notes on what you believe are the key words and phrases. Write an explanation for verses 23, 24 and 25.

2. Now turn to Luke 18:28–30 and look at the promise that is given to those who accept discipleship. How do you expect this to work out in your life?

3. These two passages will become very important as you share your life in Christ with others. Why is this true? Remember where they are and think about how you should share them with someone else.

4. Be sure to spend time in serious prayer each day. Later in this study we will examine prayer, but don't wait until then to begin to develop a great prayer life. You are God's son or daughter and he wants you to talk with him.

Day 23—Co-Crucified with Christ

1. Begin today by reading Galatians 2:20. Take a few minutes to memorize this verse.

2. The word in Greek in this verse actually means "I have been co-crucified with Christ." How do we use the prefix "co"? What is a "co-leader" or "co-worker"? And so what is the message for Christians?

3. Among other things, the crucifixion of Jesus meant he voluntarily gave up his rights for the good of others. What "rights" do you think you might have a tendency to hold on to? How do you need to give them up for others?

4. The crucifixion of Jesus meant he put others' welfare above his comfort. How can you share in his crucifixion? What was the result of his crucifixion? What will be the result of yours?

5. Why is Matthew 7:12 a description of

the "crucified life"? How are you making this part of your character?

Day 24—From Old to New

1. Turn again to Romans 6:1–4. Read and study this carefully. Each time you come to the word "we" or "us" substitute your own name. (For example, v2—"By no means. John died to sin; how can he live in it any longer?")

2. Write down some things about your old self that caused it to deserve death.

3. God has made you a "new self." How do you need to express your new self to others? How will they know you are new?

4. How do you specifically plan today to put v13 into practice?

5. Study verses Romans 6:15–23.

Day 25—Life in the Spirit

1. Before you start today's study, ask yourself a very important question: "Am I making every effort to be in close contact with other Christians?" This is crucial, and in Week Five the studies will all focus on the importance of relationships. Most of us have some tendency from time to time for various reasons to pull back from others. Spiritually, this can be fatal. Even when you don't "feel like it," stay in touch.

2. Turn to Romans 7:14–24 and read how powerless you are to live this new life without God's help. It is clear why we must "disown" the sinful nature. Especially note v24.

3. But now go on to Romans 8 where we see how we can do through Christ what is not possible alone. You were probably assured at your baptism into Christ that you would receive the Holy Spirit upon your obedience to the Gospel. Now study some of what that Spirit means in our lives. Read vv1–17, making notes on the things that impress you the most. Remember to keep substituting your own name for pronouns.

Day 26—Taking Correction

1. As you have questions about things that you are studying or things that are happening to you, seek out some of your older brothers and sisters and let them help you. They have been through many things you will go through. Lean on their wisdom and understanding.

2. When we are children, we need to be taught things we don't know, and we need to be corrected when we are wrong. You are a baby in Jesus Christ. There is much you don't know and there are some areas where you need correction. That is true of every new Christian (and every older one!). *How you take correction is going to make all the difference in your growth in Christ.*

Turn to Proverbs 2:1–8. Next look at Proverbs 12:15. Go back to 10:17. What is the message? How does this relate to the idea that we have died to the old self?

3. Write down your own attitude toward being corrected. Distinguish between those things that are left over from your earthly nature and those things that Jesus Christ is putting in your heart. Read Proverbs 15:9–10 and 12:1.

4. Go to the New Testament now and read 2 Timothy 3:16–17 and answer this question: Why are other brothers or sisters to bring the Word of God to you? What is going to be your attitude when they do?

Day 27—A New Attitude

1. Below are listed several verses. As you read them write down what you think the passage has to do with putting off the old self and putting on the new.
   a.) Philippians 2:14–15
   b.) Philippians 3:7–11
   c.) Philippians 4:4
   d.) Philippians 4:11–13

2. Write a response to the following statement: "In Jesus Christ we have all we need to maintain a great attitude." True or false? Why or why not?

3. What do these passages have to do with having a great attitude?
   a.) John 16:33
   b.) Romans 8:28
   c.) James 1:2–4

4. What will be the effect on others when you allow God to give you a great attitude in all circumstances?

Day 28—Life from Death

1. Read John 12:20–26.

2. Notice in v23 that Jesus says the time has come for him to be "glorified." What do you think of when you hear that someone is about to receive "glory"?

3. In v24 Jesus most likely surprises his disciples. He indicates that the way he will find his glory is by becoming that seed that falls to the ground and dies. What does he say will be the impact of the seed that dies?

4. How do we know that this principle of being the seed that falls to the ground and dies applies to us who are disciples of Jesus? Particularly notice v26. Why is this an exciting principle?

5. In your life right now, who do you need to "die" for so they can become a disciple?

Week Five
FAMILY

Now you are the body of Christ,
and each one of you is part of it.
1 Corinthians 12:27

This week you will study the importance of the church (the Body of Christ, the family of God) and the relationships you will have in the church. This is what the kingdom of God is all about—relationships. To be righteous means to conduct your relationships (with God and with others) in the right way.

Day 29—Jesus' Church

1. Jesus Christ, who has all authority, taught us that the church is crucial in his plan. In Matthew 16:16–18, Jesus heard Peter confess to him to be the Christ, the Son of God; and immediately Jesus said, "Upon this rock I will build my church, and the gates of Hades will not prevail against it." Jesus saw the church as the center of his plan. He wanted to build it and he intended to make it so strong that the forces of Satan could not stand against it. What Jesus counted as so important, we too must count as so important. What statements have you made or heard religious people make that discount (lessen) the importance of the church? What would Jesus say?

2. For a true picture of what the church should be striving to become every day,

look at Acts 2:40–47. What impresses you the most?

3. What can you do today and the rest of this week to contribute to this kind of life among God's people (the church)?

Day 30—New Relationships

1. As you read each of the following passages, write down something the passage teaches that must be in our relationships in the Body of Christ.

a.) John 13:34–35
b.) Ephesians 5:1–2
c.) 1 Corinthians 13:1–3
d.) Colossians 3:14
e.) Galatians 5:6, 13, 14
f.) 1 Peter 4:8, 9

2. What does it mean to love another person?

3. What does 1 John 3:16 say it means to love another person? How does this apply to our relationships?

4. What is so good and so right about loving like this? What are the results?

5. Surprise someone today with a special act of love.

Day 31—Belonging

1. Paul describes the church as the "Body of Christ." Read Romans 12:1–8. How does giving yourself first to God need to lead to giving yourself to other people in the Body of Christ?

2. Notice particularly v5 which says, "each member belongs to all the others," or "we are all members of one another." How does this fit with or conflict with the often popular idea of individualism?

3. List three things that you already know you can do for other members of the Body of Christ. Share these with someone who is close to you and get their response.

4. List at least three things that you know you need from the Body of Christ in order to grow in Christ.

Day 32—Unity

1. Read Ephesians 4:1–5. Why does it seem to you that God is so very concerned about the Body of Christ having unity and peace?

2. Turn to Romans 14:13–15:3 and read how far we should go and how much we should bend to keep the Body of Christ together. Can you think of a practical application of this passage?

3. Is there anything in your life that is so important to you that you would not give it up even if it was keeping people from coming to Jesus Christ or growing in him? If there is, look back to v21 and get help in dealing with this area of your life. What most competes against Christ in your life and why?

Day 33—Purity

1. God is greatly concerned about the unity of the church. He is also greatly concerned about the purity of the Body of Christ. We are called to a holy life and a pure life, and sin in the Body that is being hidden or ignored will destroy the power of the church.

2. Read Ephesians 4:17–5:14. List those things which are described here as improper for God's holy people.

3. How would living as "children of light" be totally different from those things you have just listed? What is the basic difference?

4. You are a young Christian, but what should you do if you see brothers or sisters falling into some sin? Read Galatians 6:1–2 and write out the principles you learned about who should help others with their sin and how it should be done.

Day 34—Encouragement

1. One of our greatest responsibilities is to *encourage* each other in the Body of Christ. Read an important statement about this in Hebrews 3:12–14.

2. According to this passage why is encouragement so needed? Judging from this passage, what kind of encouragement do you think would prove most helpful?

3. Look at Hebrews 10:24–25. What do we need to do to make our meeting times even more encouraging? Why is it discouraging for someone to miss meetings without communicating why they are not there or without getting advice?

4. Write down the names of three people you want to encourage and how you plan to do this.

5. Explain why different people are encouraged by different means.

Day 35—Conflict Resolution

1. The Body of Christ will not be a "perfect place" immune from relationship problems. Why will problems even arise in relationships that are in the church?

2. Read two important passages that tell us how to resolve problems that arise in the church.

   a.) Matthew 5:23–24 (Remember Jesus is teaching Jews here who still went to the temple to offer sacrifices; but what is the principle for us?)

   b.) Matthew 18:15–20

      (1) How is this different from the way people often handle a problem of sin? Why will step one work most of the time?

      (2) Why is step two sometimes going to be needed?

      (3) Why would the church have to sever fellowship with the person who will not repent and confess his or her sin?

3. Determine early in your Christian life that you will not complain or grumble behind someone's back. Determine that you will go to them and seek to resolve the problem with God's help.

4. You have been a Christian more than a month now. How would you evaluate the way you have handled your relationships in the Body?

5. Read 2 Corinthians 1:12. What are you appreciating about relationships that are based on God's grace and not worldly wisdom?

6. Ask someone close to you for some feedback on the conduct of your relationships so far.

7. Praise God for relationships based on Jesus and the grace of God.

Week Six
HEART

This week all of the studies will have to do with keeping our hearts pure before God and before one another. Probably you have already heard much about the importance of a great heart, but this study will help you see how to have such a heart and what the result of such a heart will be.

> *Above all, guard your heart,*
> *for it is the well spring of life.*
> Proverbs 4:23

Day 36—God Looks at the Heart

1. Read Proverbs 4:23. How would you define the "heart" that the writer is describing? And what would it mean to "guard your heart"? Read Jeremiah 17:9–10. Why did God say this about our hearts?

2. Look at 1 Samuel 16:1–7. Particularly notice v7. In terms of religion, how might our "outward appearance" be different from what is really going on in the "heart"? But what is it that God is concerned about?

3. Have you been tempted so far in your new life to put on the outward appearance without having the heart? If so, how?

4. Read Psalm 139. Especially notice David's prayer for a pure heart in vv23–24 and then spend some special time praying about your own heart.

Day 37—Heart Change

1. All the great men and women in the Scriptures had to deal with their hearts, but no one shares his heart with us and his struggle for purity of heart more than David. Psalm 32 and Psalm 51 were written by David and will be important in this week's study. Read them both carefully at this time. Make notes on those verses that seem most significant.

2. From these Psalms we can learn valuable lessons about how to come to purity of heart and how to keep the heart pure.

   a.) We must be willing to face our sin honestly and admit to ourselves what it is (51:3).

   b.) We must be broken over that sin (take seriously its effects) (51:17).

   c.) We must be willing to confess that sin (32:3–5).

   d.) We must be willing to accept forgiveness, once broken (32:11, 51:12–16).

3. Why can no one have and keep a pure heart without dealing with sin in a biblical way?

Day 38—Knowing Your Sin

1. Briefly review yesterday's study. Reread Psalm 32 and Psalm 51.

2. David struggled before he faced his sin. When are times you really don't want to face your sin? How do you usually avoid that confrontation?

3. What did David mean when he said God's hand was heavy upon him? What do you do when you feel the hand of conviction on you?

4. David said, "I know my transgressions." Are there any things in your life that you need to face honestly and say "I know that is my sin"? What will be the good of such honesty?

Day 39—Confession

1. Today's study is a continuation of the previous days. Without re-reading them, can you give a brief summary of the two Psalms (32 and 51) you have been considering?

2. When David saw sin in his life, he was broken and contrite over that sin. What does that mean?

3. David confessed his sin. Why is confession "good for the soul"? Why does it bring healing?

4. Who did David confess to? (If you said "God," think again. He wrote this Psalm of confession to be read and heard by all Israel.)

5. What did you learn earlier about confession from 1 John 1:9? Memorize this verse.

6. Look at James 5:16. You will be tempted to not let this be happening in your life, but you must remember how right it is. Also memorize this verse.

7. None of this is to write a rule that says "you must confess every sin to some other person." But isn't it clear God's people need to have a confessing attitude? Isn't it clear that hearts cannot be pure where there is hiddenness or deception?

8. What is your attitude toward confession? Do you see it as an opportunity or a burden?

Day 40—Good Fruits

1. The last several days you have studied ways to keep a pure heart. Now we want to turn specifically to the *results* or *fruits* of pure-heartedness. Again, let's consider what we learn from Psalms 32 and 51.

   a.) There is a great awareness of forgiveness and salvation.
   b.) There is a thankful, rejoicing, singing spirit.
   c.) There is a great desire to share the joy of salvation and cleansing. Look back through these two Psalms and write down the verses that illustrate these points.

2. Which of these results do you see most clearly in your own life?

3. What's the problem when these fruits aren't seen?

4. Ask someone who is very close to you in the church how they feel about your heart.

Day 41—Heart Maintenance

1. After doing the study on the heart this week, why would you say that our hearts need *continual maintenance*?

2. Look closely at 1 Timothy 1:5–7. What is implied in the phrase "wandered away from...a pure heart"?

3. Describe how this process of wandering away from purity of heart might happen in someone's life. Give some steps that might be involved.

4. What are three things you can regularly do to guard against this "wandering" in your own life?

Day 42—'Where is My Heart?'

1. Turn to Proverbs 4:23 and Jeremiah 17:9. Write out what these passages say and why you think they say it.

2. In your Christian life you will need to

learn to diagnose different "heart" conditions. Study the following:

a.) Hard heart—Proverbs 28:14
b.) Unrepentant heart—Romans 2:5
c.) Unbelieving heart—Hebrews 3:12

3. As you handle different situations in your life, learn to ask, "Where is my heart?" If you resist correction, ask "Where is my heart?" If you find yourself wanting to skip a meeting of the Body, ask "Where is my heart?" Why is it so dangerous to give in even a little to a bad heart?

4. Who is someone you know who strikes you as having a pure heart? What is it about them that you want to imitate?

5. What kind of heart did God promise to give us as we surrender our bad hearts? (See Ezekiel 11:17–19.)

6. What is the end result for the pure heart? (See Matthew 5:8.)

Week Seven
SUBMISSION

Submit to one another out of reverence for Christ.
Ephesians 5:21

This week you will study one of the keys to the Christian life. It is seldom understood and almost always rejected by those in the world, but it is something that you see perfectly in Jesus Christ, and it is something he wants to see consistently in us. It is the principle of submission.

Day 43—Different Situations

1. On the first day of our study on this topic we want to look at the different places in Scripture where submission is called for. Look up the following scriptures and list those to whom we are to be submissive.

a.) James 4:7
b.) 1 Peter 2:13–18
c.) 1 Peter 3:1–5
d.) Ephesians 5:21
e.) Hebrews 13:17
f.) 1 Peter 5:5

2. Now, to the right of each of these categories that you have written down, write the name of someone to whom you should be in submission.

3. What are some of the major problems that you have with having a submissive attitude in these relationships?

4. Why does being submissive fit with what you know about the message of Jesus?

Day 44—A Matter of Attitude

1. As you study the biblical concept of submission, one of the most important things to learn is that God wants us to have a submissive *attitude*. He does not want us to submit with resentment, resignation or bitterness. He does not want our submission to be legalistic. He wants it to come from the heart because of our trust in him, because of our confidence that he honors submission.

2. Submissiveness was an attitude found in Jesus. Read about it in Philippians 2:5–9. How do we see submissiveness in Jesus?

3. Again read about Jesus' submissive attitude in 1 Peter 2:13–21 (note particularly the first part of v13, the first part of v18, and v21).

4. Once we realize that Jesus Christ was the perfect model of submissiveness, we realize that submissiveness does not mean certain things. It does not mean (a) lack of conviction, (b) silence, (c) violating your conscience, (d) weakness, (e) inferiority.

Instead submissiveness, as we see it in Jesus, does mean (a) surrender of self-interest, (b) yielding of personal rights in order to benefit others, and (c) trusting God.

Some people think to submit means to do nothing, but we see in Jesus' life that submission meant trusting God and that is hardly "nothing."

5. In view of what we see in Jesus, which Christians should be submissive?

6. Ultimately, to whom are we to be submissive? Read James 4:7–8.

Day 45—Key to Growth

1. One of the things that all Christians need to be concerned about is their own personal spiritual growth. Why is submission such an important attitude to have in order for growth to take place? What will happen to the person who is unsubmissive?

2. Read Luke 2:51–52. Then go to Hebrews 5:7–9. How did Jesus learn what he learned?

3. What are some things that you are sure that God wants you to be learning right now, and how will a submissive attitude toward others help you to learn these things?

4. Do you feel like you have a rebellious or unsubmissive attitude about anything in your life at the present time? The tenor of God's word would strongly encourage you to open all that up to someone so you can more quickly deal with it and put it behind you. A rebellious attitude will destroy spiritual growth.

Day 46—'For the Lord's Sake'

1. Read 1 Peter 2:13 and then comment on each of the following phrases in that verse:

a.) "submit yourselves"
b.) "for the Lord's sake"
c.) "to every authority instituted among men"

2. Is the following statement true or false? "Whenever we don't have a submissive attitude, it is not for the Lord's sake but for our sake." Explain your answer.

3. Think of some times in your life when you were not submissive. How was your unsubmissiveness "for your sake" and not "for the Lord's sake"?

4. A man claiming to be a Christian once made this statement: "I submit to Jesus Christ and I submit to God, but any submission to men is way down the list, and I mean way down on the list." What do you think of his attitude? How does it fit with Scripture?

Day 47—Relationship with Leaders

1. In the Body of Christ, God has placed certain men over you. First there are elders (overseers) in the body (see Acts 20:17; 28–3 1; 1 Peter 5:1–4) and then there are others who are over you because of special responsibilities they may have been given in the fellowship. Look at what Hebrews 13:17 says about your responsibility to these Christians.

2. Do you know the names of the elders and other leaders in the congregation where you are? Have you reached out to them in any way since becoming a Christian? How

could you show them that you have a submissive attitude toward their leadership and that you want to make their work a joy and not a burden?

3. Does this passage say we have to agree with everything a leader does before we can submit to him and obey him?

4. Make sure your relationships with all your leaders are good ones. If there is ever any anger or resentment or hurt in you toward any of them, don't put off sitting down with that leader and opening up your heart. What would happen in a congregation if this did not happen?

Day 48—When We Must Not Submit

1. As we look at submission we must recognize that there will be times when we cannot specifically submit to people in what they are asking of us because to do so would be unsubmissive to God. Therefore, there are times when a Christian cannot submit. Turn to Acts 4:18–20 and Acts 5:27–30. Why did the early Christians not submit to the government in this instance?

2. Before we refuse to be submissive in any situation there are three important questions we need to ask ourselves:

a.) Do I really want to have a submissive attitude or am I looking for an excuse to be independent and rebellious?

b.) Is this really a violation of God's will or a violation of my strongly held tastes and preferences?

c.) Am I not wanting to submit because of the principle involved or some person involved? (We should never decide not to submit to someone just because we have a negative personal feeling toward them.)

3. How could you refuse to submit to some particular thing, but still maintain a submissive attitude toward the person? Example: A Christian wife is asked by her non-Christian husband to lie for him to a business partner. How can she refuse that but still maintain a submissive attitude toward her husband?

Day 49—The Blessings of Submission

1. After studying submission now for six days you should have a better picture of what true submission means, but read Philippians 2:9–11 to see the results of submission.

2. How did God bless the submission of Jesus Christ?

3. What are some specific ways that Christians will be richly blessed throughout the development of a submissive heart and attitude?

Therefore I will give him a
portion among the great,
and he will divide the spoils
with the strong,
because he poured out his life
unto death,
and was numbered with the
transgressors.
For he bore the sin of many,
and made intercession for the
transgressors.
Isaiah 53:12

Week Eight
THE FIGHT

For our struggle is not against
flesh and blood...

Ephesians 6:11

For the next week you will be studying about the spiritual battle you are engaged in and how to have victory over sin. Every person must fight the sinful desires that war against our souls (1 Peter 2:11). But God has given plans and power to ensure our victory.

Day 50—Treating Sin Seriously

1. Read the following passages looking for God's thinking about sin: Matthew 5:29–30 and 18:6–7. What would you say is the first step in the fight against sin?

2. What does God feel about religion where sin is not treated seriously? Read Jeremiah 6:13–15.

3. Turn to Psalm 36:1–2. What is the problem with the man being described here? What attitude does he really need to have toward his sin? Also read Psalm 66:18.

4. Why do you think it is unlikely that you will ever have much victory over a particular sin in your life until you hate that sin?

5. Write down some sins that you have struggles with, and then write down why those sins need to be despised and hated. Write down the effects they have on you, others and God's plans.

Day 51—The Power of Repentance

1. Read 2 Corinthians 7:8–12. Paul describes here what happens when people take their sin seriously and have godly sorrow that leads to repentance.

2. What would be the difference in godly and worldly sorrow? Why does godly sorrow have such power and bring such results?

3. Using the following diagram, write down a sin that you struggle with and the ways godly sorrow will lead you to demonstrate the attitudes that Paul describes.

God's Steps to Freedom *(2 Corinthians 7:10–11)* Repentance Steps	How to Change Specific Steps
Earnestness (Sincerity)	Fits of rage. Galations 5:19–20 I really intend to change & overcome. No excuses.
Eagerness to Clear Yourself	I will tell my closest brothers and my family my sin and my decision.
Indignation (Towards your sin)	I don't like myself when I lose control. I hate my anger.
Alarm (Urgency)	I must stop now. I cannot let this get any further.
Longing (Desire to be right with God)	James 1. I want my relationship with God to be right.
Concern (For those you have hurt)	My anger scares my wife and my children & my friends.
Readiness to see justice done	I will give up whatever I need to in order to permanently change.

4. Retain this diagram and use it to help you make changes as you see other sins that need to be dealt with.

Day 52—The Power of the Word

1. What role does the word of God play in our fight against sin? Read Psalm 119:9–11, Matthew 4:1–11, John 8:31–34.

2. What attitude must one have toward God's word in order to use it for victory over sin?

3. Look back at sins you listed in #5 on Day 50 and write down passages of Scripture that can help guard you against those sins. If you can't find what you need, ask someone for help.

Day 53—The Power of Prayer

1. What role does prayer play in the fight against sin? Read Matthew 7:7–11, Ephesians 6:10–18 (esp. v18), Hebrews 4:14–16.

2. As you pray about sin you are wanting to defeat in your life, what thoughts do you need to have about God? See the above verses and Romans 8:31–32, 1 John 2:1–2 and 3:1–3.

3. What does Jesus' example teach us about the kinds of prayers we may have to pray to win victory in our lives? Mark 1:35 and Hebrews 5:7–10.

4. In what ways have you been praying about sin you want to overcome? Who have you asked to pray for you?

Day 54—The Power of Relationships

1. What role does the Bible teach that we are to play in helping each other to live righteously and stay out of sin? Read Galatians 6:1–2, Colossians 1:28–29, 4:12, Hebrews 3:12–13, James 5:16.

2. List at least three ways that you need your brothers or sisters to help you guard your heart and your life from sin.

3. What does it say about us if we don't want help in overcoming sin, but only want to work on it by ourselves?

4. If there is some struggle with sin that you have not shared with another disciple, make a decision to do that today.

Day 55—No Temptation Too Great

1. Read 1 Corinthians 10:13. List the three promises God gives to us about overcoming sin in our lives. Why should it be such an encouragement to us to know that whatever temptation we face, it is common to man? Is there any temptation in your life that you have been reluctant to share with another Christian because you were afraid no one would understand?

2. You can see from this passage that we are not alone in our battle against sin. If you really believe that God has victory over Satan, you must not doubt the assurance of your victory over sin with God's help.

3. Read James 4:7–10. How would you describe the attitude that we are called to have here? What are some ways that you can practically come near to God?

4. How can you practically resist the devil when you face the temptation to

   a.) deceive?
   b.) lust?
   c.) have resentment?
   d.) selfishly indulge?
   e.) not care?
   f.) speak unwholesomely?

Day 56—Never Give Up

1. In the struggle against sin why do you think we might be tempted to give up?

2. Why is it worth it to never give up? Study Romans 6:15–16; 8:18; 1 Corinthians 15:56; Galatians 6:7–10; 2 Timothy 4:7–8.

3. Read James 1:12. What do you think it means to persevere under trial? How do you know if you have stood the test? Describe some area in which you need to practice perseverance. Why will this challenge require perseverance?

4. Write down why you will never give up the fight against sin no matter how challenging it might become.

5. What decisions did you make this week about dealing with sin?

Week Nine
PRAYER

The prayer of a righteous man is powerful and effective.

James 5:16

Today you begin your ninth week as a Christian. No doubt, prayer has become something very important to you, as it should be. Yet, even in this greatest of privileges you may have experienced struggles. Prayer is not natural, but like so many other facets of being a disciple of Jesus, it has to be learned. This week you will concentrate on prayer.

Day 57—Approach with Confidence

1. Think of someone in your life whom you can go to with confidence in any type of situation. How does that make you feel?

2. Read Ephesians 3:10–12 and Hebrews 4:14–16. These passages both use the word "confidence" to describe how we approach God. What does this mean to you? Of what can we be confident?

3. Why, as disciples of Jesus, are we able to come to God with such confidence?

4. When would be the only time that we could not be confident in coming to God?

5. As you pray today, thank God for Jesus who has made it possible for us to come to God without fear.

Day 58—Jesus: Man of Prayer

1. No one will have a meaningful prayer life who does not appreciate the importance of prayer, and perhaps nothing helps us see this importance more than the life of Jesus. Read Luke 5:15–16; 6:12–13; 9:18; 11:1; Mark 1:32–36; and Hebrews 5:7–10.

2. Because of these statements about Jesus, G. S. Thompson has written: "Prayer was the atmosphere in which he lived. It was the air he breathed." Robert Coleman commenting on the same scriptures has written: "Prayer was indeed the sweat and tears of His ministry. The battle of the cross was fought and won on His knees." The same author also wrote: "Jesus never got behind in His work because He never got behind in prayer."

3. Write down what the example of Jesus means to you in relationship to your prayer life.

Day 59—Surrender

1. There are certain things necessary for effective, joyful prayer. For the next several days, we want to concentrate on some of these.

2. As a disciple what should be your main objective as you pray? Read carefully Matthew 26:36–44 and 1 John 5:14–15.

3. What is wrong if an attitude of surrender to God is not at the heart of our prayers?

4. Why did Hebrews 5:7 say that Jesus was heard by God? How can you tell if your prayers are unsubmissive prayers?

5. What prayers of surrender do you need to pray today?

Day 60—Faith

1. Another key element in prayer is faith. Prayer alone without faith has no effect (read Hebrews 11:6).

2. Read Joshua 10:12–14. Faith carries our prayers to the ears of God. God listened to a man—Joshua—because he prayed believing, and the sun and moon stood still. Joshua asked for something that was impossible, yet he asked the God who makes "all things possible."

3. Read again Mark 11:22–24. What doubts have you had as you prayed? What situations seem impossible? Where do these doubts come from?

4. Read Luke 18:1–8 and Psalm 34:15. When is it important to remember these passages?

5. Read James 1:5–8. What does this say to you?

6. List three things you want to pray about *with faith*.

Day 61—'Teach Us to Pray'

The disciples asked Jesus to teach them to pray. For the next two days we want to concentrate on some practical guidelines for prayer.

1. Read Matthew 6:5–8 and Luke 5:15–16. What do these passages seem to be telling you about prayer?

2. As you look at your living situation, what arrangements must you make to have a time and place to be alone with God?

3. Read Psalm 55:17. David prayed regularly. Jesus often withdrew to pray. Why is it important for you to have a regular, set time to pray? Why is it worth the extra effort to work this out?

4. Read Ephesians 6:18 and 1 Thessalonians 5:17. Prayer is not limited to a set time and place, but should be spontaneous and continuous throughout the day. Why does God want us to "*pray continually?*" What does this mean to you? How might such a thing be done?

Day 62—Pray Like This

1. Read the prayer in Matthew 6:7–13.

2. List the several different elements that make up this prayer. Which of these do you focus on regularly? Which do you tend to neglect?

3. Many times our prayers are concentrated

on asking for certain needs to be met. Jesus teaches us to first of all focus on God and give him the honor and praise he deserves.

4. Do you have difficulty praising God? If so, use the Book of Psalms to train you. Start out with Psalm 24. Read it aloud.

Day 63—The Joy of Prayer

1. If we are to pray powerfully we must not only see the importance of prayer and the need for surrender and faith in prayer, but we must appreciate the joy of prayer. Read Philippians 1:3–6; 4:47 and 1 Thessalonians 5:16–18.

2. Why should your prayer life bring you joy? Can it do this even in the midst of trials?

3. What are some possible things that are wrong if a Christian does not see prayer as a source of joy?

4. As you close this week of study on prayer, what patterns of prayer do you have in your life at this time? What changes do you want to make?

Week Ten
DISCIPLINE

Run in such a way as to get the prize.

1 Corinthians 9:24

This week of your study will be devoted to the area of discipline. This is an important part of doing the will of God in the most effective way possible. Disciplined Christian living is *bringing all the areas of our lives under the control of Jesus Christ so that all we do fits together and contributes to our one purpose: to bring glory to God.*

When you became a Christian it was a decision to be a disciple of Jesus Christ, to put yourself under his discipline.

Day 64—The Spirit of Self-Discipline

1. Read 2 Timothy 1:7. What kind of spirit has God given us? What kind of excuses do you sometimes give for being undisciplined? Are they valid?

2. With the promise of this kind of spirit you can believe that you can become a disciplined person no matter where you are right now. Decide that from this time forward that whatever changes need to be made will be made.

3. Turn to 2 Timothy 3:16–17. What part do the Scriptures play in becoming disciplined?

4. How could a failure to be disciplined in your study of the Scriptures affect being under God's discipline or control in other areas?

5. What kind of disciplined study do you want to have after this 13-week study is over?

Day 65—Not 'Running Aimlessly'

1. Read 1 Corinthians 9:24–26.

2. What are some characteristics of discipline?

3. What is the purpose of discipline?

4. What are some characteristics of being undisciplined?

5. What does it mean to "run aimlessly"?

6. Are there any ways right now that you may be "running aimlessly"?

Day 66—Guarding Against Excess

1. There are any number of things that are not wrong in and of themselves, but to do them in excess without God's control will have a negative effect on your life and outreach.

2. What example of this does Paul give in 1 Timothy 6:6–10?

3. In the past what have been some things you might have done in excess without proper control or discipline?

4. Are there some things in your life right now that are not wrong but which could be done excessively if you are not careful?

5. Meditate on what your life would look like with the different areas under control. Get the image fixed in your mind. Now pray for God to give you the power to make that a reality. Make sure you really want it before you pray.

Day 67—Mastered by Nothing

1. Read 1 Corinthians 6:9–20. As you read keep in mind that "everything is permissible for me" and "food for the stomach and the stomach for food" were popular proverbs of the loose-living Corinthian culture that these Christians were living in.

2. What is Paul's response to each of the popular proverbs?

3. Why must disciples make the decision to "not be mastered by anything"? What will be the result if we do not?

4. What in your life right now is "mastering you" or threatens to "master you"?

5. Make a time to pray with someone about this, this week.

Day 68—Learning from the Soldier, Athlete & Farmer

1. Read 2 Timothy 2:1–7 and look for the three analogies Paul uses to characterize the Christian life.

2. What discipline is involved in being a soldier that we need in Christ?

3. What discipline involved in being an athlete do we need in Christ?

4. What discipline involved in being a successful farmer do we need in Christ?

5. As we seek to be disciplined like a soldier, an athlete or a farmer, why do we need to keep an eye on v1 and remember the grace of God?

Day 69—Spoiling the Fruit

1. Read and study Galatians 5:22–23.

2. Consider how the last element mentioned (self-control) relates to the others.

a.) Why will a lack of self-control (self-discipline) hinder your ability to love?

b.) Why will a lack of self-control interfere with peace?

c.) Why will lack of self-control often frustrate your ability to be kind, patient and gentle?

3. Self-control is a part of the fruit of the

Spirit, so that means we don't produce it on our own. What attitude must there be in our lives if God is to produce this in us?

Day 70—Discipline & Emotions

1. Self-discipline not only applies to how we use our time, money and possessions. It applies to how we handle our emotions.

2. List three emotions that need to be controlled and disciplined in your life. Find scriptures that relate to each one.

3. Turn to and read Hebrews 11:8. What emotions could have controlled Abraham in this instance? How does faith bring those emotions under control?

4. Consider these same questions as you read Hebrews 11:17–19.

5. Someone has said: "We lose control when we take control. In the same way, we gain control when we give it to God." How does this need apply to your life?

Week Eleven MONEY & MARRIAGE

Marriage should be honored by all.... Keep your lives free from the love of money....

Hebrews 13:4–5

In one passage the writer of Hebrews gives instructions about two key subjects for disciples: money and marriage (Hebrews 13:4–5). He realized that these were two areas that must be brought under the Lordship of Jesus. This week we will focus on those two areas. Money concerns us all. God's plans for marriage need to be understood whether or not we are currently married.

Day 71—The Necessity of Work

1. Money is not an evil. It is a necessity and the Scriptures teach that it should be honestly earned. Read Ephesians 4:28, 2 Thessalonians 3:6–15 and 1Timothy 5:7–8.

2. What attitudes did you have toward money before becoming a Christian? What changes have you had to make?

3. What is the impact of the irresponsible person who does not do his or her best to provide for personal financial needs?

Day 72—The Love of Money

1. Read Hebrews 13:1–5. We all must deal with money, but what attitude must we be careful not to have? Why is the love of money at cross purposes with following Jesus?

2. Read 1 Timothy 6:17–19. We are "rich" when we have the ability to meet our basic needs and then have money left over that can either be used to give us luxuries or help others. Most of us are in this category. From v18 write down three or four things we should do with our "discretionary money."

3. If we are not disciplined in the way we handle money, what will happen to our ability to share? Who will we not be able to share with?

4. Read Romans 13:8. Unmanageable and unresolved debt is a major problem for many people in our world. What is to be the disciple's attitude toward debt?

5. Write down at least three negative effects that will be present when we have a problem with debt?

6. What were your financial habits before becoming a Christian? What changes have you made? If your financial house is not in order, if debt is a major factor in your financial picture, do not wait any longer about getting help. Tell one of your leaders you need to talk. God can help you to victory if you are humble and open.*

Day 73—Righteous Use of Money

1. In this study we want to look at two places our money needs to go as disciples of Jesus. First read Luke 14:12–14 and Matthew 25:31–46. How important is it to God that we give to the poor? In what ways can you do this right now? If you just don't know where to begin, ask someone for advice. Find out what organized efforts there are in your congregation. But whatever you find, do it.

2. Read Philippians 4:14–16. Paul describes here the way the church in Philippi supported him as he spent his life spreading the gospel of Jesus. It is right for those who have received instruction in the Word to support those who bring the Word to them (Galatians 6:6). Without the generous giving of Christians we would not have seen the gospel taken around the world in recent years. Without continued generous giving, we will not see the mission completed.

3. How much of your income is being used to help the poor and to spread the gospel? God's Old Testament people under a far less glorious covenant were required to give 10% and beyond. What would faith lead you to do today under the covenant brought by Jesus?

Day 74—Generosity

1. Read 2 Corinthians 8:1–7. What would be necessary for someone in extreme poverty to "well up in rich generosity"? What steps would enable you to become more generous in your giving?

2. According to 2 Corinthians 9:6–11 what will be the joys of generosity?

3. How are you making your decisions about your giving? Do you see your giving as being generous? What sacrifices would you have to make to be more generous?

Day 75—Marriage in a New Light

1. For the rest of this week we will focus on marriage. Read Genesis 1:26–31 and 2:15–25.

2. Who is the designer of marriage? What did he plan for the marriage relationship?

3. What happens today when people forget that God is the originator of marriage? What problems does that lead to? What does it have to do with the divorce rate in most countries of the world?

4. If you are married, what do you have now that you are a Christian that you did not have before becoming one? How are you letting it change your outlook on your relationship?

Day 76—A Perfect Plan

1. Read Ephesians 5:21–33. What is *God's* plan for marriage?

2. Why is v21 such a crucial introduction to this section?

3. If the wife follows God's plan for her

and the husband God's plan for him, write out what kind of interaction this will lead to?

4. True or false? A husband or wife is relieved of his or her responsibility here if the other person does not hold up their end of the bargain? Explain your answer.

Day 77—Honoring Marriage

1. Read 1 Peter 3:1–7. What would you say is the basic message here for the wives? For the husbands?

2. If you are married, how does this passage personally challenge you? Share that conviction with your spouse.

3. Read 1 Corinthians 7:1–6. The Christians in Corinth were thinking that they might have more "spiritual" marriages if they refrained from the sexual relationship. What was Paul's answer? What attitude is he saying each marriage partner should bring to the sexual union? For more on the biblical view of sex in marriage read Song of Songs in the Old Testament.

4. Read Hebrews 13:4. In what way can you give honor to marriage if you are married? If you are not?*

Keys to a Great Marriage

1. Seek first the kingdom of God and his righteousness (Matthew 6:33). Build the marriage on God, his truth and his heart.

2. Get discipled. Be open and let others into your lives. Get input, advice and perspective from others who can be objective about your relationship (Colossians 1:28–29).

3. Treat each other with great respect (Ephesians 5:21–33, 1 Peter 3:1–7). Do not tear down the other person or try to "win." When you "win," your marriage always loses.

4. Love unconditionally (1 Corinthians 13). Don't love on the basis of performance but on the basis of a decision.

Week Twelve GROWTH & DIRECTION

I press on toward the goal.
Philippians 3:14

In this week you will be studying passages from God's word that will help you keep on growing as a disciple, help you learn to discern God's will and help you make spiritual plans that God can bless.

Day 78—Keep on Growing

1. Many seem to believe that the normal thing is for a person to grow as a Christian to a certain point and then level off. Read the following passages and see what you think:
   a.) Hebrews 5:11–14
   b.) 2 Peter 1:5–8
   c.) 1 Peter 2:1–2
   d.) 2 Peter 3:17–18

2. Look at Ephesians 3:14–19. How much is there to know? Who has learned enough?

* A helpful resource on marriage from Illumination Publishers is *Friends and Lovers: Marriage As God Designed It* by Sam and Geri Laing (www.ipibooks.com).

3. It has been said that as Christians we either grow or dry up. Do you think this is true and if so why?

Day 79—Going After It

Spiritual growth is something you must go after. The following are four keys to growth.

1. *Make a Decision to Grow.* Very seldom does any significant growth occur without this decision. Read Philippians 3:7–12. What is Paul's attitude toward growth? Notice especially vv10 and 12. How are you answering this question right now: "In my own life, what am I willing to give up in order to grow"?

2. *Concentrate on Specifics.* Change takes place not in the vague or general but in the specific. "I want to be like Jesus." Okay! But how?

3. *Push Yourself to Grow.* We need to be so willing to put ourselves in situations where we must grow and where we must depend on God for his help. Read 1 Timothy 4:7. Why is the word "train" an important word here? When an athlete trains what does he do? What are some ways you can be pushing yourself to grow right now? (Think about areas where growth does not at all come naturally for you.)

4. *Have a Vision for What You Can Become.* Read 2 Peter 1:3–11 and realize that you can become everything that Jesus would have you to become. What is the promise that we have in v3? End your time today by reading Philippians 1:6.

Day 80—Not Growing? Take Inventory

1. If we are not growing then what does that mean? Read each of the following passages and complete this statement for each:

If I am not growing then it may mean that...

a.) John 12:24
b.) Ephesians 4:15
c.) Philippians 3:12–14
d.) Hebrews 12:1–2
e.) 1 Corinthians 9:19–23

2. Which of these passages most describes something that is holding growth back from you? Share your conviction with someone today.

(Note: Look ahead to Day 85 in your study and make sure you can get one of the items mentioned in point No. 1 by the time you reach this point in your study.)

Day 81—Knowing God's Will

All of us make plans. Hopefully we have some dreams for our lives, some goals. How can we know whether or not we're doing God's will? How can we know that decisions we are making align with God's will? The next four studies will deal with this topic.

1. Read Romans 12:1–2. What does this passage teach about knowing God's will? The word here for transformed is the word "metamorphosis." The usage of this word implies a radical or drastic kind of change. What are some ways in which God has had to radically change you in order to make known his will to you?

2. Read 1 Thessalonians 5:16–17. Sometimes God's will is difficult to discover in our lives but always we know some right things to do. It is always right to be joyful, to pray continually and to give thanks. Think back over the last week. Are there some times when this

was not your attitude? Why will this attitude help you see other aspects of God's will?

3. Read Ephesians 5:8–17. How does tolerating darkness in our lives keep us from knowing God's will? Why are we being foolish?

4. Read Philippians 1:9–11. If we want to discern what is best, then we must be letting our love abound more and more. So often, when we are struggling, when we have doubts or questions, when we don't know what God is trying to say to us, the best thing we can do is look for a way to serve someone. In what ways can your love abounding more and more?

Day 82—The Importance of Plans
1. Read Psalm 20:1–5. From v4 we can draw two conclusions:
   a.) God wants his people to have plans, and
   b.) when his people have godly plans, he wants to bless those plans.

2. Why do you think that many religious people have no real plans for their spiritual development, but at the same time have various plans for other aspects of their lives?

3. If we don't have plans, then obviously God cannot make those plans succeed. It is, of course, possible to over-plan or to plan so much you can't possibly get to it all. But we all need plans—plans that God can bless. Write down elements in your plan for future growth in God's Kingdom.

Day 83—The Desires of Your Heart
1. Psalm 37:1–11. Look especially at v4 and make a list of the desires of your heart that you know are God's desires as well.

2. Look at v5. Can you give some specific examples of how you need "to commit your way to the Lord." What is the promise made to you in v6?

3. Look at v8. What kind of problems do you get into if you begin to "fret" over your plans?

4. Describe the difference you want your faith to make in your life—as you make decisions and go through trials.

Day 84—Your Heart at Peace
1. Read Philippians 4:4–7. What words do you read here that relate to your life?

2. What is Paul saying that we can do once we have committed our present and our future to God? What is he saying God will do for us once we have made that commitment?

3. As you seek to grow and please God with a lifetime of service, you will be challenged. There will be hardships. There will be pain. There will be trouble. But look at what Jesus said about this in John 16:33. Life is difficult. Right? But what else is true?

4. Read about the ultimate result of your growth as a Christian in Romans 5:1–5. In what way will our "hope" not disappoint us? Read 1 Peter 1:3–5.

Week Thirteen
HOW TO STUDY
A STUDY OF COLOSSIANS

Let the word of Christ dwell in you richly.

Colossians 3:16

As we come to the last week of this guided study, the Letter to the Colossians has been selected for in-depth study. The study you do this week will give you a vision for the kind of study you can regularly have taking other books from the Bible as the object of your study.

Day 85—Introduction & Background

1. From a study Bible, Bible dictionary or commentary read about the background of Colossians. Understand what concerns motivated Paul to write this letter.

2. Read Colossians 1:1–8 underlining key phrases as you read.

3. a) What qualities did Paul see in the lives of these Christians that caused him to be so thankful for them?
   b) Where did he see these qualities coming from?
   c) How are you showing these qualities in your relationships with others?

4. Read 1:9–14, underlining key phrases as you read.

5. a) List the things Paul was praying would be found in the lives of these disciples.
   b) What kind of life is pleasing to God in every way? Where is your heart in regard to these things?

6. What overall purpose do you think Paul had in writing what he did in the introduction to this letter (vv1–13)?

Day 86—The All-Sufficiency of Jesus

1. Read Colossians 1:15–18, underlining key phrases.

2. Knowing the Colossian Christians may be under the influence of those who have an inadequate view of Christ, what message is Paul wanting them to understand about Jesus Christ?

3. Given what Paul says here, what understandings of Jesus are totally inadequate?

4. What is the personal significance of v17 for your life? How do you share this with other people who know you?

5. Read 1:19–23, underlining key phrases.

6. a) God wants to "reconcile" all of us to himself (vv19 and 22). What does this mean God really wants from us?
   b) How does the price he was willing to pay for such reconciliation need to affect us?
   c) From v22, what impact does it have on you to know that you can stand before God through Christ "*without blemish and free from accusation*"?
   d) According to v23 what is the key to remaining in such a state?

7. Read 1:24–27 and continue in your readings to underline key phrases.

8. What impact does the idea of "*Christ in you*" have on your life?

Day 87—A Heart for Others

1. Read Colossians 1:28–2:15.

2. a) What passion did Paul have? For what goal was he giving all he had, as God blessed him?
   b) How does God want to use you in the same way?
   c) What will you do today to fulfill this passage in your life?
   d) How will you let others help you toward being "perfect in Christ"?

3. a) Paul talks in these verses about "struggling" for his brothers and sisters. What struggles will we have to willingly accept in order to help others get where they need to be?
   b) What is the secret to Paul's ability to keep up the struggle?

4. a) Read 2:6–15 and start taking careful note of the false ideas of which Paul is warning the disciples to be aware.
   b) Someone is probably telling the Colossians that they need Christ *plus* philosophy for the full life. What is Paul's answer and warning?
   c) What such philosophies are trying to influence you?

5. From vv9–15, why would you say you do not need Christ *plus* anything else to find your life?

Day 88—Watch Out for False Teaching

1. Read Colossians 2:16–23, looking for other misleading teachings that the Colossians were being tempted to fall into. Look for at least three major false teachings.

2. What do vv16–17 say to the person today who thinks we should keep the Sabbath and observe Old Testament regulations?

3. What is the basic problem with the person described in v18?

4. Does the word "asceticism" have meaning to you! If it does not, look it up in a dictionary.

5. Apparently some were teaching that asceticism was the way to spirituality—denying our bodily needs and harshly treating the body (vv20–23). What does the Bible say?

6. Why do you think people are often vulnerable to exotic teachings about how to become spiritual? What do they fail to understand about Christ?

Day 89—Off with the Old, On with the New

1. Read Colossians 3:1–17.

2. What reason does Paul give in vv1–3 for living a new and different life?

3. What things that "*belong to your earthly nature*" still need to be "put to death"? What does that language communicate to you? Dare you be that radical?

4. Of the qualities listed with which to "*clothe yourselves*" which one is most missing from your present character or lifestyle? Do you believe God can add it to your life? Do you want it? What do you plan to do? Why?

Day 90—Everyday Relationships

1. Read Colossians 3:18–4:2. Compare with Ephesians 5:21–6:9.

2. What do all these things talked about here have in common?

3. Why is it so important that these relationships we are in, usually on a daily basis, be conducted so differently?

4. How many of these are specifically addressed to you, and how can you demonstrate the spirit that Paul describes in these relationships? (Realize the master/slave directives are parallel to employer/employee or teacher/student relationships.)

5. Why does God give us instructions like this? What will be the results of obedience?

Day 91—For the Rest of Your Life
1. Read Colossians 4.

2. Earlier you studied vv2–6. Go back to your notes on Day 6 and see what you wrote down. What do you think you have learned about this in last 12 weeks?

3. Why is Epaphras a great example for us? What characterized his approach to prayer? Why is his approach to prayer often a necessary one? What are some issues in your life that require nothing less?

4. Write out v17 putting your name in where you see the name "Archippus." How would you respond to receiving such direction from an apostle. How does it make you feel?

5. This is the last day of your guided study. At this point you need to formulate plans for continuing your own personal Bible study. There are many ways for you to proceed. One suggestion is to pick a certain gospel, letter, etc., and work your way through it verse by verse. Use the type of study done in Colossians and study books like 1 John, 1 Peter or Philippians in the same way. Perhaps you want to study a certain theme in the Bible like "trust" or do some character studies of men and women in the Bible.

6. Whatever you decide to do, have a specific plan. Beware of the "lucky dip" method that involves just letting the Bible fall open somewhere each day. That may be often used but it is unproductive. Write down what you plan to study next.

As you leave this study, you should not think that you are through looking at these ideas. You will need to come back to them again and again. Many have worked through this material after being Christians and then have done it again a year or two later, finding that after a time of growth the concepts get even richer.

May God bless you in your future study of his will for your life! Make being with God every day for the rest of your life a joyful habit that you would not think of living without!

As a deer pants for streams of
water,
so my soul pants for you,
O God.
My soul thirsts for God, for the
living God.
When can I go meet with
God?

Psalm 42:1–2

Other Helpful Studies

Introduction to God

"The God who made the world and everything in it is the Lord of heaven and earth and does not live in temples built by hands. And he is not served by human hands, as if he needed anything, because he himself gives all men life and breath and everything else. From one man he made every nation of men, that they should inhabit the whole earth; and he determined the times set for them and the exact places where they should live. God did this so that men would seek him and perhaps reach out for him and find him, though he is not far from each one of us. 'For in him we live and move and have our being.' As some of your own poets have said, 'We are his offspring.'

"Therefore since we are God's offspring, we should not think that the divine being is like gold or silver or stone—an image made by man's design and skill. In the past God overlooked such ignorance, but now he commands all people everywhere to repent. For he has set a day when he will judge the world with justice by the man he has appointed. He has given proof of this to all men by raising him from the dead."

Acts 17:24–31

God first revealed himself through the creation. Therefore, many of his key features are self-evident when we look at what was created. These include his glory, his creativity, his love, his governing providence and traits of a parental figure.

The entire family of man descended from one couple and we are all God's offspring. While Scriptures apply the masculine tense to God, both man and woman were created in his image as equals.

Our world reflects the work of a designer far more than just reflecting the self-will of any particular species to survive. Believers have the privilege to choose from various models of origins in order to explain the connection of science with sacred literature. Every Christian will personally determine which model upholds the sacredness of Scripture while satisfying his or her personal faith and reason.

The Lord holds all things together in creation and weaves his own story in human history as a trail that leads us to him. This story reveals the fact that we will each stand before God and give an account of the life we were given. Our greatest reasons for confidence for on that day will be his "atoning sacrifice for our sins" and "because in this world we are like him."

INTRODUCTION: This study is limited to broad yet compelling features of God. The objective here is to see the relational aspects of God behind creation and human affairs.

1. **God's Creativity** (Genesis 1:1, 20–21, 26–27)
   a. The "heavens and the earth" (v1) reveal God's creativity as well as the creatures of the sea (v21). The massive star formations vs. the minuscule but beautiful seahorse.
   b. We were made in his image, both men and women (vv26–27).

2. **God's Glory** (Psalm 19:1–6)
   a. Creation speaks, broadcasting a story (vv1–2) that cannot be ignored (v3).
   b. What does it tell? Read the Illustration from "Octavius on God As a Glorious Parent" (at the end of this study).
   c. Creation reports of God's majestic features (vv5–6).

3. **God's Engineering** (Job 39:13–18)
   a. Consider the ostrich, lays eggs in the open ground (v14).
   b. Lacks ability or wisdom to protect young yet the species survives (vv15–17).
   c. It even thrives among competition and is not threatened by environment (v18).

4. **God's Vastness** (Psalm 8:3–5)
   a. Something happens when one considers how huge God's handiwork is (v3).
   b. Read the illustration, "From Us to the Universe" (at the end of this study).
   c. It is humbling that God cares for us like this even though we are so small (vv4–5).

5. **God's Omnipotence** (Jeremiah 31:35–36)
   a. Omnipotence = universal "power" and authority.
   b. God's purposes prevail and Israel is a perfect illustration. The order of the universe are the decree that is tied in with Israel's survival (vv35–36)
   c. Ancient Israel was a very small nation hemmed in by three larger nations (Assyria, Babylon, Egypt).
   d. The Scriptures contain a great delivery story for the underdog nation (reference of God's power for Israel. Psalm 68:34–35). The other nations tried to destroy and had sometimes collaborated against ancient Israel.
   e. This is not political validation for modern Israel, but it means God is in control.

6. **God's Providence** (Acts 17:24–31)
   a. He arranged national events showing providence (foresight, guardianship and care).
   b. Human decisions seem autonomous when they may actually be guided, allowed or pre-conceived by God (vv24–26). (Nations behave as if they control their steps.)
   c. His purpose is to have us reach out for him (vv27–31).
   d. God has his own storyline that is weaved throughout history of the nations.

7. **God's Omnipresence** (Psalm 139:7–8, Hebrews 4:13)
   a. Omnipresence = always present everywhere.
   b. The all-seeing eyes of God reveal everything, both good and bad (v13).
   c. Cannot run or hide. We will give an account to this great God (v13).

8. **God is Love** (1 John 4:7–10, 16–17)
   a. God models love through providing

the ultimate gift (vv7–10).

b. We gain confidence as we resemble him in this most important trait (vv16–17).

c. His consistent love is a selfless love, not manipulative or arbitrary. Parents influence someone's view of God.

9. Additional Features

God is *light* (1 John 1:5–7), *kind* and *stern* (Romans 11:22), a *consuming fire* and *jealous* (Deuteronomy 4:24), *merciful* (Deuteronomy 4:31), a *righteous judge* (Psalm 7:11), and he is *just* (2 Thessalonians 1:6).

CONCLUSIONS: God has made it clear that he wants to be known. State your own conclusions about these amazing traits. What do you think and feel about God?

Illustration:
Octavius on God As a Glorious Parent

"Now, if entering a house you found everything well arranged and adorned, you would surely believe that a master governed the house. You would also recognize that the master was greater than all the things in the house. Therefore, when you look upon the house of the universe—the heavens and the earth, its laws, and its order—believe that there is a Lord and Parent of the universe far more glorious than the stars themselves and the other parts of the universe."

(Octavius, second century, Rome)

Illustration:
From Us to the Universe

– If metropolitan Chicago was leveled and each of Earth's six billion inhabitants was given two square yards in this city there would be room to spare. We are but a tiny part of our planet.

– Approximately one million Earths would fit within the mass of our sun. The sun is just one of a 100 billion stars in our small-to-average-sized galaxy.

– The next closest galaxy (Andromeda) would take 2,200,000 years for our light to reach.

– Besides asking how many grains of sand in the universe, we can ask, "How many universes in a grain of sand?" In 2002, the famous Hubble Space Telescope took a million-second core sample of "empty" space—equivalent to looking through a grain of sand at the end of your outstretched arm—and saw 10,000 galaxies. Extrapolated to the rest of the sky, this number implies 250 billion galaxies. The previous estimate was 10 billion galaxies. Scientists wonder if there is even an edge to the universe or if it is expanding without limit.

– One translation of Isaiah 66:1–2 reads, "I live in heaven; it is my throne; I made the earth. It's a footstool before My throne. I am bigger than you are even capable of thinking. I am God."

Steve Staten
Chicago, Illinois

To learn more abou the nature of Christ read *In Christ,* by John M. Oakes

Evidences for Jesus

1. Matthew 16:13
   A. Who do you personally say Jesus is?
   B. Jesus claimed to be the Son of God (John 5:24; 8:23–24; 10:30; 14:6–7).
   C. What are the possibilities? Was that claim true or false?
      1) If false, then Jesus either
         a) Was a mythical character that didn't exist: Legend.
         b) Knew that his claims were false: Liar.
         c) He didn't know his claims were false: Lunatic.
      2) If true, then Jesus is Lord.
      3) Comments:
         a) Extra-biblical manuscripts prove Jesus to be a historical figure, therefore he was not a legend.
         b) Jesus' teachings and the impact of his life make it impossible to entertain the possibility that Jesus was either a liar or lunatic. Would the greatest ethical teachings in the world have come from a liar or from a lunatic?
         c) We must not conclude that Jesus was simply a good moral teacher. That option is not open to us, because it would mean Jesus lied when he claimed to be the Son of God.
         d) There is strong evidence to support the fact that Jesus is clearly Lord, the Son of God as he claimed. Let's look at the evidence.

2. Evidences
   A. Miracles: Attested to by numerous eyewitnesses (John 20:30–31).
   B. Prophecies fulfilled:
      1) Born of a virgin: Isaiah 7:14; Matthew 1:18, 24, 25
      2) House of David: Jeremiah 23:5; Luke 3:23, 31
      3) Born in Bethlehem: Micah 5:2; Matthew 2:1
      4) Ministry to begin in Galilee: Isaiah 9:1; Matthew 4:12–13, 17
      5) Betrayed by a friend: Psalm 41:9; Matthew 10:4; Matthew 26:49–50
      6) Sold for 30 pieces of silver: Zechariah 11:12; Matthew 26:15
      7) Wounded and bruised: Isaiah 53:5; Matthew 27:26
      8) Bones not broken: Psalm 34:20; John 19:32–33
      9) Crucified with thieves: Isaiah 53:12; Matthew 27:38
      10) Resurrection: Ps. 16:10; Acts 2:31
      11) There are more than 400 Messianic prophecies. Jesus fulfills them all! The probability that any man might have lived and fulfilled just 8 prophecies is 1 in 10 to the 17th power or 1 in 100,000,000,000,000,000.
   C. Jesus' life and teaching: His teachings surpass human wisdom while his life exemplifies them perfectly (John 7:17).
   D. The Resurrection: This is perhaps the most convincing of all the evidences. Was Jesus raised from the dead? The response is critically important. Read 1 Corinthians 15:12–19.
      1) The Prediction: Matthew 27:62–66. Jesus' predictions about his own resurrection were so well known that guards were posted at the tomb. This raised the question: Did he really die? Perhaps he passed out on the cross and was later revived.
      2) The Death: John 19:31–34.

Professional executioners would not make such a basic error as to think a live person was dead. Jesus was clearly dead. But perhaps they visited the wrong tomb and mistakenly thought he was raised.

3) The Wrong Tomb
   a) The tomb was near the cross: John 19:38–42.
   b) Mary saw where he was buried. Pilate knew where to send the guards: Matthew 27:61–66. They didn't visit the wrong tomb. So let's visit the tomb.
4) The Empty Tomb: Matthew 28:11–15. Was the tomb empty? If not, the Jews would have produced the body. The fact that they tried to explain away the empty tomb shows that it was empty. So, was the body stolen as they claimed?
5) The Stolen Body: It would have been incredibly difficult for anyone to steal the body considering the huge stone and the Roman guards in front of the tomb. There are two possibilities: Someone other than the disciples stole the body; therefore, the disciples were deceived and wistfully hallucinated the risen Christ. OR the disciples stole the body and hoaxed the resurrection.
   a) Someone other than the disciples stole the body. John 20:19–29. Disciples are scared and hiding, having earlier fled at Jesus' arrest. Was this a mass hallucination? Thomas, the skeptic, touched Jesus. This was no hallucination to Thomas. But perhaps the resurrection was all a hoax, the second possibility...
   b) The disciples stole the body. Acts 4:12–13. Remember the cowardly disciples? (Matthew 26:56). Peter who denied Jesus? They are now men of remarkable courage. Something has happened. In fact, according to early church history, each of the disciples died a martyr's death, except John:

Peter—crucified head downward
Thomas—speared to death
James—beheaded by Herod (Acts 12:1–2)
Matthew—martyred
Andrew—crucified
James—crucified
Philip—martyred
Jude—shot with arrows
Simon the Zealot—crucified
Bartholomew—flogged to death
Matthias—axed to death

   Why did these men endure such atrocities? Who would suffer and die for a lie that gains them nothing? When men are all alone and under pressure, they crack. These men did not. Why not?

6) These men had seen Jesus raised from the dead: 1 Corinthians 15:1–6. In fact, over 500 people at once saw the resurrected Jesus.
   Indeed, Jesus has been raised. The proof is logical and overwhelming.

3. Conclusion: Christianity is true and reasonable: Acts 26:24–29. Jesus is the Son of God! Now what remains is to make the decision to follow him.

Man's Wisdom / God's Wisdom

1. Everyone on earth is asking the question in one form or another: How Can I Really Live?

2. The Bible says there are two ways to answer that:

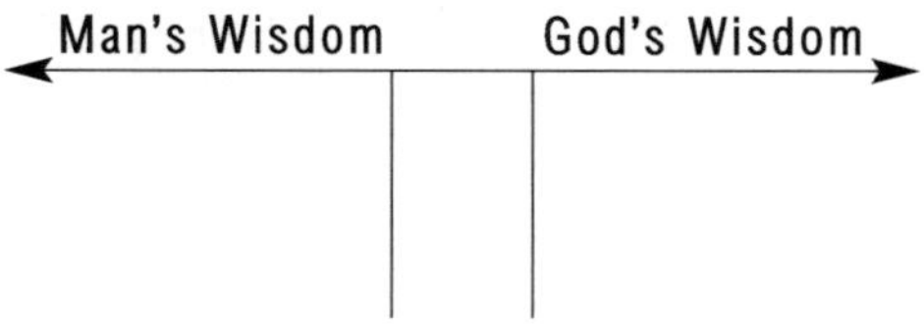

1 Corinthians 1:18-20

A. Where does the cross belong? Wisdom of man or wisdom of God?
B. How does man, in his wisdom, view the cross?
C. How does God, in his wisdom, view all of man's wisdom?
D. If I think you are a fool and you think I am a fool, what will be true about our relationship?
E. What is the relationship then between the wisdom of man and the wisdom of God? We are dealing with two things going in opposite directions, two things totally opposed to one another. (See James 4:4.)

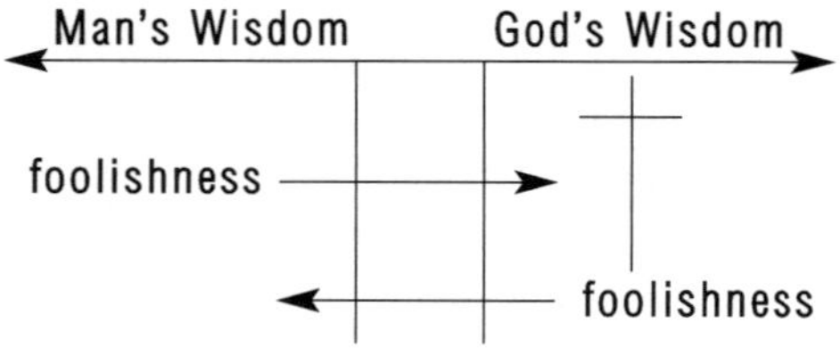

1 Corinthians 3:18-20

F. What does "he must become a 'fool,' and he can become wise" mean?
G. Again, what is the strong message? God's wisdom and man's are total opposites.
H. You cannot straddle the fence. The gulf is too wide.

Matthew 16:13-23

I. What does "Peter rebuked Jesus" mean?
J. What was Jesus' response?
K. Where does "man's wisdom" really come from? Satan. Jesus is clear. No wonder it is the opposite of God's wisdom.

L. Important question: What is man's wisdom about "how to really live"? What do you learn from television, from the streets, from movies, from the talk shows? What is the world telling us we must do to really find life? "Look out for number one." "Get what you want." "Get the power, the pleasure, the control you want." "Get the money." "Protect yourself." "Guard your rights." "Maintain your independence." "Get a good lawyer." Etc.

What then is at the center of man's wisdom?

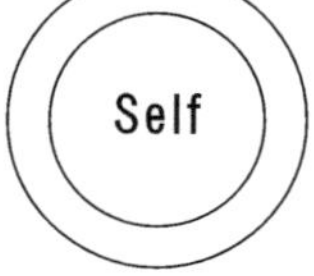

3. Matthew 16:24-26
What is Jesus' message? What is his wisdom about how to really live? Just the opposite of the world's message. Definitely a radical message.
   A. Deny self? What does this mean?
      1) *Arneomai* in Greek means to "disown." A strong word. What does it mean if you disown your son or daughter? How much support? How many letters. The word here is an usually strong form of this verb. Aparneomai. The "ap" prefix means utterly.
      2) Jesus is saying we have all lived on man's side. We have all put self at the center. Now we need to totally disown that old person and turn to an opposite way of living.
   B. "Take up the cross." What does this mean. What were crosses for? Death. Put to death the old life. Don't defend it. Don't support it. Put it to death.
   C. "Follow me." Why is it impossible to do this without doing the things mentioned above. Note: It is impossible to follow Jesus without meeting his conditions of discipleship.
   D. What does Jesus say the bottom line will be for people who live on man's side? He who "saves" his life (guards it and protects it) will lose it.
   E. What is the bottom line for those foolish people who "lose their lives for his sake"? They will find their lives. They will really live. Jesus' own life, death and resurrection is proof of what he taught. This is how to find life.

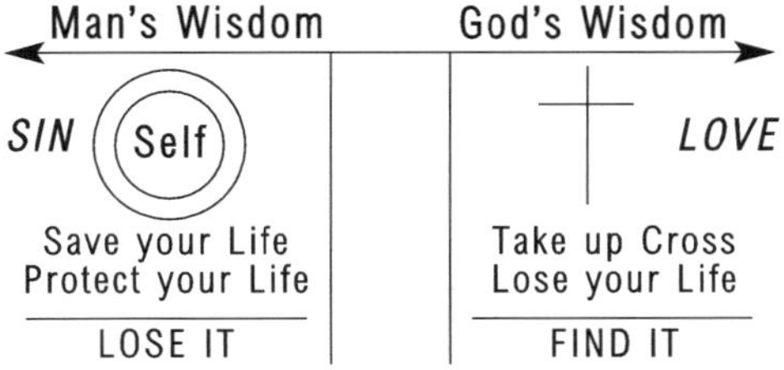

4. Additional thoughts
   A. What is everything on the left side of the diagram called? Sin.
   B. What is everything on the right side called? Love. Love for God and love for others. Living for God and living for others.
   C. How have you lived according to man's wisdom? What are your greatest tendencies in this direction?
   D. When did you make the decision to renounce man's wisdom and commit yourself to following God's plan?
   E. Which side was Peter on? Which side would Jesus say you are on? Which do you want to be on?

5. Later, you can look at the following diagram and show that repentance and baptism bring forgiveness of all of man's sin (left side of the diagram) and power through the Holy Spirit to live out God's plan (right side of the diagram.)

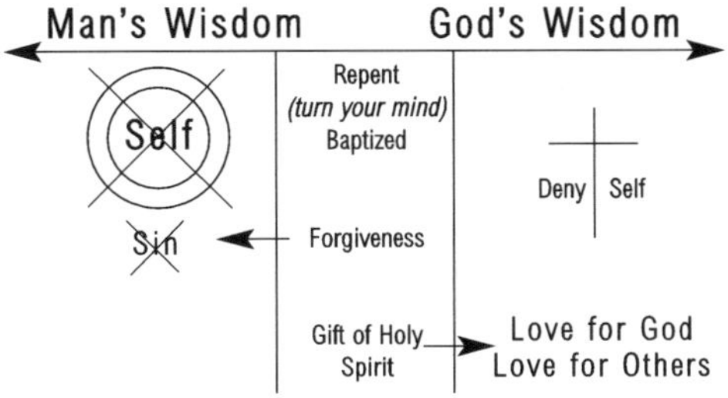

NOTE: See completed diagram on the following pages.

How Can I Really Live?

Satan → WORLD'S WISDOM

foolish →

Get what you want.
Get what you need.
Protect what is yours.
Hold on to what is yours. (Get a good lawyer!)
Look out for "Number One."
Have It your way.
Maintain independence.

Can be very religious and still on this side.
(Matthew 15: 7-9)

Self

SAVE YOUR LIFE
LOSE IT

This side: What the Bible calls "Sin"

GOD'S WISDOM

← foolish

Deny Yourself
(Greek: utterly disown)

Take Up the Cross
(death to old self)

Follow Me

God

LOSE YOUR LIFE "FOR MY SAKE"
FIND IT

This side: What the Bible calls "Love"

Loving God
Loving Others
(Matthew 22:36-40)

How have you lived according to man's wisdom? What are your greatest tendencies in this direction? When did you make the decision to renounce man's wisdom and commit to following God's plan? Which side was Peter on? Which side would Jesus say you are on? Which do you want to be on?

How Can I Really Live?

Satan

WORLD'S WISDOM

GOD'S WISDOM

foolish

Acts 2:38

Repentance (Greek metanoia): "turn the mind." Turn away from the world's wisdom. Disown your old life.

Baptism – Put the old life to death.

Receive the forgiveness of sin for the life you lived over here.

Receive the Hold Spirit for the power to live the new life.

Get what you w
Get what you ne
Protect what is yo
Hold on to what is yours.
...!)
Look out for "Numb
Have It your w
Maintain indepen

Can be very religious and st
(Matthew 15: 7

Deny Yourself
k: utterly disown)

ke Up the Cross
eath to old self)

Follow Me

Self

God

SAVE YOUR L

LOSE IT

LIFE "FOR MY SAKE"

FIND IT

This side: What the Bible calls "Sin"

This side: What the Bible calls "Love"

Loving God
Loving Others
(Matthew 22:36-40)

The Grace of God

1. **2 Corinthians 5:10**—Do you feel confident about standing before the judgment seat of Christ? Why or why not? In this study we will learn how we can be completely confident about standing before God.

2. There are more than 110 specific references to the grace of God in the New Testament and many other times when the concept is alluded to. Grace is a major biblical theme.
   - A. **Acts 14:26**—What does "the grace of God" mean to you?
   - B. **Acts 20:24**—Why was the message of Jesus called "the gospel of God's grace"?

3. There are two basic ways that people could be saved (be accepted by God):
   - **A. Works model**—Earning our place with God by doing all the right things.
     - 1) Here the standard is perfection.
       - a) **James 2:10**—To even fail at one point is to be guilty of all. One sin would keep one from being saved by works.
       - b) **Galatians 5:3**—Written to those taking certain works and making them the standard for salvation.
       - c) **Romans 3:23**—Based on the works model everyone falls short, and no one will be right with God.
     - 2) If God made anything less than perfection acceptable, where do you think he should draw the line? 95? 90? 80? 65? How fair would God be to save the person who made a 65 on the morality scale and condemn the person just a point behind at 64? God can have only one performance standard—perfection!
   - **B. Grace model**—God giving us salvation as a gift that we have not earned and do not deserve.
     - 1) Here your perfection or performance is not the issue. The issue is what Christ has done.
       - a) **Romans 3:22–25a**—"Justified" (declared not guilty) freely by his grace
       - b) **Romans 4:4–8**—Why is the person who comes to Christ totally saved? (Because the righteousness of Christ is "credited" to his or her account.)
       - c) **Colossians 1:21–23**—How does God view a person who has been reconciled to him through Christ? Holy, without blemish and free from accusation! Is such a one really without blemish? Why does God view him or her this way?
     - 2) This grace was made available only because Jesus was willing to pay the enormous price that had to be paid for sin.
       - a) **2 Corinthians 8:9**—He became poor for our sakes.
       - b) **Hebrews 2:9**—He experienced death for all men.
       - c) **1 Peter 1:18–19**—We are redeemed, not with perishable things, but with the precious blood of Christ.
       - d) **1 John 4:8–10**—What does all this mean? God loves us! He loved us so much he sent Jesus

to die for our sins so we might be saved by grace!

4. If salvation is not by works but by grace, is everyone saved?
   A. **Hebrews 2:9**—Who did Jesus die for?
   B. **1 Timothy 2:3–5**—How many does God want saved?
   C. **2 Thessalonians 1:6–10**—Are all people going to be saved? If Jesus died for all and wants to give grace to all but not all are going to be saved, what does that tell us?
   We must accept his offer. We must receive the pardon. We must say "Yes, I want the relationship with God that comes by grace."
   Illustration: A pardon that is not accepted does not become a pardon.
   D. **Acts 2:36–39**
   How did Peter tell his listeners to put their faith in Christ and accept the grace of God?
      1) Repentance—turning to Christ and away from the world.
      2) Baptism—giving God your old life to bury, so by grace he can raise up a new life.
   What gifts did he promise that God would freely give?
      3) Forgiveness of sins—because we have trusted in what Jesus did.
      4) The Holy Spirit—to help us live the new life.
   E. **Romans 1:5; Galatians 5:6**—Biblical faith is never alone. What always goes with it? Is it possible to trust Christ and not obey him?

5. Who can be ***completely confident*** about his or her salvation?
   A. The person who has accepted God's grace and puts faith in Christ just as these people did in Acts 2.
   B. The person who keeps his or her faith in Jesus and never leaves him.
   Colossians 1:22–23; Hebrews 3:14
   Confidence rests on what Jesus has done. If we are responding in faith to him, it is his work that saves us—not our own performance. Our performance will vary. His work of salvation never does. He redeems us. He justifies us. He reconciles us. We are secure.

6. What is the only right response to "salvation by grace?"
   A. **1 John 3:1**—Rejoicing and amazement
   B. **1 Corinthians 15:9–10**—Total commitment to Jesus

7. Have you accepted God's grace? Are you saved by his grace?

For more informaton about grace read *The Guilty Soul's Guide to Grace*, by Sam Laing

One Another Relationships

Gordon Ferguson, McKinney, Texas

Introduction

1. The New Testament is full of passages which regulate the Christian's attitudes and behavior toward others in the Body of Christ.

2. These teachings come in many forms, and all of these forms are equally valid and helpful.

3. However, the phrases "one another" and "each other" are found numerous times in the context of Christian relationships, and in order to narrow down the topic into manageable portions, we are going to examine only the passages which contain these specific phrases.

4. As we will see, the religion of Jesus Christ is definitely a one-another religion.

5. First, these passages will be written out as they appear chronologically in the N.T.

6. Second, they will be outlined according to subject into these three categories: the atmosphere of peace; the attitudes of love; and the actions of encouragement.

The N.T. Passages in Chronological Order

Mark 9:50—"Salt is good, but if it loses its saltiness, how can you make it salty again? Have salt in yourselves, and be at peace with each other."

John 13:34—"A new command I give you: Love one another. As I have loved you, so you must love one another."

John 13:35—"By this all men will know that you are my disciples, if you love one another."

John 15:12—"My command is this: Love each other as I have loved you."

John 15:17—"This is my command: Love each other."

Romans 12:10—Be devoted to one another in brotherly love. Honor one another above yourselves.

Romans 12:16—Live in harmony with one another. Do not be proud, but be willing to associate with people of low position. Do not be conceited.

Romans 13:8—Let no debt remain outstanding, except the continuing debt to love one another, for he who loves his fellowman has fulfilled the law.

Romans 14:13—Therefore let us stop passing judgment on one another. Instead, make up your mind not to put any stumbling block or obstacle in your brother's way.

Romans 15:7—Accept one another, then, just as Christ accepted you, in order to bring praise to God.

Romans 15:14—I myself am convinced, my brothers, that you yourselves are full of goodness, complete in knowledge and competent to instruct one another.

Romans 16:16—Greet one another with a holy kiss. All the churches of Christ send greetings.

1 Cor. 1:10—I appeal to you, brothers, in the name of our Lord Jesus Christ, that all of you agree with one another so that there may be no divisions among you and that you may be perfectly united in mind and thought.

1 Cor. 7:5—Do not deprive each other except by mutual consent and for a time, so that you may devote yourselves to prayer. Then come together again so that Satan will not tempt you because of your lack of self-control.

1 Cor. 11:33—So then, my brothers, when you come together to eat, wait for each other.

1 Cor. 12:25—so that there should be no division in the body, but that its parts should have equal concern for each other.

1 Cor. 16:20—All the brothers here send you greetings. Greet one another with a holy kiss.

2 Cor. 13:12—Greet one another with a holy kiss.

Gal. 5:13—You, my brothers, were called to be free. But do not use your freedom to indulge the sinful nature; rather, serve one another in love.

Gal. 5:15—If you keep on biting and devouring each other, watch out or you will be destroyed by each other.

Gal. 5:26—Let us not become conceited, provoking and envying each other.

Eph. 4:2—Be completely humble and gentle; be patient, bearing with one another in love.

Eph. 4:32—Be kind and compassionate to one another, forgiving each other, just as in Christ God forgave you.

Eph. 5:19—Speak to one another with psalms, hymns and spiritual songs. Sing and make music in your heart to the Lord,

Eph .5:21—Submit to one another out of reverence for Christ.

Phil. 4:2—I plead with Euodia and I plead with Syntyche to agree with each other in the Lord.

Col. 3:9—Do not lie to each other, since you have taken off your old self with its practices

Col 3:13—Bear with each other and forgive whatever grievances you may have against one another. Forgive as the Lord forgave you.

Col 3:16—Let the word of Christ dwell in you richly as you teach and admonish one another with all wisdom, and as you sing psalms, hymns and spiritual songs with gratitude in your hearts to God.

1 Thes. 3:12—May the Lord make your love increase and overflow for each other and for everyone else, just as ours does for you.

1 Thes. 4:9—Now about brotherly love we do not need to write to you, for you yourselves have been taught by God to love each other.

1 Thes. 4:18—Therefore encourage each other with these words.

1 Thes. 5:11—Therefore encourage one another and build each other up, just as in fact you are doing.

1 Thes. 5:13—Hold them in the highest regard in love because of their work. Live in peace with each other.

1 Thes 5:15—Make sure that nobody pays back wrong for wrong, but always try to be kind to each other and to everyone else.

2 Thes. 1:3—We ought always to thank God for you, brothers, and rightly so, because your faith is growing more and more, and the love every one of you has for each other is increasing.

Hebrews 3:13—But encourage one another daily, as long as it is called Today, so that none of you may be hardened by sin's deceitfulness.

Hebrews 10:24—And let us consider how we may spur one another on toward love and good deeds.

Hebrews 10:25—Let us not give up meeting together, as some are in the habit of doing, but let us encourage one another—and all the more as you see the Day approaching.

Hebrews 13:1—Keep on loving each other as brothers.

James 4:11—Brothers, do not slander one another. Anyone who speaks against his brother or judges him speaks against the law and judges it. When you judge the law, you are not keeping it, but sitting in judgment on it.

James 5:9—Don't grumble against each other, brothers, or you will be judged. The Judge is standing at the door!

James 5:16—Therefore confess your sins to each other and pray for each other so that you may be healed. The prayer of a righteous man is powerful and effective.

1 Peter 1:22—Now that you have purified yourselves by obeying the truth so that you have sincere love for your brothers, love one another deeply, from the heart.

1 Peter 3:8—Finally, all of you, live in harmony with one another; be sympathetic, love as brothers, be compassionate and humble.

1 Peter 4:8—Above all, love each other deeply, because love covers over a multitude of sins.

1 Peter 4:9—Offer hospitality to one another without grumbling.

1 Peter 5:5—Young men, in the same way be submissive to those who are older. All of you, clothe yourselves with humility toward one another, because, "God opposes the proud but gives grace to the humble."

1 Peter 5:14—Greet one another with a kiss of love. Peace to all of you who are in Christ.

1 John 1:7—But if we walk in the light, as he is in the light, we have fellowship with one another, and the blood of Jesus, his Son, purifies us from all sin.

1 John 3:11—This is the message you heard from the beginning: We should love one another.

1 John 3:23—And this is his command: to believe in the name of his Son, Jesus Christ, and to love one another as he commanded us.

1 John 4:7—Dear friends, let us love one another, for love comes from God. Everyone who loves has been born of God and knows God.

1 John 4:11—Dear friends, since God so loved us, we also ought to love one another.

1 John 4:12—No one has ever seen God; but if we love one another, God lives in us and his love is made complete in us.

2 John 1:5—And now, dear lady, I am not writing you a new command but one we have had from the beginning. I ask that we love one another.

I. The Atmosphere of Peace

A. The commands:

1. Be at peace.
   a. Mark 9:50—"Salt is good, but if it loses its saltiness, how can you make it salty again? Have salt in yourselves, and be at peace with each other."
   b. 1 Thes. 5:13—Hold them in the highest regard in love because of their work. Live in peace with each other.
2. Live in harmony.
   a. Rom. 12:16—Live in harmony with one another. Do not be proud, but be willing to associate with people of low position. Do not be conceited.
   b. 1 Pet. 3:8—Finally, all of you, live in harmony with one another; be sympathetic, love as brothers, be compassionate and humble.

B. The attitudes:

1. Negatives to avoid.
   a. Judgmental: Rom.14:13—Therefore let us stop passing judgment on one another. Instead, make up your mind not to put any stumbling block or obstacle in your brother's way.
   b. Conceited and envious: Gal. 5:26—Let us not become conceit-

ed, provoking and envying each other.

2. Positives to pursue.
   a. Submissiveness: Eph. 5:21—Submit to one another out of reverence for Christ.
   b. Humility: 1 Pet. 5:5—Young men, in the same way be submissive to those who are older. All of you, clothe yourselves with humility toward one another, because, "God opposes the proud but gives grace to the humble."

C. The actions:

1. Negatives to avoid.
   a. Depriving one's mate of the sexual relationship: 1 Cor. 7:5—Do not deprive each other except by mutual consent and for a time, so that you may devote yourselves to prayer. Then come together again so that Satan will not tempt you because of your lack of self-control.
   b. Destroying of each other: Gal. 5:15—If you keep on biting and devouring each other, watch out, or you will be destroyed by each other.
   c. Lying: Col. 3:9—Do not lie to each other, since you have taken off your old self with its practices.
   d. Slander and grumbling: James 4:11, 5:9—Brothers, do not slander one another. Anyone who speaks against his brother or judges him speaks against the law and judges it. When you judge the law, you are not keeping it, but sitting in judgment on it. / Don't grumble against each other, brothers, or you will be judged. The Judge is standing at the door!

2. Positives to pursue.
   a. Agree with each other:1 Cor. 1:10; Phil. 4:2—I appeal to you, brothers, in the name of our Lord Jesus Christ, that all of you agree with one another so that there may be no divisions among you and that you may be perfectly united in mind and thought. / I plead with Euodia and I plead with Syntyche to agree with each other in the Lord.
   b. Bear with each other: Col. 3:13—Bear with each other and forgive whatever grievances you may have against one another. Forgive as the Lord forgave you.
   c. Fellowship with one another: 1 John 17—But if we walk in the light, as he is in the light, we have fellowship with one another, and the blood of Jesus, his Son, purifies us from all sin.

II. The Attitudes of Love

A. Love's commitment.

1. Seen in its devotion: Rom. 12:10—Be devoted to one another in brotherly love. Honor one another above yourselves.
2. Seen in its description. (From *agape* unless otherwise noted.)
   a. The command: John 13:34—A new command I give you: Love one another. As I have loved you, so you must love one another. (See also John 15:17; 1 John 3:11, 3:23; 4:7; 2 John 1:5.)
   b. The extent:
      (1)To increase and overflow: 1 Thes. 3:12—May the Lord make your love increase and overflow for each other and for

everyone else, just as ours does for you. (See also 2 Thes. 1:3.)

(2) To come deeply from the heart: 1 Pet. 1:22—Now that you have purified yourselves by obeying the truth so that you have sincere love (*phileo*) for your brothers, love one another deeply, from the heart. (See also 1 Pet. 4:8.)

c. The obligation:

(1) A continuing debt: Rom. 13:8—Let no debt remain outstanding, except the continuing debt to love one another, for he who loves his fellowman has fulfilled the law.

(2) As taught by God: 1 Thes. 4:9—Now about brotherly love (phileo) we do not need to write to you, for you yourselves have been taught by God to love each other.

(3) To keep on loving: Heb. 13:1—Keep on loving (*phileo*) each other as brothers.

(4) Because God first loved us: 1 John 4:11—Dear friends, since God so loved us, we also ought to love one another.

d. The demonstration:

(1) That we are his disciples: John. 13:35—By this all men will know that you are my disciples, if you love one another

(2) That men might see God in us: 1 John. 4:12—No one has ever seen God; but if we love one another, God lives in us and his love is made complete in us.

B. Love's respect.

1. Shown by honoring: Rom. 12:10—Be devoted to one another in brotherly love (*phileo*). Honor one another above yourselves.
2. Shown by accepting: Rom. 15:7—Accept one another, then, just as Christ accepted you, in order to bring praise to God.
3. Shown by equal concern: 1 Cor. 12:25—so that there should be no division in the body, but that its parts should have equal concern for each other.

C. Love's mercy.

1. Shown by compassion: Eph. 4:32—Be kind and compassionate to one another, forgiving each other, just as in Christ God forgave you.
2. Shown by kindness: 1 Thes. 5:15—Make sure that nobody pays back wrong for wrong, but always try to be kind to each other and to everyone else. (See also Eph. 4:32.)
3. Shown by forgiveness: Col. 3:13—Bear with each other and forgive whatever grievances you may have against one another. Forgive as the Lord forgave you. (See also Eph. 4:32.)

III. The Actions of Encouragement

A. Instructing one another.

1. Competency to counsel: Rom. 15:14—I myself am convinced, my brothers, that you yourselves are full of goodness, complete in knowledge and competent to instruct one another
2. Communicated in singing: Eph. 5:19—Speak to one another with psalms, hymns and spiritual songs. Sing and make music in your heart to the Lord.
3. Carried out in wisdom given by God: Col. 3:16—Let the word of Christ dwell in you richly as you teach and

admonish one another with all wisdom, and as you sing psalms, hymns and spiritual songs with gratitude in your hearts to God.

B. Serving one another.
   1. Freedom to serve: Gal. 5:13—You, my brothers, were called to be free. But do not use your freedom to indulge the sinful nature; rather, serve one another in love.
   2. In hospitality.
      a. By waiting and sharing: 1 Cor. 11:33—So then, my brothers, when you come together to eat, wait for each other.
      b. Without grumbling: 1 Pet. 4:9—Offer hospitality to one another without grumbling.

C. Encouraging one another.
   1. The specific commands for it.
      a. Use God's promises: 1 Thes. 4:18—Therefore encourage each other with these words.
      b. Build up one another: 1 Thes. 5:11—Therefore encourage one another and build each other up, just as in fact you are doing.
      c. Make it daily: Heb. 3:13—But encourage one another daily, as long as it is called Today, so that none of you may be hardened by sin's deceitfulness.
      d. Encourage to give up no meetings: Heb. 10:25—Let us not give up meeting together, as some are in the habit of doing, but let us encourage one another—and all the more as you see the Day approaching.
   2. The warmth in it. Rom. 16:16—Greet one another with a holy kiss. All the churches of Christ send greetings. (See also 1 Cor. 16:20; 2 Cor. 13:12; 1 Pet. 5:14.)
   3. The challenge of it. Heb. 10:24—And let us consider how we may spur one another on toward love and good deeds.
   4. The healing from it. James 5:16—Therefore confess your sins to each other and pray for each other so that you may be healed. The prayer of a righteous man is powerful and effective.

For more informaton about love read *Love One Another—The Importance and Power of Christian Relationships*, by Gordon Ferguson

Character Studies for Teens

These studies are designed to help teens have a good understanding of God and his love and to encourge them to imitate God's qualities. In addition, the studies can help them to see their need for Jesus and his grace, since it is impossible to live these qualities out to perfection. Understanding their inadequacy in living these out can lead to a felt need and deep appreciation for God's grace. This will lead to an even deeper understanding of who he is, how he fits into their lives...and hopefully a desire to live for him in reponse.

It is our prayer that, while there is no single, guaranteed formula for studying with teenagers, these character studies will provide extra help for tailoring your studies to meet the needs of each individual teen.

Phil and Kris Arsenault
Boston, Massachusetts

How to Use the Character Studies

The purpose is to teach the teenagers about God and his character and to motivate them to become more like him in their character.

In studying with the teenager, it is essential that you, as a leader, allow the teenager to answer the questions. Draw their hearts out by allowing them to respond (Proverbs 20:5). After they have responded, add what you see is also important and continue to ask stimulating questions to be sure they understand. Have a conviction that shallow and generic responses are unacceptable. When you ask a question, an example of a shallow response is, "I don't know the answer." Ask them if they would like to know, and help them search for the answer. Examples of generic responses are "I need to obey," "Because God says so," "The Bible," etc. Ask them why they need to obey, why God says so, and continue to ask these types of questions until you have truly drawn their hearts out. Help them to see that a relationship with God is not knowing the right information or doing things "because I have to." Rather, out of a sincerely loving relationship between the teen and God, they should want to do what God asks. They need to obey out of a willing spirit through an overflow of their personal love for God (Acts 13:22).

At the end of each study, we've asked that the teenager take some time at home to write what they have learned from the study. They need to bring their essay to the next study for you to read. This will assist you in determining how much the teen is really learning and how much they are connecting with God. It also helps draw out the teen's heart through their own words.

Feel free to add your own scriptures, discussion or examples to the studies to most effectively meet the needs of the teenager you are working with.

Pray at the end of each study.

Finally, believe in each teen you are studying with—even when it takes months or years for them to connect with God in a heartfelt way. God's word will not return to him empty (Isaiah 55:11), and each study will plant seeds which will help them to see how much they need God in order to take on his character.

1
Honesty

To the leader of the study:

Honesty is a critical character trait to have as a teenager. One of the tendencies in the sinful nature of a teenager is to lie. Lying manifests itself in half-truths, exaggeration and deceit. The goal of this study is to free teens from the trap of lying and to help them see that honesty is absolutely God's way.

The more open you are about your life, the more open the teenager will be.

Intro

Ask:

1.) Why do teens lie?

Some answers:

a.) afraid of getting in trouble

b.) want to look good in front of others

c.) ashamed and embarrassed about something—Leader of the study should share some lies they have told and why they told them—even from their teen years.

2.) Who do teens lie to?
   a.) authority figures (parents, teachers, ministry leaders, etc.)
   b.) friends
   c.) siblings

3.) What do they lie about?
   a.) performance (i.e., report cards, chores, Bible reading, sports performance, homework, etc.)
   b.) treatment of others

• The goal of this study is to get you to see that honesty is what God wants from you and that when you are honest, you are like God.

The Scriptures

Psalm 139:1–18, 23–24

Name some different things God knows about you.

Why does it make sense to be honest all the time?
   a.) God knows and sees when we even just think about lying.
   b.) God knows and sees when we tell half-truths, when we exaggerate, when we're deceitful and when we blatantly lie.

• *Bottom line:* God knows everything about us. Lying to others instantly leads to lying to ourselves and ultimately, lying to God.

John 8:44

What can you learn from this scripture?
   a.) Lying is Satan's language.
   b.) Satan is the father of lies.

Bottom line: Satan is behind every lie.

Mark 7:22

How would you define "deceit"?
   a.) shading the truth
   b.) not telling the whole truth, usually to make yourself or a situation look better
   c.) not saying what you are really thinking, not being open (giving answers like "Fine," "okay," or "I don't know" when you know there's more in your heart than those)

• *Bottom line:* Saying what you are really thinking is very important because that's the only way you can get the spiritual help you need to be able to change your heart.

Personal Heart-Check Questions

1.) When are you most tempted to lie?
2.) Are you willing to make honesty your goal?

Practical Applications

James 5:16

When you lie:
   a.) Confess it to the person you lied to.
   b.) Confess it to your parent(s) and/or teen leader.
   c.) Tell them that you are sorry and you want to change.
   d.) Then, go on your way happily and joyfully because you did what was right before God.

Please take some time to write about what you've learned from this study, some things you have done or will do differently, and how all this will help you be a disciple someday or how it will help you be a better disciple if you already are one.

2
Humility

To the leader of the study:

Humility is essential in beginning and maintaining a relationship with God. Pride, the opposite of humility, is often difficult to see in oneself and difficult to define in one's character. It can be described as stubbornness toward God and his word and others, or as independence from God or others.

Try to use specific examples of interactions you've observed between the teenager and others that show a lack of humility and share from your own life as well.

Intro

1.) What is pride?
- a.) being stubborn
- b.) thinking you are better than others or above others
- c.) thinking your ideas are best and that things should always go your way
- d.) not admitting wrongdoing or apologizing—leader of the study should share how they were prideful as a teenager

2.) What do you think humility is?

possible negative responses:
- a.) being whimpy and letting people walk all over you
- b.) letting people tell you what to do
- c.) having no opinions

possible positive responses:
- a.) listening to input and getting help from God and others
- b.) taking correction well
- c.) apologizing for sin

- The goal of this study is for you to see your pride so that you can humbly accept and respond to the word of God.

The Scriptures

Philippians 2:5–8

How was Jesus humble?
- a.) He was God but became a man.
- b.) He became a servant when he could've been a ruler.
- c.) He died for others!

- *Bottom line:* To be like Jesus is to be humble.

Ephesians 4:2–3

How does God want us to get along and be unified with others?
- a.) be completely humble and gentle (no selfishness)
- b.) deal patiently with people
- c.) focus on our love for others so that we can bear with their faults

- *Bottom line:* To get along with others, we must put ourselves aside—that's what Jesus has done for us.

1 Peter 5:5–6

How can humility be like clothing?
- a.) put it on everyday before you go outside
- b.) not a natural part of us—has to be put on (thought about)
- c.) should be the first thing people see about us

What is in store for the humble person?
- a.) grace
- b.) "lifted up"—growth and blessing
- c.) relief because his burdens and anxieties will be carried by God instead of himself
- d.) better relationships (As God opposes the proud, so do other people!)

• *Bottom line:* The humble person is on God's team.

Personal Heart-Check Questions

1.) Do you see the pride in your life? When is it hardest for you to be humble?

2.) Are you willing to change your prideful ways and attitudes and be humble toward God and others? Be specific about what ways and to whom.

Practical Applications

Isaiah 66:2b

God is fired-up about the humble person and the humble person totally respects what the Bible says. Humility is not being phony by not expressing your opinions, but humility is considering others before yourself and having the loving, selfless attitude of Christ even when you express your own opinions.

To be humble when you sin:

a.) accept full responsibility

b.) make no excuses

c.) do not be defensive

d.) apologize humbly and rejoice in being pleasing to God and like Jesus

When others sin against you:

a.) tell them in a respectful way (don't give in to fear or intimidation)

b.) focus on your love for them and not on what they have done to you

c.) forgive them and forget about it, moving on to being even better friends

Write a one-page description of how you have seen your pride and how you can turn it into a humility that will make you ready to study the Bible to become a Christian.

3
Grace

To the leader of the study:

The understanding of grace is the foundation for a love-motivated relationship with God, rather than one that is works-motivated. Often teens raised in the church can be little Pharisees in the making, knowing the requirements of the Christian life, but missing the heart motivation. Similarly, overachievers (in the world or in the kingdom) are valued by others and value themselves based on their performance. The goal of this study is to build security, self-esteem and worth based on God's forgiving love and not on their Christian duty or perfect performance.

Your personal examples and analogies will make the difference in their understanding of a potentially broad and complex concept.

Intro

Ask:

1.) What is grace?

Some answers:

a.) undeserved forgiveness

b.) an "in spite of" kind of love

c.) acceptance even without perfect performance

d.) real love

(Give some examples and analogies from your own life.)

2.) Where does grace come from?

a.) a Christian receives the substitution of Jesus' righteousness for their sinfulness (2 Corinthians 5:21)

b.) after baptism, the blood of Jesus covers over my sins, allowing me to be justified: "just as if I'd never sinned" (1 John 1:7)

input=our part	G	output=God's view
sin	R	forgiveness
imperfection	A	perfection
filthy heart	C	a sinless heart
	E	

- *Bottom line:* Grace is almost too good to be true, but it is! The goal of this study is to help you to see the real God who loves you and how valuable you are to him. He valued you at the cost of his only Son, whom he gave up so that there could be grace to forgive your sins and restore your relationship with him.

The Scriptures

Psalm 103:8–10

What are some sins in your life?

What do you deserve for them?

a.) punishment (grounding, removal of privileges, jail, etc.)

b.) not being trusted by people

- *Bottom line:* God sees everything that we do and think, and he knows what we deserve. Yet, it is his grace that gives us forgiveness rather than punishment.

Romans 8:1–2

What does "no condemnation" mean?

a.) no punishment

b.) not feeling "in the doghouse"

c.) not feeling like God and others are looking down on you

- *Bottom line:* We can never earn grace. Grace comes through Jesus' sacrifice for our sins and frees us from the condemnation that we deserve because of our sins.

1 Corinthians 15:9–11

What is Paul because of grace?

a.) a forgiven man

b.) a Christian

What effect did God's grace have on Paul?

a.) He worked hard for God.

b.) He lived his whole life for Christ (Philippians 1:21).

c.) He was a very grateful man.

- *Bottom line:* Grace completely changes our lives.

Personal Heart-Check Questions

What should God's grace produce in you? Does it?

How should you respond to God's grace? Will you?

Practical Applications

Decide that you will live for God because of his grace and not to earn his grace.

Write a one-page letter to God expressing your understanding of his grace (using a personal example from your life) and your gratitude for his grace.

4
Purity

To the leader of the study:

Our society exalts sexual immorality, and it's raging out of control. Teenagers have hormones that are newly active, and they can let them rage out of control. However, God has made it clear that he wants our natural sexual desires to be expressed only within the marriage relationship.

In the Bible the term "purity" is most often referring to sexual purity, but it also is used to refer to being free from contamination by worldliness in general. Contaminated water is undrinkable, just as a contaminated heart is unacceptable to God. The purpose of this study is to help teenagers to understand and embrace God's convictions about purity.

Share some of your challenges with purity when you were a teen.

Intro

1.) Have you, or has anyone you know, had food poisoning? Do you know what happens?

Since the food is contaminated and poisonous, the body does everything possible to flush the poison out! It's really gross, but if the poison is not removed, the person could die.

2.) What are some ways teenagers are impure in everyday life?
- a.) lustful thoughts/fantasies and "the second look"
- b.) watching movies or TV shows with sexually explicit scenes and themes
- c.) reading pornographic magazines or visiting pornographic sites on the Internet
- d.) listening to or telling dirty jokes
- e.) flirting (desiring attention from the opposite sex and acting or speaking in such a way as to get it)
- f.) sexual immorality
- g.) masturbation

• The goal of this study is to help you to take hold of God's convictions about purity of heart and life. It will also help you see that following God's plan is always the most fulfilling in the long run. Being contaminated and poisoned by the world will damage your soul. God has a great plan for your life and is excited about watching it unfold for you in his time!

The Scriptures

1 Thessalonians 4:3–8

What are some things we need to do to stay pure?
- a.) avoid sexual immorality
- b.) have control over our own bodies

• *Bottom line:* God has high standards for us to be totally different from people in the world. We need to have the same expectations for ourselves that God does. He doesn't call us to anything that is not possible. When we are impure, we hurt God and ourselves and, if someone else is involved, we hurt them.

2 Timothy 2:22

What are "the evil desires of youth"?

sensual pleasures like sex and drugs and wild living

Why do you think God says these evil desires have to do with youth?
- a.) They are new experiences, so they appeal to curiosity.
- b.) Teenage bodies are changing sexually.
- c.) The "young, wild, free, indestructible" mentality can take hold of young people.

What does it mean to "flee" from something?

to desperately run away, usually from something dangerous (a murderer, etc.)

What does it mean to "pursue" something?

to go after it with all your heart

• *Bottom line:* We have the right to choose where we spend our energy in life—whether on worldly goals or on spiritual ones. God calls us to run away from what our human nature screams for us to go after: destructive, worldly desires, activities and thoughts. We must, instead, go after the challenge of being godly in a godless world.

Ephesians 5:3–5

How much is a hint?

What does God say to replace impurity with?

What does it mean to have no inheritance?

• *Bottom line:* God takes purity very seriously!

Personal Heart-Check Questions

How are you different from your friends in the world?

Are you willing to change your life, thoughts, and habits to be radically pure?

Practical Applications

Read Psalm 119:9. Remember that when you are tempted, the Word will help you to resist sin. Memorize scriptures about purity/impurity to have ready for when you are tempted with this sin.

Read James 5:16. Confess your sin to someone who can help you. Remember that God loves you and forgives you! Next time, ask advice about movies, times with boys and girls together, dates, etc.

Please take some time to write about what you have learned about purity from this study. Include ways you can change and what you can do differently from now on.

5
Respect

To the leader of the study:

In today's society, respect is in a sad state of affairs. We see a lack of respect in the classroom, in athletics and against those given authority by the government. But that's the world and it's different for those who love God. There must be an uncompromising, relentless expectation of young teenagers to respect those they are called to respect. Every aspect of disrespect must be challenged in their lives from this study. I do believe deep in their hearts they do want to respect others. Help draw it out of them.

Intro

Ask:

1.) What does respect mean?

Some answers:

a.) look up to

b.) admire

c.) listen to

The answer: To feel or show honor or esteem for; hold in high regard.

• The goal of this study is to help you see how important respect is to God and to teach you who needs to be respected.

The Scriptures

Mark 12:28–30

Best place to start is respect for God.

How do you show respect for God? By loving God with all you've got and seeking to obey him.

How do you love God with all your heart and soul (emotions)? Mind and strength (actions)?

a.) share your heart with him in prayer

b.) do all God asks of you

c.) serving God (i.e. by being a servant to others)

d.) finding out, by studying, how to be with God in heaven

e.) think about God and what Jesus would do in every situation

• *Bottom line:* You show respect for God by honoring him by who you are, what you say and how you live. Your respect for God will directly cause you to respect others, as he commands.

Ephesians 6:1–3

Respect your parent(s).

How should you honor and show respect for your parents?

a.) obey them right away without complaining

b.) love them unconditionally

c.) listen attentively and look them in the eyes when they speak

d.) be open with them (share your heart with them)

e.) appreciate and value them for who they are and all they do for you

f.) have respectful body language

• *Bottom line:* Any disrespect for your parent(s) needs to change. The result of respect is that it brings joy to God and joy to your family.

1 Peter 2:17

Name others you absolutely need to respect.

a.) sibling(s)

b.) leaders in the church

c.) teachers in school

d.) coaches of athletic teams

e.) policemen and other government officials

f.) people running clubs/activities you're part of

1 Thessalonians 5:12

Why should you respect spiritual leaders?

a.) They've been given a responsibility and you should make their responsibility a joy.

b.) It builds your spiritual character to respect others.

c.) God says so.

Romans 13:1–7

Respecting rules, regulations, laws and guidelines

Why wouldn't you follow these?

a.) To have an unfair advantage over someone

b.) Because you're rebellious

Why should you follow these?

a.) God expects you to.

b.) It builds your spiritual character.

c.) You contribute to order rather than participate in disorder.

Name some rules, regulations, laws and guidelines you need to follow at home, at school and at other people's houses.

• *Bottom line:* The fact of life is that there are rules, regulations, laws and guidelines to follow everywhere you go. God expects us to follow them as long as it doesn't contradict the Bible. You must repent of any disrespectful attitude in any of these areas.

• *Overall bottom line:* Romans 12:10. Respecting others and respecting rules will show how spiritually mature you are. Also, the more you respect people and rules, the more respect you will get back from others.

Personal Heart-Check Questions

Would God say he feels like you respect him? Would your parents?

To whom are you most tempted to be disrespectful? How will you repent?

What rules, regulations, laws or guidelines are you most tempted not to follow? How will you repent?

Practical Applications

Please take some time to write about what you learned and what you will do differently.

Note to leader of study: If a teen has an extreme problem with respect, he may have an extreme problem with respecting himself. Please do an appropriate follow-up study on that subject.

6
Righteousness
(No Matter What)

To the leader of the study:

Righteousness is one of the most unpursued qualities of Jesus. To be righteous is to be like Jesus. The goal of this study is to challenge and inspire the teens to seek righteousness with all their hearts.

You must be open about your life to facilitate openness in the teenager.

Intro

Ask:

1.) Describe "righteousness" in your own words.

Some answers:

a.) doing the right thing

b.) being obedient to God and parents

c.) obeying laws

2.) When is it most challenging to be righteous?

a.) during peer pressure

b.) when things are hard

c.) when you just don't feel like obeying

d.) when you don't understand

• The goal of this study is to help you to biblically define righteousness and to help you see your need to be righteous in every situation no matter what.

The Scriptures

1 John 3:7

Who is righteous?

a.) Those who do what is right.

b.) Those who are not led astray.

c.) Those who imitate Jesus.

James 2:21–22

What made Abraham righteous?

a.) He offered Isaac.

b.) He obeyed God.

c.) He obeyed with faith.

• *Bottom line:* To be righteous is to do what is right and to obey God's commands.

Matthew 26:38–39

How was Jesus feeling?

overwhelmed, sad or sorrowful, "This is hard," "I do not want this."

How did Jesus respond to his feelings?

a.) He was open about them in prayer.

b.) He was willing to do God's will.

c.) He made a decision to obey, no matter what.

• *Bottom line:* We must do what is right even when we do not feel like obeying God.

Acts 5:28–29

Why were the apostles being persecuted?

a.) They filled the city with the words of Jesus.

b.) They made people feel guilty about hurting Jesus.

How did they handle the persecution?

a.) They were bold.

b.) They obeyed God no matter what.

c.) They did what was right or righteous.

• *Bottom line:* In the face of persecution or peer pressure, we must do what God says.

Personal Heart-Check Questions

Is righteousness a daily goal in your life?

In which areas are you most tempted to be unrighteous?

Practical Applications

Matthew 6:33

Start every morning by seeking God first.

a.) Pray to be righteous.

b.) Be open about areas of weakness.

c.) When unsure of what to do, ask, "What would Jesus do?"

Please take some time to write about what you learned from this study about righteousness, some things you have done or will do differently, and how an understanding of this can strengthen your relationship with God.

7
Training Yourself to Be Godly

To the leader of the study:

A teen embarking on studying the Bible must have the maturity to follow through with the life-changing decisions that they will make throughout the study series. One way that their maturity can be discerned is by their efforts to train themselves in godliness through their personal Bible study and their conduct around other teens. Look for signs that they are taking their spiritual progress into their own hands and not waiting for others to do all of the initiating.

The goal of this study is to help them to see their need to be self-motivated in their relationship with God and the pursuit of their studies. Hopefully they will come away with the confidence that they can mature in their character quickly.

Intro

Ask:

1) What is involved in training? (athletic, spiritual)

a.) repetition

b.) learning the basics

2) How will you train yourself to be godly?

a.) consistent, daily times with God in Bible study and prayer

b.) sharing your faith daily

c.) having self-control in challenging situations

• The goal of this study is to help you to see that your spiritual progress depends on your willingness and effort to build your relationship with God on the foundation that has been laid by others. God wants each of us to take personal responsibility to mature and grow. To be godly requires self-discipline and seriousness in heart and mind.

The Scriptures

1 Peter 2:2–3

What does it mean to "crave"?

a.) to have an intense desire

b.) can't wait to get it

What is "pure spiritual milk"?

a.) the Bible and prayer

b.) godly advice from parents, teachers and leaders

c.) Christlike examples

- *Bottom line:* What we desire, we pursue. You must cultivate an appetite for a godly character by "tasting" the goodness of the Lord through your personal Bible study and imitating godly qualities in others.

1 Timothy 4:12

What example can you set for other teens?

a.) Bible study and prayer being daily and life-changing

b.) daily evangelism with faith

c.) home life (Christianity starts in the home!)

d.) serving without hesitation

e.) speaking to others to build them up and not tear them down, whether it's a challenge or an encouragement; giving from your heart in all conversations

f.) acting maturely in church (not silly or immature)

g.) being real and sincere in your motivation to become a Christian

- *Bottom line:* Even though you are young, you can inspire others by your godly example.

Personal Heart-Check Questions

What areas do you see that you need to mature in?

Are you willing to take responsibility for seeking to change in these areas?

Practical Application

Keep a journal for your quiet times so that you can remind yourself of the things you are learning and growing in.

Decide that you will be an example to the other teens when you are in the fellowship.

Go over the studies we are doing so that you can be sure to put the things you are learning into practice.

Write a one-page essay describing the areas that you need to grow in and what you will initiate to see them change.

8

What's Your Dad Like?

IMPORTANT NOTE: Ask the teen to write out their view of God before you get together to study the Bible. When you sit down to study, ask them to give you their essay, and hold on to it until the end.

To the leader of the study:

Teenagers' view of their dad will affect how they view God. In order to be in a healthy relationship with God, teens must understand what God is like and begin to love him deeply.

Special notes: Even if the teen's dad is not with the family, he still has a presence and an impact on his child's life. Use the introduction time to draw out how the teen feels about him, whether present or absent. Also, be sure to encourage teens who don't have a great example in a dad that God is the perfect Dad for them.

Open your time together by sharing about your own dad.

Intro

1.) Think about your own dad. Pretend I've never met him or heard about him. Describe him to me.

Some sample questions to help the teen:

What does your dad love to do? Hate to do? What are some of his best character traits? Worst? How do you know how he feels about you? When is he most proud of you? What makes him mad?

The Scriptures

Luke 15:11–24

What is the son like before he leaves?

a.) selfish—took his dad's money before he was even dead
b.) very sinful—reckless, wild, sensual

Even though the son was really mean to his father when he left, how did the father respond when the son returned?

a.) excited
b.) gave him gifts
c.) called people together to celebrate

• *Bottom line:* God is a compassionate and loving Father who desperately wants to be with us. He is not a judgmental God, waiting to zap us for every mistake. He is not an uncaring God, laughing at our pain. He wants to welcome each one of us home in our relationship with him.

John 8:1–9

What was Jesus' reaction to this woman's embarrassing, humiliating sin? (Keep in mind that Jesus' character is the exact representation of God's character.)

a.) sensitive to her embarrassment
b.) treated her sin like any other—not, "Oh, I can't believe you did that!"
c.) totally forgiving, even though that sin was punishable by death

• *Bottom line:* Forgiveness is part of God's character. Understanding our need for forgiveness and God's willingness to totally forgive us helps to draw us closer to him, to love and appreciate him more.

Hebrews 12:5–11

How does this passage say it feels to be disciplined?

a.) like hardship
b.) painful
c.) unpleasant

Why does God discipline?

a.) for our good (to keep us from walking on evil paths)
b.) so we can learn lessons in order to make better decisions in the future
c.) so we can be secure that he loves and cares for us

What is our Dad in heaven like?

a.) He unconditionally loves.
b.) He forgives all of our sins.
c.) He disciplines us for our good.
d.) He believes in us and wants us to live happily ever after.

Jeremiah 29:11

This passage sums up how God takes care of us when we seek him.

Personal Heart-Check Questions

Do you want to be closer to God?

Let's read your essay now. Is your view of God different now than when you wrote this?

Do you see any relationship between how you personally view your earthly father and how you view your heavenly Father?

Are you willing to open wide your heart to God and let him be the Father to you that he wants and needs to be?

Practical Application Questions

Please write about what you learned

about God and the Father he wants to be in your life. How do you feel about it? How can it strengthen your walk with him?

Pray every day to see God as the Bible describes him, not as you feel or think he is.

9
Who Are You Living to Please?

To the leader of the study:

People-pleasing is predominant among teens. As they develop a stronger sense of their own identity, they seek approval and acceptance from others. Christian-parented teens are commonly motivated by people-pleasing to study the Bible. They feel a great deal of pressure to study the Bible to please their Christian parent(s), siblings and friends. They can strive to give the "right" responses to questions—not necessarily their own true heartfelt responses.

Intro

Ask:

1.) Whose approval is important to you? Who do you want to please or get approval from?

Some answers:

a.) myself
b.) parents, teachers
c.) teen leaders and older disciples
d.) friends

2.) Why?

a.) to be accepted, liked, popular
b.) to feel good about myself
c.) because if feels good to be praised

• The goal of this study is to help you to see the importance of pleasing God and seeking praise and approval from Him.

The Scriptures

John 5:41–44

What is Jesus teaching in this Scripture?

a.) We need to follow his example by focusing on getting praise from God, not people.
b.) We will please who we love.

• *Bottom line:* These people knew the truth but did not follow it because of peer pressure. They cared more about their reputation with people than they cared about doing what was right before God.

Galatians 1:10

What does Paul tell us about the difference between pleasing people and pleasing God?

They are opposites!

When are you tempted to do the God-pleasing thing but with people-pleasing motives?

a.) going to church
b.) obeying parents just because they said so, not because we want to please God
c.) serving, but wanting recognition for all you do by peers or leaders

• *Bottom line:* When we strive to please God, we may not be popular with the world, but keep in mind that man's approval is temporary, while God's approval is eternal!

Mark 12:14

What does it mean to be "swayed by men"? Who are you most likely to be swayed by?

What does "integrity" mean?

a.) sticking to your convictions no matter what

b.) doing what you said you would do and doing it on time

- *Bottom line:* Jesus was not swayed by men because he saw them from a spiritual perspective. We need to imitate this quality in him.

2 Corinthians 5:9–10

Why should we care about trying to please God?

a.) It doesn't just happen—it has to be a set goal.

b.) We all (every single person, whether we believe in God or not) will be accountable for our lives.

c.) Jesus died for us, and we need to live to please him.

Personal Heart-Check Questions

Can you relate to the people-pleasing Pharisees in any way?

Have you counted the cost of studying the Bible? Becoming a Christian will affect your reputation with your non-Christian friends.

What do your lifestyle and your priorities say about how much faith you have in God?

Practical Applications

Make three columns on a page. In the first column, list all the activities you are involved in—everything, including studying the Bible, school activities, free time, etc. In the next column, write the reason you think you participate in it. Ask others who know you well to tell you why they think you are involved. Allow them to point out the areas where they see you "loving praise from men rather than from God," and write their insights in the third column. Be honest and encourage honesty! Bring the list to your next study and review it with your teen leader. This will help you to see who you are living to please and decide to please God instead.

After thinking about this study, take some time to write about what you learned about yourself.

10

Relationships with the Family

To the leader of the study:

Family relationships are second only to your relationship with God. It is an absolute must that a teen's heart for his or her family is in the right place. There needs to be a deep abiding love and respect for parent(s) and a strong, inseparable love for each sibling. From this study there needs to be a distinct change in the teenager's relationship with family members.

Note: This is not a study about the weaknesses of parent(s) or sibling(s). Hear the teenager out if he or she feels the need to voice some of the weaknesses so you don't frustrate them. Then you, the teen leader, go back and respectfully talk those issues out with the parent(s). Strongly emphasize to the teenager that this study will focus specifically on what he or she needs to change.

Intro

Ask:

1.) What are your greatest strengths and weaknesses in your relationships with your family?

Some answers:

Strengths	Weaknesses
a.) cheerful	a.) irresponsible

b.) loving
c.) affectionate

b.) disrespectful
c.) independent

Proverbs 23:22–26

2.) What do you think will bring the greatest joy to your parent(s)?

a.) listening to them
b.) living by the truth
c.) changing how you live at home

- The goal of this study is for you to begin to change your dynamics in your relationship with your family. The results will bring greater joy to your family.

The Scriptures

John 19:25–27

As Jesus was dying on the cross, what are some words you would use to describe how he looked after his family?

a.) compassion
b.) love
c.) care

- *Bottom line:* If Jesus shows that kind of care for his family, especially making sure his mother was taken care of, while dying on a cross, we need to daily care about our own families by being righteous and loving toward them.

1 Thessalonians 5:12–13

Who should you respect?

a.) those who work hard
b.) those over you in the Lord (Your parents fit into these categories!)

How can you show greater respect for your parent(s)?

a.) listen right away
b.) obey right away
c.) verbally express to them frequently that you love and respect them or write it to them in cards or letters.

- *Bottom line:* You've been given so much by your parents. You need to give back by showing the respect they deserve and God expects you to have for them.

Ephesians 4:29–5:1

How do you get along with each sibling? (Go through each one.)

In your relationship with your sibling(s), what should you get rid of?

a.) bitterness
b.) rage
c.) anger
d.) any bad feelings

How should you treat your sibling(s)?

a.) with encouragement
b.) with kindness
c.) with compassion

- *Bottom line:* In God's eyes, there is no such thing as sibling rivalry. You must treat all your physical brothers and sisters with so much love that this love is only surpassed by your love for God and your parent(s).

Personal Heart-Check Questions

What needs to change the most in your relationship with your family?

How will you go about changing these things starting today?

Practical Applications

Apologize specifically to your sibling(s) about how you've fallen short and express to them how you want to be different.

Write a one-page letter to your parent(s) about how grateful you are for them, and how you will specifically change to show a greater respect for them (Ephesians 6:1–2 and 1 Thessalonians 5:13: obey, honor and hold them in the highest regard).

Thirteen Follow-up Studies for New Christians

We understand the imperative, methods, and urgency of evangelism. We teach it, preach it, and know what it means to be a "minister of reconciliation." And yet we have a chronic weakness. Too often we see conversion as the end of the process of evangelization, rather than as the middle. What, the middle? Yes, the middle! Our work is certainly not finished when we have influenced someone to obey the gospel (Romans 1:5, 16:26, 2 Thessalonians 1:8). Obedience to the gospel is an ongoing process. Spiritual maturity (Ephesians 4:16) cannot be achieved in just a few Bible study sessions. In fact, to lead someone to the point of faith, repentance, and baptism without ongoing study and discipleship is careless (2 Peter 2:20-22)! The result of this weakness: a poor retention rate. Certainly we will want to do all that we can to keep faithful those who have confessed Jesus as Lord.

These studies have been designed to remedy that, to be used after baptism. The order in which you make use of them will vary. Perhaps you will want to come up with your own studies. In the meantime, take these as a suggestion, as a model. To aid you in bringing the principles to life, several practical suggestions have been added to most of the studies.

I. The Basis: Relationship with God

1—Prayer: Speaking to God

What could be more natural between two people who love each other than to communicate? Surely one would expect to see an enormous amount of communication between a man and the God he loves with all his heart, soul, mind and strength. And yet this is far from what we observe! Communication of this sort is not natural; it must be learned. There are many hindrances—all of which Satan will gladly use in his campaign to keep us off our knees. Yet they can all be overcome, if we are willing to rely on God and give prayer the priority it deserves.

Priority

- Mark 1:35—Jesus found time to pray.
- He finds a place free from distraction.
- He finds a time free from distraction.
- Suggested: Psalm 42:1, 63:1, Luke 6:12, Hebrews 5:7.

Learning process

- Luke 11:1-13—It's not natural (even Jesus' apostles had to be taught).
- Develop structure in your prayer life.

Hindrances

- 1 Peter 4:7—Lack of concentration. May wish to pray aloud.
- Psalm 66:18—Lack of personal righteousness.
- Luke 18:1-8—Lack of persistence.
- 1 John 5:14—Prayer contrary to God's will.
- Mark 11:24—Lack of faith.
- Suggested: Matthew 6:5, John 9:31, 14:13-14, Ephesians 6:18, Colossians 4:2-4, James 5:16-17.

Conclusion

- Philippians 4:6-7—Give worries to God.
- Jeremiah 20:21b—God is looking for people who will devote themselves to be close to him. Take up the challenge!
- Psalm 5:3—Have a daily prayer time.
- Suggested—1 Thessalonians 5:17, 1 Peter

5:7, 1 John 5:14.

Practicals
- Set a time and length to pray every day.
- Write out a prayer list.

Fasting
- Often associated with prayer in the Bible.
- Matthew 6:17-18—shows that this is expected of Christians.
- Suggested: Nehemiah 1:4, Isaiah 58, Joel 2:12, Acts 14:23.

2—Bible Study: Listening to God

Assisting young Christians to become rooted in consistent and productive personal Bible study is one of the top priorities of those helping them to mature in Christ. This is an excellent way to take our stand against Satan and his schemes, wielding "the sword of the Spirit" (Ephesians 6:18). Let us listen to God's voice.

Introduction
- Matthew 4:4—"Every word." Comparable to physical bread, therefore essential. If you don't stay in the word, you won't stay in the faith.

Work at your Bible study
- 2 Peter 3:15-16—Possible to distort scriptures to own destruction. Tremendous responsibility on us personally to stick with the truth.
- Yes, some passages are difficult to understand—but not impossible! (2 Corinthians 1:13). Strive to comprehend them first, before asking others what they mean.
- 2 Timothy 2:15—Becoming a well-equipped workman (3:17), not being ashamed, developing competence in teaching God's word to others.
- 1 Peter 3:15—Equipped for evangelism: not just Bible knowledge, but being able to answer questions, helping others, gently and respectfully.
- James 1:22-25—It is useless to study the Bible without apply it to our lives.
- Suggested: Psalm 1:2-3, 119 (entire), Ezra 7:10, Isaiah 66:2b, Matthew 24:35, Romans 15:4, 1 Corinthians 10:11, Colossians 3:16, 2 Timothy 2:7.

Practicals
- Have a set time to study your Bible daily. Spend daily time in the word (Joshua 1:8, Acts 17:11, Deuteronomy 17:18-20).
- Write down the convicting points and pray about them.
- Do well in church classes; make the most of any available local teaching programs.
- For first time Bible readers, focus on the New Testament until you are familiar with it, then read Old Testament.

3—Faith, Works & Grace: Balance

One of the greatest travesties in the church today is that new Christians are taught to depend on self, to struggle up the road of salvation by works. This is an acquired deficiency, learned through observation of "older" Christians. Such an orientation undoes the work of the cross. Equally sad, however, is the school of thought that prides itself on having arrived at a true understanding of grace, only to condone and even encourage lukewarm commitment. We must strike the balance—hence this study.

Faith
- Hebrews 11:6—We need faith to please God, but what is faith?
- James 2:14-16—Faith is more than intellectual belief—it results in action. Compare verses 20-24 with Genesis 22. Note the interrelationship between faith and obedience.

Works
- Ephesians 2:8-10—The Bible clearly teaches that we are not saved by our own effort, but this doesn't mean that God doesn't expect anything from us. It is an unearned gift, but it is conditional on obedience (2 Kings 5:1-15).

Grace
- Titus 3:5—We're saved not because of our righteous deeds, but by his mercy.

- Grace is unmerited favor or mercy. But the fact that we do not deserve it does not mean that we can do as we like (Jude 4).
- 1 Corinthians 15:10—Grace impacts.
- Titus 2:11-14—It is because of grace that we strive to live self-controlled, upright and godly lives.

II. The Church: The Body of Christ

4—Relationships in the Body

When one enters the community of the redeemed, relationships are radically transformed! Instead of having ourselves as the centre of our focus, we are to "consider others better than ourselves" (Philippians 2:3). However, implementation of these biblical principles will never occur as long as we retain a defective concept of fellowship and the body. Church is not something we attend; it is an opportunity to tend to needs. And there are many needs to be tended to! If young Christians are not grafted into the body in a functional way, they may well be reclaimed by the world. And if that is what happens, we are failing (1 Corinthians 2:12-15). The most crucial time for integrating the young convert into the local church is the first few weeks—and even days.

Why different from the world's relationships?
- John 13:34-35—Jesus commands us to love each other as he has loved us. This quality of love shows we are Christians.
- Mark 3:35—We are Jesus' brothers and sisters if we do God's will. Because of this common purpose, Christian relationships transcend even blood relations.

How are they different?
- 1 Peter 1:22—Our love for each other must be sincere and from the heart.
- 1 John 3:16—Jesus is our example. Our love for others can be measured by how much we are willing to sacrifice for them.

What does this mean in practice?
- 1 Thessalonians 5:12—Different people have different needs.
- 1 John 3:17—Meet material needs.
- Colossians 1:28—Let's be concerned about each other's spiritual well being.

Conclusion
- Ephesians 4:29—Be edifying.
- Ephesians 5:21—Be submissive not only to leaders (Hebrews 13:17), but also to each other (Ephesians 5:21).
- Suggested: Acts 2:42-47, 4:32-35, Romans 12:5, 1 Corinthians 12:12-27, Hebrews 10:24-25, 13:1-2, James 1:19.

Practicals
- Make it a point to phone and email other Christians.
- Spend time with other believers in order to build relationships (Hebrews 3:12-14).
- Pray for each other daily.
- Introduce yourself to at least one new person in each service for the next month.
- Write cards to your brothers and sisters.

5—The Church: Three Aspects

We demand book, chapter and verse for all our doctrines and practices and rightly so. How does a young Christian respond when he sees practices he hasn't seen in his life? He is not used to weekly communion, and certainly not to sacrificial contributing. This study provides scriptural explanation for these three practices in the New Testament Church.

Communion (Lord's Supper, Eucharist)
- Matthew 26:26-29—Passover supper (Jewish background). Bread is the body of Christ, wine is blood.
- 1 Corinthians 11:23ff—Jesus instituted the Lord's Supper. It is a proclamation of the Lord's death until he comes. Examine yourself before eating.
- Acts 20:7—Christians came together in order to break bread.
- It appears from the evidence of the NT and that of church history that the Christians broke bread together at least once a week.
- Suggested: Exodus 12 (historical background), Mark 12:12-26, Luke 22:7-20, John 6:48-58, Acts 2:42.

Contribution (for needs of the church)
- Matthew 6:21—Your treasure is where your heart is.
- Matthew 6:24—Cannot serve both God and money, so make sure that God is first.
- Proverbs 3:9-10—Are you honoring God with your money? Give him the "firstfruits" of your income. Be responsible when you are away; leave your contribution behind.
- 1 Corinthians 16:1-2—A collection to meet the needs of the poor is biblical.
- 2 Corinthians 8:1-15—Advance planning.
- 2 Corinthians 9:6ff—Good material on sacrificial giving...
- Suggested: Exodus 36:6-7, Mark 12:41-44, Luke 6:38, 1 Timothy 6:5-10, 17.

Confession of sin (e.g. coming forward in response to the preached message)
- James 5:16—Public confession. No private "confessional" in the Bible. Ask spiritual people to pray for you. Their prayers will be effective.
- Proverbs 28:13—You will not prosper if you keep sins inside.

6—One-another relationships: God's Plan

Although you will not find a doctrine of "discipling partners" explicitly spelled out in the New Testament, it is indisputable that the scriptures teach the necessity of one-another relationships. The importance of ongoing discipleship should be clear to someone before he makes Jesus Lord. This study aims to cultivate an attitude of openness on the part of the young Christian to input, as well as to remind him that, in the final analysis, it is the responsibility of the one who has confessed Jesus as Lord to persevere in his Christian growth.

Discipleship is not a human expedient; it is a clear command of God (Matthew 28:19).

Levels of discipling
- Hebrews 3:12—Others disciple us.
- Hebrews 4:12—The Word disciples us.
- Hebrews 5:12—We disciple ourselves.
- Hebrews 6:12—We are discipled by the faithful examples of biblical figures.
- Hebrews 12:12—God disciples us too.

Being discipled
- 2 Timothy 2:2—The teaching process: a chain reaction.
- Colossians 1:28-2:1—The goal is maturity/completeness/perfection. There will be difficulties in any relationship, but try to realize that the challenges you receive are made in love. This is hard work.
- Proverbs 10:17—Attitude of openness to correction. If you have the wrong attitude, you will lead others astray.
- Proverbs 11:14—Ask for advice.
- Proverbs 12:15 and 15:12—Cherish challenge and ask for help.

Discipling yourself
- Hebrews 5:11-14—Don't be slow to learn. By constant use (habit), train yourself. You are responsible for how you do spiritually. You cannot blame your sins on others.

Practicals
- Arrange a time to meet each week with an older, more mature Christian.
- Strive for daily contact.

III. The Work: Becoming Like Christ

7—Hindrance: The Heart

The Bible speaks of the heart as the governing center of the whole man—intellectual, physical, and psychological, and thus a man's heart makes him what he is and gives rise to all his thoughts and actions. It is imperative that a young disciple be taught to guard his heart, to keep it sensitive and open to God's word.

Introduction
- 1 Samuel 16:7—God sees the heart.

Problems of the heart
- Jeremiah 17:9—Deceitfulness: in the sense of feelings and impulses. Deceitful with regard to discerning the truth, or what is best.
- Mark 7:21—Sinfulness: the heart is the source of sin, and evil desires.

- Hebrews 3:12—Hardening: hearts can become hard, become unbelieving and turn away from God.

The remedy
- Jeremiah 29:13—Seek God with all our heart. This verse applies to everyone!
- Psalm 51:17—Cultivate a penitent heart, which responds quickly to God's Word.
- Psalm 119:11—Hide God's Word inside.
- Proverbs 3:5-6—Trust in the Lord with all our hearts.
- Ezekiel 11:19-20—The Lord has placed his Spirit in our hearts to lead us.

Conclusion
- Proverbs 4:23—Guard your heart! It is the source of our spiritual life.
- Suggested: Genesis 6:5, 2 Chronicles 16:9, Psalm 51:10, Proverbs 14:12, 28:26, Ezekiel 18:31, 1 John 3:20.

Practicals
- Pray for a pure heart.
- Confess sin; be humble.
- Write out verses that address your heart.

8—Laziness, Idleness, Discipline

How many of us have had great dreams for how God was going to use us—how he would mold us into what he wanted us to be—and just when the going got rough, and the process became painful, we resisted, and perhaps even took a couple of steps backwards! Few of us are naturally disciplined; discipline must be learned. And yet without it, how do we suppose we will really grow? Surely that is fantasy! Discipline, therefore, must be built into our Christian lives from the earliest moment.

Introduction
- 1 Timothy 4:7—Train yourself to be godly. Physical training (sports) is of limited value, but spiritual training is immeasurably valuable. The Christian life is a process of training in righteousness.

Laziness
- Hebrews 6:12—Don't become lazy. Laziness is a constant threat to the life of every Christian, young or old. Imitate those who are patient, faithful and disciplined. Look for good examples; learn from them. Realize laziness is a sin!
- Suggested: Proverbs 12:1, 24:30-34, 26:13-16.

Idleness
- 1 Thessalonians 4:11ff—Be constructive members of society and of the church. Hard-working people win the respect of others. Try not to be dependent on anybody (do not go into/remain in debt). Both unemployment and underemployment can be detrimental to spiritual growth.
- 2 Thessalonians 3:3ff—Follow the example of disciplined people. Don't be a "busybody"—appearing busy but not really achieving anything.

Discipline
- Heb 12:11-12—No discipline pleasant, but it yields a more satisfying life.
- Suggested: 1 Corinthians 9:24-27, 2 Timothy 2:4-6, Heb 5:14.

Practicals
- Make a timetable of how you use your time. Get some suggestions.
- Set some goals.
- Spend time with a disciplined person and learn from him or her.
- If you are not a punctual person, make an effort to be early.
- Read *The Disciplined Life* by Richard Taylor.

9—Evangelism, Boldness, Tact

When it comes to evangelism, few young Christians possess both boldness and tact. We are tempted towards one extreme or the other: so tactful we say little, if anything, or so bold that tact is thrown to the wind. Boldness comes via prayer, and tact is developed through observation of those who are diplomatic. In view of the crippling effect of fear on new Christians—and old—and considering the number of tactical errors that are made by all, is why we need a separate lesson on this important subject.

Evangelism

- 2 Corinthians 5:10-21—Because we know and fear God, we try to persuade others. We are Christ's ambassadors and God has given to us the ministry of reconciliation. It is not an option.
- Acts 8:1, 4—The early Christians were evangelistic—not just the leaders!
- 1 Peter 2:9-10—We are all a royal priesthood. There is no "clergy" today!

Boldness

- Romans 1:16-17—The gospel is nothing to be ashamed of because it has the power to save.
- Luke 9:23-26—If we're ashamed of Jesus, he will be ashamed of us.
- Acts 4:29-31—Pray for boldness! God will answer your prayer.

Tact

- Matthew 10:16—Need to be wise/shrewd in our evangelism.

- Negatives:
  Proverbs 12:18—Beware reckless words.
  Prov. 25:17—Avoid too frequent contact.
  Proverbs 27:14—Don't be rude.

- Positives:
  1 Corinthians 9:20-23—Accommodate yourself to your hearer.
  Titus 2:10—Make the gospel attractive.
  1 Peter 3:15-16—Gentleness & respect.
- Suggested: Matthew 7:6, 2 Tim. 2:23-26.

Practicals

- Be friendly and start conversations wherever you go. The Lord will use this.
- Invite people to church.
- Improve one area of your life in order to make the gospel more attractive.

10—Service with a Smile

When Jesus came to the earth, he came as a suffering servant (Mark 10:45). And he is still a servant, since he always lives to intercede for us (Hebrews 7:25). In following the Master, this is one area that we dare not play down, no matter how unglamorous it may seem. For, as Jesus taught us, the road up is the road down.

- Matthew 20:26-28—The way up is the way of service, opposite the way of the world. Jesus came to serve, not to be served.
- Philippians 2:3-8—Do nothing out of selfish ambition or vain conceit. Consider others better than yourselves—then you'll look to see others' needs met. For Jesus to come to earth was the supreme act of self-humiliation. We need to imitate this selfless example in our everyday lives.
- Luke 17:7-10—When we have served, our attitude should be that we have done our duty. No complaining (Philippians 2:14); no expectation of reward.
- Colossians 3:23-24—Serve with all your heart! Realize that you are serving the Lord Christ, not men.
- Suggested: Psalm 100:2, Proverbs 3:27-28, John 13:1-17, Galatians 6:2, 10, Ephesians 6:7-8, Philippians 4:4-5.

Practicals

- Learn to serve without being asked.
- When asked to help in a particular way, be responsible! for example, duties such as children's ministry, ushering, communion, teaching, clean-up, office duty, and food preparation.

IV. Other Needs: Following God's Way

11—Academics: Obstacle or Opportunity?

God certainly expects excellence of Christian students: if not excellent results, at least excellent effort. Too often (undisciplined) students become Christians and then use evangelism or "church" as an excuse for mediocre performance. We must help students to see academics as a God-given responsibility. There is nothing "unspiritual" about studies.

Clear commission

- 1 Corinthians 7:25—God called us to be

Christians as students for a reason! We have a responsibility to glorify God in academics and evangelism.

- Colossians 3:22-23—Attitude is more important than aptitude. Academics are a vital part of your "spiritual" life. For consistent motivation, work for God, not self.

Evangelistic example

- 1 Thessalonians 4:11—A consistent example has an impact! Classmates will be drawn to those who can help others.
- Mark 7:37—People were amazed by Jesus' all-around excellence. You will amaze family and friends if you excel in all areas. "Ministry through academics, not in spite of academics."

Powerful preparation

- James 1:2-4—Persevering with academics leads to spiritual maturity: discipline, focus, faith.
- Suggested: Proverbs 6:6, 18:9, Philippians 2:14-16, 1 Timothy 3:7, 4:15-16.

Practicals

- Seek input in the area of academics.
- Get input from professors, classmates.
- Attend every lecture. This is important for your example.
- Take good notes, and catch up on missed lectures.
- Go through homework within a day of receiving it and plan how you will get it done.
- Keep current at all times! For conscience's sake, as well as for practical reasons.
- Aim to get rest, especially before exams.

12—Christian Marriage: A Cord of Three Strands

God's Word and power provide us with everything we need for happy, godly, fulfilling lives in every area (2 Tim 3:17, 2 Peter 1:3, John 10:10). The area of marriage is crucial, and if marriage is not going well, serious spiritual problems will also be present. Indeed, Christian marriage is one arena in which disciples of Christ will dramatically outshine the many worldly examples surrounding them.

God's plan

- Marriage meets many of our deepest needs (Genesis 2:24, Proverbs 18:22).
- Marry a Christian! (1 Corinthians 7:39).
- Marriage is for life (Matthew 19:9).
- Take advice! (Proverbs 15:22)

Worldly v. spiritual marriages

- Communication

  1. Time together (meals, spiritual talks, unscheduled time)
  2. Listening (especially for husbands)
  3. Express, don't suppress feelings
  4. No resentments (Colossians 3:13)
  5. Co-ordinate schedules; communicate clear your plans to each other!
  6. Communication may increase conflict; expect it, don't avoid it!
- Selfishness

  1. Harsh husbands? (Colossians 3:19) Husbands must serve their wives, being considerate (1 Peter 3:7). Husbands should help in housework, cleaning, taking care of children...
  2. Nagging wives (Prov. 21:19, 25:24, 27:15). Wives must be submissive (Col. 3:18, 1 Pet 3:5-6).
  3. Weak husbands? (henpecked) The man must be the spiritual leader (Eph 5:22-33).
- Hospitality

  1. Is home life centered only around each other, life in a cozy, selfish, private world?
  2. Hospitality is God's will (1 Peter 4:9)! Open your home.
  3. Use hospitality in evangelism.
  4. This is the husband's responsibility more than the wife's (1 Timothy 3:4)!
  5. An untidy home isn't inviting! (Proverbs 24:30-34)
- Spirituality

  1. Talk about spiritual things together.
  2. Pray with spouse daily.
  3. Don't "protect" each other when there is lukewarmness or compromise (Acts 5:1-11); speak the truth in love! (Ephesians 4:15).
- Romance

1. Don't deprive one another (1 Cor. 7:5).
2. Remember cards, flowers, presents...

- Input
  1. Do you strive to get input?
  2. Every marriage needs help!

Practicals

- Pray together every day!
- Share your faith together.
- Work on the church classes together. Expect the best of each other!
- Spend time showing your love for each other and really communicating.
- Read and discuss 1 Corinthians 13.
- Read Song of Songs to one another!
- Pray daily that you will be able to study with one couple together.
- "Double dates."
- Discuss your schedules together.
- Plan an overnight trip together
- Read a book on marriage and discuss it.

13—The Christian Family: Parents and Children

The family following God's Word is a happy, communicative, warm, loving, committed and fruitful family. Just as Christian marriage is God's wise plan for men and women to love and live together, so the Christian family is both God's answer to the ungodliness and selfishness of society and his plan for character development in his most precious gift to parents: their children.

Spiritual focus

- Chain of command (Christ—husband—wife—children)
- If you want a great family life, get help!
- Aim to have an evangelistically fruitful family!

Bringing up children

- Basic need for security and happiness:
  1. Time—you need to set priorities!
  2. Affection—without it, they will become insecure, cold, introverted, awkward around strangers.
  3. Spiritual examples (parents)—Ephesians 6:4, Deut 6:7.
- Discipline—it's loving to give it (Proverbs 23:13-14). Discipline is training.
  1. Always encourage (Colossians 3:21)
  2. Discipline is essential
     a. God commands it (Proverbs 22:15, 29:15, 17, 19, 21)
     b. The husband is chief discipler.
     c. Wife and husband should agree on the "rules," lest the children pick and choose whom to obey!
     d. Areas of training (Proverbs 22:6)
        - Respect toward authority
        - Moodiness
        - Speech and openness
        - Affection
        - Manners
        - Tidiness
     e. Regular spiritual times with each child!

Other Important Matters

- Regular, consistent family devotionals.
- Be on time to church. Allow extra time, particularly considering the children. Plan to come early!
- Pray with the children before they go to bed.
- Have a weekly family time.
- If you have Christian children, work with the pre-teen or teen ministry. Embrace feedback. Don't be defensive.

Practicals

- Create a simple system of allowances and incentives for the children.
- Take the whole family out evangelizing. Reach out to other families as a family.
- Ask Christians you respect to recommend helpful books.

Follow-up Studies: Closing Considerations

Follow-up studies can be covered at the rate of about one or two per week over the period of a few months. Depending on the needs, they may be used in any order. And, by all means, do not consider that your work with a young Christian ends after the follow-up studies have been completed! No, for you are still only in the middle.

Part Two

Resources

Medical Account of the Crucifixion

The Passion of Christ from a Medical Point of View

C. Truman Davis, M.D., M.S.
Reprinted with Permission from *Arizona Medicine*, March 1965

In this paper, I shall discuss some of the physical aspects of the passion, or suffering, of Jesus Christ. We shall follow Him from Gethsemane, through His trial, His scourging, His path along the Via Dolorosa, to His last dying hours on the cross....

This led me first to a study of the practice of crucifixion itself; that is, the torture and execution of a person by fixation to a cross. Apparently, the first known practice of crucifixion was by the Persians. Alexander and his generals brought it back to the Mediterranean world—to Egypt and Carthage. The Romans apparently learned the practice from the Carthaginians and (as with almost everything the Romans did) rapidly developed a very high degree of efficiency and skill in carry it out. A number of Roman authors (Livy, Cicero, Tacitys) comment on it. Several innovations and modifications are described in the ancient literature; I'll mention only a few which may have some bearing here. The upright portion of the cross (or stipes) could have the cross-arm (or patibulum) attached two or three feet below its top—this is what we commonly think of today as the classical form of the cross (the one which we have later named the Latin cross); however, the common form used in Our Lord's day was the Tau cross (shaped like the Greek letter Tau or like our T). In this cross the patibulum was placed in a notch at the top of the stipes. There is fairly overwhelming archeological evidence that it was on this type of cross that Jesus was crucified.

The upright post, or stipes, was generally permanently fixed in the ground at the site of execution and the condemned man was forced to carry the patibulum, apparently weighing about 110 pounds, from the prison to the place of execution. Without any historical or biblical proof, medieval and Renaissance painters have given us our picture of Christ carrying the entire cross. Many of these painters and most of the sculptors of crucifixes today show the nails through the palms. Roman historical accounts and experimental work have shown that the nails were driven between the small bones of the wrists and not through the palms. Nails driven through the palms will strip out between the fingers when they support the weight of a human body. The misconception may have come about through a misunderstanding of Jesus' words to Thomas, "Observe my hands." Anatomists, both modern and ancient, have always considered the wrists as part of the hand.

A titulus, or small sign, stating the victim's crime was usually carried at the front of the processions and later nailed to the cross above the head. This sign with its staff nailed to the top of the cross would have given it somewhat the characteristic form of the Latin cross.

The physical passion of the Christ begins in Gethsemane. Of the many aspects of this initial suffering, I shall only discuss the one of physiological interest: the bloody sweat. It is interesting that the physician of the group, St. Luke, is the only one to mention this. He says, "And being in agony, He prayed the longer. And his sweat became as drops of blood, trickling down upon the ground."

Every attempt imaginable has been used by modern scholars to explain away this phrase, apparently under the mistaken impression that this just doesn't happen.

A great deal of effort could be saved by consulting the medical literature. Though very rare, the phenomenon of Hematidrosis or bloody sweat, is well documented. Under great emotional stress, tiny capillaries in the sweat glands can break, thus mixing blood with sweat. This process alone could have produced marked weakness and possible shock.

We shall move rapidly through the betrayal and arrest; I must stress that important portions of the passion story are missing from this account. This may be frustrating to you, but in order to adhere to our purpose of discussing only the purely physical aspects of the Passion, this is necessary. After the arrest in the middle of the night, Jesus was brought before the Sanhedrin and Caiphas, the High Priest; it is here that the first physical trauma as inflicted. A soldier struck Jesus across the face for remaining silent when questioned by Caiphas. The palace guards then blindfolded Him and mockingly taunted Him to identify them as they each passed by, spat on Him, and struck Him in the face.

In the morning, Jesus, battered and bruised, dehydrated, and exhausted from a sleepless night, is taken across Jerusalem to the Praetorium of the Fortress Antonia, the seat of government of the Procurator of Judea, Pontius Pilate. You are, of course, familiar with Pilate's action in attempting to pass responsibility to Herod Antipas, the Tetrarch of Judea. Jesus apparently suffered no physical mistreatment of the hands of Herod and was returned to Pilate.

It was then, in response to the cries of the mob, that Pilate ordered Bar–Abbas released and condemned Jesus to scourging and crucifixion. There is much disagreement among authorities about scourging as a prelude to crucifixion. Most Roman writers from this period do not associate the two. Many scholars believe that Pilate originally ordered Jesus scourged as his full punishment and that the death sentence by crucifixion came only in response to the taunt by the mob that the Procurator was not properly defending Caesar against this pretender who claimed to be the King of the Jews.

Preparations for the scourging are carried out. The prisoner is stripped of His clothing and His hands tied to a post above His head. It is doubtful whether the Romans made any attempt to follow the Jewish law in this matter of scourging. The Jews had an ancient law prohibiting more than forty lashes. The Pharisees, always making sure that the law was strictly kept, insisted that only thirty–nine lashes be given. (In case of miscount, they were sure of remaining within the law.) The Roman legionnaire steps forward with the flagrum (or flagellum) in his hand. This is a short whip consisting of several heavy, leather thongs with two small balls of lead attached near the ends of each.

The heavy whip is brought down with full force again and again across Jesus' shoulders, back and legs. At first the heavy thongs cut through the skin only. Then, as the blows continue, they cut deeper into the subcutaneous tissues, producing first an oozing of blood from the capillaries and veins of the skin, and finally spurting arterial bleeding from vessels in the underlying muscles. The small balls of lead first produce large, deep bruises which are broken open by subsequent blows. Finally the skin of the back is hanging in long ribbons and the entire area is an unrecognizable mass of torn, bleeding tissue. When it is determined by the centurion in charge that the prisoner is near death, the beating is finally stopped.

The half-fainting Jesus is then untied and allowed to slump to the stone pavement, wet with His own blood. The Roman soldiers see a great joke in this provincial Jew claiming to be a king. They throw a robe across His shoulders and place a stick in His hand for a scepter. They still need a crown to make their travesty complete. A small bundle of flexible branches covered with long thorns (commonly used for firewood) are plaited into the shape of a crown and this is pressed into His scalp. Again there is copious bleeding (the scalp being one of the most vascular areas of the body). After mocking Him and striking Him across the face, the soldiers take the stick from His hand and strike Him across the head, driving the thorns deeper into His scalp. Finally, they tire of their sadistic sport and the robe is torn from His back. This had already become adherent to the clots of blood and serum in the wounds, and its removal, just as in the careless removal of a surgical bandage, causes excruciating pain...almost as though He were again being whipped—and the wounds again begin to bleed.

In deference to Jewish custom, the Romans return His garments. The heavy patibulum of the cross is tied across His shoulders and the procession of the condemned Christ, two thieves and the execution detail of the Roman soldiers, headed by a centurion, begins it slow journey along the Via Dolorosa. In spite of His efforts to walk erect, the weight of the heavy wooden cross together with the shock produced by copious blood loss, is too much. He stumbles and falls. The rough wood of the beam gouges into the lacerated skin and muscles of the shoulders. He tries to rise, but human muscles have been pushed beyond their endurance. the centurion, anxious to get on with the crucifixion, selects a stalwart North African onlooker, Simon of Cyrene, to carry the cross. Jesus follows, still bleeding and sweating the cold, clammy sweat of shock. The 650-yard journey from the fortress Antonia to Golgotha is finally completed. The prisoner is again stripped of His clothes—except for a loin cloth which is allowed the Jews.

The crucifixion begins, Jesus is offered wine mixed with Myrrh, a mild analgesic mixture. He refuses to drink. Simon is ordered to place the cross on the ground and Jesus is quickly thrown backward with His shoulders against the wood. The legionnaire feels for the depression at the front of the wrist. He drives a heavy, square, wrought-iron nail through the wrist and deep into the wood. Quickly, he moves to the other side and repeats the action, being careful not to pull the arms too tightly, but to allow some flexibility and movement. The patibulum is then lifted in place at the top of the stipes and the titulus reading "Jesus of Nazareth, King of the Jews" is nailed in place.

The left foot is pressed backward against the right foot, and with both feet extended, toes down, a nail is driven through the arch of each, leaving the knees moderately flexed. The victim is now crucified. As He slowly sags down with more weight on the nails in the wrists, excruciating, fiery pain shoots along the fingers and up the arms to explode in the brain—the nails in the wrists are putting pressure on the median nerves. As He pushes Himself upward to avoid this wrenching torment, He places His full weight on the nail through His feet. Again there is the searing agony of the tearing through the nerves between the metatarsal bones of the feet.

At this point, another phenomenon occurs. As the arms fatigue, great waves of cramps sweep over the muscles, knotting them in deep, relentless, throbbing pain. With these cramps comes the inability to push Himself upward. Hanging by His arms, the pectoral muscles are paralyzed and the intercostal muscles are unable to act. Air can be drawn into the lungs, but cannot be exhaled. Jesus fights to raise Himself in order to get even one short breath. Finally carbon dioxide builds up in the lungs and in the blood stream and the cramps partially subside. Spasmodically, He is able to push Himself upward to exhale and bring in the life-giving oxygen It was undoubtedly during these periods that He uttered the seven short sentences which are recorded:

The first, looking down at the Roman soldiers throwing dice for His seamless garment, "Father, forgive them for they know not what they do."

The second, to the penitent thief, "Today thou shalt be with me in Paradise."

The third, looking down at the terrified, grief stricken, adolescent John, (the beloved Apostle), He said, "Behold thy mother," and looking to Mary, His mother, "Woman, behold thy son."

The fourth cry is from the beginning of the 22nd Psalm, "My God, my God, why hast thou forsaken me?"

Hours of this limitless pain, cycles of twisting joint-rending cramps, intermittent partial asphyxiation, searing pain as tissue is torn from His lacerated back as He moves up and down against the rough timber. Then another agony begins. A deep crushing pain deep in the chest as the pericardium slowly fills with serum and begins to compress the heart.

Let us remember again the 22nd Psalm (the 14th verse), "I am poured out like water, and all my bones are out of joint; my heart is like wax, it is melted in the midst of my bowels." It is now almost over—the loss of tissue fluids has reached a critical level—the compressed heart is struggling to pump heavy, thick, sluggish blood into the tissue—the tortured lungs are making a frantic effort to draw in small gulps of air. The markedly dehydrated tissues send their flood of stimuli to the brain.

Jesus gasps His fifth cry, "I thirst."

Let us remember another verse from the prophetic 22nd Psalm: "My strength is dried up like a potsherd, and my tongue cleaveth to my jaws; and thou has brought me into the dust of death."

A sponge soaked in Posca, the cheap, sour wine which is the staple drink of the Roman legionnaires, is lifted to His lips. He apparently does not take any of the liquid. The body of Jesus is now in extremis, and He can feel the chill of death creeping through His tissues. This realization brings out His sixth words—possibly little more than a tortured whisper.

"It is finished."

His mission of atonement has been completed. Finally He can allow his body to die.

With one last surge of strength, he once again presses His torn feet against the nail, straightens His legs, takes a deeper breath, and utters His seventh and last cry, "Father into thy hands I commit my spirit."

The rest you know. In order that the Sabbath not be profaned, the Jews asked that the condemned men be dispatched and removed from the crosses. The common method of ending a crucifixion was by cruxifracture, the breaking of the bones of the legs. This prevents the victim from pushing himself upward; the tension could not be relieved from the muscles of the chest, and rapid suffocation occurred. The legs of the two thieves were broken, but when they came to Jesus they saw that this was unnecessary, thus fulfilling the scripture, "not one bone shall be broken."

Apparently to make doubly sure of death, the legionnaire drove his lance through the fifth interspace between the ribs, upward through the pericardium and into the heart. The 34th verse of the 19th chapter of the Gospel according to John: "And immediately there came out blood and water." Thus there was an escape of watery fluid from the sac surrounding the heart and blood from the interior of the heart. We, therefore, have rather conclusive postmortem evidence that Our Lord died, not the usual crucifixion death by suffocation, but of heart failure due to shock and constriction of the heart by fluid in the pericardium.

Thus we have seen a glimpse of the epitome of evil which man can exhibit toward man—and toward God. This is not a pretty sight and is apt to leave us despondent and depressed. How grateful we can be that we have a sequel: A glimpse of the infinite mercy of God toward man—the miracle of the atonement and the expectation of Easter morning!

To learn more about the impact of the cross read *Thirty Days at the Foot of the Cross,* edited by Tom and Sheila Jones

You Made the Right Decision

(Especially for new Christians)

Thomas Jones
Nashville, Tennessee

> *But you are a chosen people, a royal priesthood, a holy nation, a people belonging to God, that you may declare the praises of him who called you out of darkness into his wonderful light. Once you were not a people, but now you are the people of God; once you had not received mercy, but now you have received mercy.*
>
> 1 Peter 2:9–10

My new Christian friend, this is written especially for you to help you understand what you have done and what you have become. Some time ago, you did what few in this world ever do. You made a decision that few have the courage to make. You left one life behind and burst into a new life, whose architect and designer is God. You turned your back on the "wisdom of this world," on that which you had been taught for years, on that which had become such a part of you that you didn't know for a very long time that there was any other way to be, and you reached out and embraced the wisdom of God. You did what few have the integrity and the guts to do.

Not even those who skydive or climb mountains or race into battle do something as daring as you did. You left the familiar, the normal, the traditional and the expected and you cast your lot with a radical. You didn't do it to be a rebel, because he didn't do what he did to be a rebel. You did it because it is right. You did it because he is right.

You did it because you came to your senses. You did it because your eyes were opened. You did it because you saw that it is not in man to direct his own steps. You did it because you saw and understood that apart from God we can do nothing. You gave yourself to Jesus Christ. You stood before others and you said for all to hear, "Jesus is Lord." Those words of yours echoed all the way to the corners of glory and into the dungeons of demons, because you stood face to face with the truth about God, the truth about yourself and the truth about this world, and you had the heart and the humility to admit how much you needed him.

My friend, you did the right thing. You put your faith in the right person. You committed to the right cause. And you will not be sorry.

From Old to New

Oh, yes, you were a sinner. You were dead in your trespasses and sins. You followed the ways of the world and, yes, even the evil one who rules the dominion of darkness. You gratified the cravings of your sinful nature. You followed its desires and thoughts. And you will never be able to look down on anyone and say, "Well, at least I wasn't *that* bad." You were bad and you must never forget that. Your need for a savior was no less than the child-killer you read about in the newspaper or the sorry-looking figure you see in handcuffs on the evening news. Oh, your mother may have told you how nice you were and friends may have said you were wonderful, but none of them knew much about God's standards—his radical standards—his right and true standards. But you looked at and studied those standards with an open heart and saw yourself for the first time, and you cried out with the apostle, "Wretched man (or woman) that I am."

But then, by the grace of God, you made a right and courageous choice. You looked up into his eyes and said one of the most important words anyone can ever say to God. You said, "Help!" Like the Roman centurion, like the Canaanite woman, like the invalid at the pool, you said, "I need help." You said, "I need your help." And then God looked back at you and said, "I will help. I am in the helping business. I am in the saving business. I am in the redeeming business. I am in the forgiving business." And then God worked a miracle. He took a sinner who was lost in an empty way of life, traveling toward hell and without hope, and he made you new. And that is what you are today. You are new. You don't belong to the old any more. You belong to the new.

You confessed, "Jesus is Lord" and went down into the water. You were buried with Jesus in baptism and your old life was consigned to the grave (and by way, let it stay there). You came out of the water and are not the same. A new Spirit is filling you up. Heaven's view of you has changed and now your view of everything can change. Once you looked at things from a human point of view. Now you do so no longer. Everything Jesus did has now been applied to your life. Everything he achieved has been credited to your account. When God looks at you today, it is as though he is looking at Jesus. Incredibly, you stand before him without spot or blemish and free from accusation (and this remains true for as long as you live if you continue in your faith). The old has passed away. The old you is gone. The old record of sin is gone. The old sentence of death is gone. All things have become new.

Take some time to just let that soak in. It is so amazing that you won't get it quickly. In fact, only in heaven will you surely understand it all.

Challenges Ahead

You have probably already learned that new does not mean perfect—at least not yet. (Perfect also must wait for heaven.) You are new, but there is still a lot of old around to deal with. You are new but you are not finished. There is still a great spiritual battle to be fought. You are on the right side. You have been given the right weapons. But there are some intense times ahead. One thing is for sure: Jesus never promises that following him will be a cushy ride. He promises life and joy and peace, but he also talks plainly about sacrifice, crosses and persecution. He lets you know plenty of times that being new in an old world means there is a price to pay. But you counted the cost and with eyes wide open made your decision, and now by the grace of God you can keep paying the price as long as it takes.

Along the journey, you will have some great victories. You are fighting with a God who knows how to win. You will see amazing things. You've seen love, but you will see much more. You will see love that overcomes sin and love that overcomes hurt and love that never quits. You will have that kind of radical love for others and you will be loved with that kind of love. You are in a kingdom that is advancing around the world. You are in a church that is tearing down walls of division and bringing people together, and you will be a part of that. You will contribute to all this. God will take your talents, energize them with his Spirit and use you to make a difference in the lives of others.

God has a plan for your life and it will

come true as you stay with him. He did not go to all the trouble of creating the world, choosing a nation, bringing a savior and giving us a Bible to let it all fizzle in the twenty-first century. What he starts he finishes, and what he started with you, he will finish. The bottom of the ninth and the fourth quarter always belong to God. He finishes, and he finishes strong.

But bear in mind that you will have some tough days. God allows them. Don't be surprised when they come. Don't despair if they come more often than you think they ought. Somehow they're all part of his plan to build your character. You'll have days when the demons of doubt will pound on your faith. You'll have days when the demons of fear will chip away at your courage. You'll have days when the demons of selfishness will try to undermine your commitment. You'll have days when the demons of fatigue will tell you God expects too much. Your old life died with Christ in baptism, but the demons didn't take that same bath. You have a new mind and new heart but the demons haven't given up on reclaiming you for their cause.

Sometimes, they'll dress up in sheep's clothing and present their case in a dozen smooth and attractive ways. Sometimes they'll come dressed like football linebackers and try smashing you into hopelessness. Their minds are fertile with schemes to distract and discourage disciples. But mark this down: No day will ever be so tough that you cannot make it through and no demon so strong that you cannot overcome him. God just will not let it be any other way. You are his son or his daughter, and he will make sure that no matter how hot the fire, no matter how cold the wind, no matter how tough the disappointment, no matter how perplexing the question, he will always provide a way out—a way of escape—a way back to the one and only road that leads to heaven. Just make up your mind that you will never, never, never quit on God, and you can be sure that he will never quit on you.

Vital Principles

Being a disciple of Jesus is really a matter of taking very simple ideas and relentlessly applying them. And relentless means daily. Remember how often the word "daily" shows up in your Bible. Understand what this is saying about what we all need. Never think you can be an exception.

Your conviction that you needed help brought you to God in the first place. Now, let him hear from you every day how you need his help. Make your prayer life a priority. Do it now as a young disciple. Give it the place that it deserves—at the top of your "to do" list, at the center of your existence. But don't ever do it just to check it off. Don't do it to fulfill a duty. Do it because every day of your life as long as you live you will need help from God. Fight off the distractions, shake off the drowsiness, break out of the routine, do something unusual, but whatever it takes, claim your birthright. You are a child of the King. Walk with him every day. Lay every tough decision before him. Cast all your anxieties on him. Intercede with him for every person he is putting in your life to love. No matter how much you learn. No matter how much you do. No matter how many other great things others may say about you, learn to be a man of prayer or a woman of prayer and stay that way as long as you live.

And then, treasure your Bible. Expose your mind and your heart to it every day. In a world of shifting opinions and changing standards, it is your only safe guide to truth. When powerful feelings of sentimentality pull you toward compromise and an unbiblical broadmindedness, the Bible will remind you that God means what he says. But beyond that you need the Bible's wisdom, its vision, its direction—and you need it fresh every day. If Jesus lived by every word that came from the mouth of God, how can we be any different?

And then look around you and see the family you are in. Be grateful for your physical family, but realize that this new spiritual family is even more of God. Here is where you will see godly examples. Here is where you will get godly advice. Here is where you will give and receive the love that Jesus said would get the attention of the world. And it needs to happen how often? There's that word again—daily. But, remember, we haven't gotten to perfection yet. Your spiritual family is still on earth, not in heaven, which means you will have to forgive even as you will need to be forgiven. You will need to be forbearing, even as you will need others to be forbearing of you. But love this family. Treat it just the way God does.

And then, never forget the importance of the mission. Fulfilling the mission must be daily like the others. God has a strategy of getting his miracles into more offices, more neighborhoods, more cities, and more countries. You are at the center of his plan. He called you to fish for men and women, to go and help others become what you have become. You can think of a dozen reasons why you can't do it. But understand this: Your circumstances will change, your opportunities will change, your energy will change, your challenges will change. But your mission will not change. In every situation, you will still be Christ's ambassador and God will still be seeking to make his appeal through you. In many ways, being faithful here may be your greatest challenge, but aren't you grateful someone was faithful to you? Aren't you glad someone didn't make an excuse but found a way to get into your life and share with you that Jesus is Lord? Aren't you glad someone gave you a lot of time and stayed with you until you got it? Because that person did that for you, you can now do it for someone else. What that will mean to them and to you can hardly be described.

And so, my new Christian friend, you did the right thing. You have the right King. You are on the right road. You have the right friends. You are singing the right song and you are reading the right book. Never forget what you were, how you got here and who you belong to.

If you want to learn more about following Jesus read *Letters to New Disciples*, by Tom A. Jones

Using the Psalms to Pray

To help you use the Psalms as outlines, guidelines and inspiration for prayer, all of the 150 Psalms are categorized below; there are no duplications.

I. Kindling wood for the fires of prayer when it's tough to get started

A. When unmotivated (inspiring prayers)

Psalm 1	Psalm 19	Psalm 27
Psalm 91	Psalm 103	Psalm 107

B. When feeling faithless (great reminders of the basis of our faith):

Psalm 48	Psalm 74	Psalm 77
Psalm 78	Psalm 81	Psalm 105
Psalm 106	Psalm 111	Psalm 119

II. Learning how to worship, praise and give thanks to God

A. Adoration and praise, worship and thanks

Psalm 8	Psalm 9	Psalm 24
Psalm 29	Psalm 45	Psalm 47
Psalm 87	Ps 92–93	Ps 95–96
Ps 98–99	Psalm 100	Psalm 104
Psalm 113	Psalm 117	Ps 133–135
Psalm 136	Ps 146–150	

B. Special affection to God (some of the most intimate prayers)

Psalm 18	Psalm 42	Psalm 63
Psalm 84	Psalm 116	Psalm 139
Psalm 145		

III. Where to turn in the Psalms when feeling overwhelmed or discouraged

A. When overwhelmed (need to trust God)

Psalm 16	Psalm 17	Psalm 20
Psalm 28	Psalm 33	Psalm 37
Psalm 57	Psalm 62	Psalm 112
Psalm 122	Psalm 125	Psalm 143

B. When afraid (need your fears calmed)

Psalm 23	Psalm 34	Psalm 46
Psalm 55	Psalm 56	Psalm 118

C. When feeling guilty about sin and needing to get open and confess

Psalm 32	Psalm 38	Psalm 43
Psalm 88	Psalm 130	Psalm 141

D. When feeling disciplined by God

Psalm 6	Psalm 44	Psalm 60
Psalm 66	Psalm 85	Psalm 89
Psalm 102	Psalm 108	Psalm 137

E. How to cry out to God for help

Psalm 3	Psalm 10	Psalm 12
Psalm 26	Psalm 70	Psalm 82
Psalm 86	Psalm 132	Psalm 142

IV. God, help me to overcome!

A. When fighting worldliness

Psalm 11	Psalm 49	Ps 52–53
Psalm 58	Psalm 73	Psalm 101

B. When struggling with sin

Psalm 4–5	Psalm 7	Psalm 13

Psalm 25	Psalm 31	Ps 39–41
Psalm 65	Psalm 79–80	

C. When dealing with persecution

Psalm 2	Psalm 22	Psalm 54
Psalm 59	Psalm 64	Psalm 69
Psalm 83	Psalm 94	Psalm 109
Psalm 120	Psalm 129	Psalm 140

D. How to humble yourself before God

Ps 14–15	Psalm 36	Psalm 50
Psalm 51	Psalm 71	Psalm 75
Psalm 76	Psalm 90	Psalm 97
Psalm 114	Psalm 128	Psalm 131

V. How to rely more on God for victory

A. God gives the victory!

Psalm 21	Psalm 30	Psalm 35
Psalm 67	Ps 126–127	Ps 144

B. God enables us to lead (when need courage, confidence)

Psalm 61	Psalm 68	Psalm 72
Psalm 110	Psalm 115	Psalm 121
Psalm 123	Psalm 124	Psalm 138

Jeff Chacon
Tampa, Florida

For more informaton about Psalms read *THRIVE—Using Psalms to Help You Flourish,* by Douglas Jacoby

For more informaton about Psalms read *Into the Psalms* by Rolan Dia Monje

A Biblical Guide to Help You Work Through Your Past

Introduction

A. What is the world's way of dealing with hurt, pain, injustice and abuse?

–anger	–hold a grudge
–hatred	–pull heart away
–resentment	–run away
–bitterness	–ignore it and hope it goes away
–revenge	–justify all these behaviors

1. The problem is that these "solutions" don't work. They are like putting a Band-Aid on a major wound. Instead of helping, they only make the problem worse because the heart is allowed to harden over a long period of time.
2. Jesus is the only one who can heal us of our hurt and pain. He stands ready to do it (see the account of the "bleeding woman" in Mark 5:25–34 for reference), but we must do it his way.

I. God's way is that you face the truth.

A. John 8:31–32
1. Only the truth will set you free.
2. Many of us grew up in dysfunctional families where "touchy subjects" were not openly discussed.
3. Must be willing to face the truth, no matter how painful, in order to be healed

B. Action
1. On a piece of paper, write:
What ___________ *did to hurt me:*
2. Then list things—the facts, not the feelings yet.
   a) Ex: *My father hit me several times as a child.*
   b) Ex: *My brother sexually abused me at least 10 different times from the ages of 10–15.*
   c) Ex: *My mother belittled me and abused me verbally, saying things like: "You'll never amount to anything," etc.*

II. You must feel the hurt.

A. Action
1. On paper describe how each fact made you feel.
   a) Ex: When my father hit me, I felt angry at him and wanted to hit him back, or even kill him at times.
   b) Ex: When my brother abused me, I felt confused, dirty and guilty.
   c) Ex: When my mother belittled me, I felt discouraged and depressed.
2. Write down how you responded to each hurt, what you did.
   a) Ex: I resented my dad privately and silently. We still aren't close.
   b) Ex: I hated men because of what my brother did to me.
   c) Ex: I have become an overachiever because of what my mom said to me. I am constantly trying to prove her wrong about me.

III. You must free your heart.

A. Recognize that God will judge the perpetrators, so you don't have to.
1. God is just, and he will judge all of us appropriately on Judgment Day. Therefore, no one is getting away

with anything.

2. David took comfort in knowing that God would judge his enemies with justice, that he would be vindicated on Judgment Day, and so may we (Psalm 10, Psalm 17, Psalm 26, Psalm 31 and others).
3. In Romans 12:19 God says, "It is mine to avenge; I will repay."

B. Recognize that God will judge you for your attitude and actions toward them as well.
   1. Take responsibility for your sinful responses, and repent!
   2. Anger, resentment, bitterness and hatred are all sins, no matter what the cause, and must be repented of (read Ephesians 4:31–32, Colossians 3:8, 2 Timothy 3:3, 1 Peter 2:1).

C. *Action:* Write out your sins and a paragraph of apology to God.

D. *Action:* Forgive the perpetrators for the things listed earlier and for how they made you feel, as you want God to forgive you. (NOTE: In some cases it may not be best to talk to the person, but to simply forgive them in prayer. Get advice.)
   1. Matthew 6:14–15: If you don't forgive them, God won't forgive you!
   2. Matthew 5:44: Jesus commands us to love our enemies.
   3. Matthew 18:21–35: You can forgive because God has forgiven you for so much.

F. *Action:* Surrender the hurt and pain to God emotionally—1 Peter 2:18–25 (esp. v23)—Jesus entrusted himself and his victimizers to God, who judges justly.

G. *Action:* You may want to seal up these papers and put them in a drawer, or throw them away, or burn them as a symbol of your letting go of the past once and for all.

H. *Action:* Get grateful, and establish a new relationship with the person if possible.

I. *Action:* List as many good memories and positive qualities about that person as possible. Focus from now on those things. Write a letter or call them, if appropriate, to share your gratitude for them.

J. Some good books to read:
   1. *You're Someone Special* by Bruce Narramore
   2. *Family Dysfunctions* by Dale and Anita Ryan
   3. *A Tale of Three Kings* by Gene Edwards
   4. *Trusting God: Even When Life Hurts* by Jerry Bridges

IV. Conclusion

A. You can be freed from the baggage of the past. There is hope!

B. The whole process described in this study can take just a day or two. (*NOTE:* It can be done even if perpetrator is deceased because it depends on you, not them.)

C. Harboring a lack of forgiveness toward someone is a sin against God. So, you must repent of this to be right with God.

I wrote the following poem after freeing my heart from the past in 1992:

WE NEVER PLAYED CATCH

We never played catch
or tried to walk on a wall.
He didn't come to my games
when I used to play football.

All I wish was I knew him,
and that he knew me.
But now it's too late—
I'm almost 33.

No, not too late,
because...there really are three.
There are three Daddys now:
him, God and me!

To Ty, Ky and Ry
I'm the one they see.
The past is the present
and the future's up to me!

Cool! We'll play catch, we'll ride bikes,
and we'll talk all the time!
Ya, most of all...
we'll spend a lot of time.

And we all have God.
There is justice you see,
because everyone can have
the perfect Daddy.

He's loving and loyal
and where he really shines
is he's really good
at just "spending time."

I forgive you, Dad,
as I hope they'll forgive me.
And I thank you, Father,
for giving me three.
—Jeff Chacon (4/25/92)

Jeff Chacon
Tampa, Florida

Read more from Jeff Chacon about keeping your vision for the future. *Dare to Dream Again,* by Jeff Chacon

The Purpose of the Lord's Supper

Tom A. Jones, Nashville, Tennessee

By the time you read this, it is likely that you will have taken the Lord's Supper (sometimes called "communion" from the KJV translation of 1 Corinthians 10:16) with other Christians at least several times. In some cases, some of you who have been Christians for years will have taken it hundreds of times. To keep his death, burial and resurrection in our minds and hearts, and to keep this reality in the midst of the life of the church—his body, Jesus first broke bread and drank the cup with his disciples and then told them simply that whenever, or as often as, they did this, to do it in remembrance of him (1 Corinthians 11:23–26).

The New Testament does not give us any more specific instructions about how to observe the Lord's Supper, but as we study various passages about it we can clearly see six key words or phrases that help us stay focused on the purpose of this time together as a body. As we examine these, we will see that in the Lord's Supper, we focus on the past, the present and the future.

1. The first word is "remembrance."

In 1 Corinthians 11:23–24, Paul writes, "For I received from the Lord what I also passed on to you: The Lord Jesus, on the night he was betrayed, took bread, and when he had given thanks, he broke it and said, 'This is my body, which is for you; do this in remembrance of me.' The Hebrew notion of remembrance means more than that a past event is *recalled*. It means that the event is *reexperienced*. For Jews, Passover is a reparticipation in the events of Exodus, not just a distant recollection. The Greek word that is used here actually implies this same thing.

For Christians the Lord's Supper is a reexperiencing of the cross. As we take the bread we are to seek to reexperience that event

- Where Jesus was despised and rejected by men
- Where he took up our infirmities and carried our sorrows
- Where he was pierced for our transgressions and crushed for our iniquities
- Where by his wounds we were healed
- Where the Lord laid on him the iniquity of us all

For some of us this is why a movie like *The Passion of the Christ* was so powerful. It helped us to reexperience what Jesus did for us and to remember that "atonement" and "redemption" are not just theological words but that Jesus, who knew no sin, really did become sin for us so that in him we might become the righteousness of God.

But why would God want us to remember or reexperience? Why do people say we must not forget the Holocaust? Why do they say we must remember September 11? Why remember "slavery"? Isn't it true that remembering gets you in touch with important realities?

In this case it would be

- The seriousness of sin
- The depth of God's love for us
- The kind of God he is
- The sacrificial spirit and heart of Jesus

2. The second word is "covenant."

In 1 Corinthians 11:25 Paul wrote, "In the same way, after supper he took the cup, saying, 'This cup is the new covenant in my blood; do this, whenever you drink it, in remembrance of me.'" God shows his grace in relating to his people by initiating covenants with them. The Old Testament story can be related as the story of God making covenants with his people and responding to them out of that covenant relationship. The New Testament can be described as the fulfillment of the Old Testament covenant in the establishment of God's new covenant in Jesus Christ.

Covenant has everything to do with one thing: *relationship*. And so in the Lord's Supper we celebrate the *new covenant* and we celebrate our *present* relationship with God based on blood, offered to us by grace. We have a living relationship with God because of what Jesus did that allows us to come into the "Holy of Holies." We call the second part of our Bible the New Testament. "Testament" is a translation of the word *diatheke*. The better translation of that would be "covenant." The books of Matthew through Revelation are the new covenant scriptures. They are not so much the new covenant itself but the scriptures that describe for us the new covenant. The new covenant is the relationship we now enjoy with God because of the fact that Jesus laid down his life for us.

3. The third word is "fellowship" or "participation."

Here is what Paul says in 1 Corinthians 10:16: "Is not the cup of thanksgiving for which we give thanks a participation in the blood of Christ? And is not the bread that we break a participation in the body of Christ?" The word for "participation" is the Greek word *koinonia*. This is the same word used in Acts 2:42 where we are told they devoted themselves to the fellowship. The cup we drink is a fellowship in the blood of Christ. The bread we break is fellowship in the body of Christ. It is a "*sharing together in*" the body and blood of Christ as the *new covenant community*. The Lord's Supper is a time to celebrate and focus on the fact that the body and blood of Jesus have brought us into fellowship with him and into fellowship with each other.

By the way, it is from this passage that we get the word "communion." The KJV translates this passage "is not the cup of thanksgiving a communion in the blood of Christ?" The word "communion" doesn't appear in most of the recent translations.

As you read 1 Corinthians 11 carefully, here is what you see: The failure to understand that the connection of fellowship and the Lord's Supper was at the heart of the Corinthians' problem with their observing it. Listen to Paul's words in 1 Corinthians 11:28–30: "A man ought to examine himself before he eats of the bread and drinks of the cup. For anyone who eats and drinks without recognizing the body of the Lord eats and drinks judgment on himself. That is why many among you are weak and sick, and a number of you have fallen asleep." If we don't consider carefully the context here, we will miss the fact that their failure to "recognize the body of the Lord" is failure to recognize the church and one's relationships with other disciples.

Jesus' death was not just to forgive us of our sin and bring us to God. It was to bring us into a relationship with each other. The Lord's Supper then is to be a *fellowship meal*. It is to be a time for us to celebrate how God brought us out of our sin and into relationship with him and with each other.

With this in mind, there are two things that will completely ruin the Lord's Supper: (1) not being *resolved* and (2) not being *involved*. Allowing unresolved conflicts in relationships with others destroys the fellowship. Not being involved in the lives of others is to not "recognize the body of the Lord."

4. The fourth phrase is "his coming."

In 1 Corinthians 11:26, Paul says, "For whenever you eat this bread and drink this cup, you proclaim the Lord's death until he comes." In the Lord's Supper we are not just looking back and not just thinking about the present. We also are thinking about the future. "Until he comes." He is coming back. He will bring all things to an end. And as the new covenant community, we will sit down with him at the great feast.

It has been pointed out that for many westerners the idea of heaven is sitting on a cloud with a harp, but the Biblical view of heaven is a great supper and great banquet (Luke 13:29). And so how does the New Testament end? Hear these words from Revelation 19:9:

> *Then the angel said to me, "Write: 'Blessed are those who are invited to the wedding supper of the Lamb!'" And he added, "These are the true words of God."*

And so in Scripture we see three great suppers: (1) There is what we call the "Last Supper" when Jesus first broke the bread and drank the cup with the disciples and told them to continue to do this. (2) There is the Lord's Supper, which the church continues to observe as it remembers his death and focuses on what it means to us in the present. (3) And finally, there is the wedding supper of the Lamb which will take place when he comes again. As we break the bread and drink the cup now, we look forward to the great supper of the victorious Lamb.

5. Next is the phrase "personal examination."

Again we look at the words of Paul: "Therefore, whoever eats the bread or drinks the cup of the Lord in an unworthy manner will be guilty of sinning against the body and blood of the Lord. A man ought to examine himself before he eats of the bread and drinks of the cup" (1 Corinthians 11:27–28).

In light of what Christ has done and how he has brought me by this sacrifice and grace into this body of believers, I need to examine myself. But examine what? My heart, my faith, my commitment to God, my attitude, but especially in 1 Corinthians 11, my commitment to others, the kind of fellowship and relationships I have with others in the body.

And what if that examination reveals sin and the need for change? Praise God! His grace is sufficient. Remember you are examining yourself in the context of grace. The Lord's Supper, if it is anything, is a place to remember grace. Whatever we find, can be forgiven and dealt with and changed if we have a heart that is eager to repent.

6. The final word is "thanksgiving."

Looking again at Paul's words, "For I received from the Lord what I also passed on to you: The Lord Jesus, on the night he was betrayed, took bread, and when he had given thanks, he broke it and said, 'This is my body, which is for you; do this in remembrance of me'" (1 Corinthians 11:23–24). The Greek word for "thanks" here is the word *eucharisteo* from which comes the word "Eucharist." Jesus is described as giving thanks as he broke the bread with his disciples. How much more do we need to be giving thanks as we break the bread and drink the cup in remembrance of what he has done for us?And so the NIV translates 1 Corinthians 10:16: "Is not the cup of thanksgiving for which we give thanks a participation in the blood of Christ?" What are some of the things we need to be thankful for as we eat and drink? Is it not all of the things we have looked at: (1) What he did for us, (2) the relationship he gives us in the new covenant, (3) the fellowship it brings us into with him and others, (4) the future he promises us, and (5) the freedom to be honest about our lives, knowing there is grace and power to help us change.

So, should the Lord's Supper be a time of serious reflection or joyful fellowship and celebration? While the greatest emphasis would seem to be on the latter, the former should also be there.

The Lord's Supper: 'Moscow Style'

From *In Remembrance of Me* by Andy Fleming, © 2018 by Illumination Publishers, available at www.ipibooks.com.

After just five days of sharing our faith on the streets, we held the first service of the church in Moscow on July 14 with 268 in attendance. From that very first meeting, the Lord added daily to our number those who were being saved (Acts 2:42), and during the next twelve months we saw 850 people baptized into Christ. Although it had been our practice in other places to celebrate the Lord's Supper during our public Sunday worship service, the sheer numbers of visitors initially made this impractical. Instead, after our regular worship service, comprised of singing, praying, testimony and preaching, we would have about an hour of fellowship before we would gather the members together again.

At this much smaller meeting, usually accompanied by some of the more eager visitors, the disciples would celebrate the Lord's Supper in small groups there in our rented hall or in nearby parks.

I will never forget taking a small group to the park right under the Kremlin wall in early September of 1991 and breaking bread and sharing the fruit of the vine together. Soldiers stood nearby at their stations, Muscovites were strolling in the afternoon sun, and there in a little corner garden of the park, disciples of Jesus circled together singing softly and thanking God in prayer—remembering the incredible sacrifice of Jesus Christ.

By January of 1992, winter conditions, combined with economic recession due to the collapse of the USSR, moved us into another pattern. After our regular Sunday service we would go back to our apartments, scattered throughout Moscow, for a fellowship meal of soup and bread, followed by the Lord's Supper. For many of our poorer members, these meals not only provided a time of awesome fellowship, but also actually satisfied a true physical need. Among all my memories of our eight years of ministry in Moscow, these house church meetings are among some of the most dear and vivid. With twenty or so people jammed into our small living room and half the people seated on the floor, we first shared our soup and bread together, and then remembered Jesus in the Lord's Supper. It was awesome!

For more about the
Lord's Supper read
In Remembrance of Me,
by Andrew C. Fleming

Parents Who Make a Difference

I. Many battles to fight in God's kingdom, but the battle for our own children is one of the most important.

II. 1 Samuel 30:1–6

A. Note verse 6. Although David was such a hero, the men were ready to kill him when their own families were threatened.

B. David was out fighting battles, but the home front was left unprotected.

C. As leaders, what we do with our own sons and daughters will determine what we are able to do in helping the children of other disciples.

III. Sad situations with parents today.

A. Ignorance is one of the big culprits, lack of knowledge of the Bible and its principles.

B. The other main culprit is arrogance—knowing the principles and not putting them into practice, thinking that somehow it will work out anyway or being too self-absorbed to pay the price of training the family.

IV. Ephesians 6:1–4—Wherever we are, we must do all that we can to offset the mistakes we have made.

A. This is a faith issue for some of us who have lost hope.

B. Back in 1 Samuel 30, David found strength in the Lord and delivered the children by the power of God.

C. The men of David were tempted to become embittered, as we are when our children are not doing well, but we have a choice in the matter. Take responsibility and do everything you can do to help them.

D. Differences to make in our children

1. Spiritually—Get them "in the Lord." Nothing else is more important.
2. Emotionally—Do not exasperate your children, and meet their emotional needs. Emotional happiness and maturity comes as a result of the right kind of "nurturing" (as some versions translate Eph. 6:4).

V. The ten commandments of effective parenting

A. Develop the child's relationship with God (1 Chronicles 28:9).

1. Kids will not pick it up by osmosis. They must be trained.
2. Much more is involved than making them go to church. If they don't like church, they don't know God.
3. Illustration—David training Solomon by showing him where he wrote the various Psalms and why.
4. You must set the example and share your own struggles and victories.
5. My conversation with my son Sam when his cousin fell away: Get determined and not discouraged. (Blair has been restored and said that Sam had a big influence on him.)
6. Early morning quiet times together.

B. Show the importance of family over everything but God (Deut. 6:4–7).

1. Sam said that he could always interrupt a meeting if he really needed help. (Can your child reach you when he has a need?)
2. Getting up early with Sam really made an impact on him and demonstrated the importance of family.

C. Become your child's best friend.

1. David and Solomon; Paul and Timothy; God and Moses; all of these were best friends.
2. Kids don't remain little kids, but they can remain best friends.
3. Vulnerability is a key ingredient,

and getting involved in their world is another.

4. Both praise and correction must be clear. God said of Jesus, "This is my Son, whom I love; with him I am well pleased" (Matthew 17:5). Do you express this to your children or only point out their needs to improve?

D. Allow them the freedom to make mistakes (Colossians 3:12–14).

1. In the Colossians passage, these qualities are all applied when mistakes are made.
2. Sam made comments about how he felt that he would be corrected but never rejected.
3. We cannot stifle our kids—they must be able to express what is really in their hearts and lives.
4. When the discipline is over, the incident must be in the past. Grace must be demonstrated.

E. Teach lessons from real life situations with the Bible in hand.

1. Show how the principles apply. Mistakes can be stepping stones to victories.
2. Correction with explanation and direction.
3. Attitudes must be the focal point of the correction, not simply the outward action.

F. Respect must be built both ways (1 Peter 2:17).

1. As the children age, they cannot be treated as toddlers.
2. Treat them with respect by being honest and up-front.
3. Embarrassing situations must be avoided, which calls for getting input from the kids themselves.
4. For all of us, being treated with respect is a key.
5. Let kids make some decisions, and more as they age.
6. Be humble and vulnerable when you have messed up.
7. Team decisions are extremely healthy and productive. Give the kids the opportunity for input.

G. Be affectionate and expressive to the children (2 Corinthians 6:8–10).

1. Some men especially have a difficult time being expressive, even with their wives, to say nothing of the children.
2. Jesus is our role model, not our parents who may have set the wrong example.
3. "I love you more than you love me" is a friendly competition in the Shaw family.

H. Notice that they are growing up.

1. Make the adjustments and make the use of the limited opportunities.
2. Provide a "no regrets" atmosphere.

I. Provide confidence through a godly marriage.

1. Nothing provides more security.
2. Your marriage is the greenhouse of security, the thermostat of their happiness and the model of their future families.

J. Encourage the success of each child (Romans 12:3–21).

1. The Romans qualities all contribute to success.
2. Encouraging each child in his or her own gifts is the most important issue here.
3. Let them be who they are, and help them develop themselves.

Wyndham Shaw
Boston, Massachusetts

Helping the Physically Challenged Disciple

I. Realities

A. People have physical challenges. Sickness is a reality. Disabilities are realities.

B. Chronic illnesses and other chronic physical challenges take an emotional and relational toll on those who have them and on those who live with them.

C. Studies have shown that an estimated thirty to thirty-five percent of the adult population faces some on-going physical challenge (PC). This means two things:

1.) We all have a substantial number of PC people to work with.

2.) Being PC is still a minority status (with all the challenges that brings).

D. As people age, PCs increase, and so, as our churches age, we will have more PC issues to deal with, not less.

E. Illness can mask other problems or can be used deceitfully.

1.) Psychosomatic illness does exist.

2.) Hypochondria is real.

3.) Some people do exaggerate illness or pain in order to manipulate others, to excuse themselves from activity or to avoid responsibility.

4.) Some people have a real illness, but for various reasons don't really want to get well.

F. Working effectively with people always takes into consideration all of the realities.

II. Biblical Teaching

Not only must we take into consideration the realities, but we also must take into consideration biblical teaching ("the whole counsel of God") and the qualities of Christian character.

A. Compassion is vital.

1.) It is found in God in abundance (Psalm 103:13, Psalm 116:5).

2.) It is not found in most of us naturally, but must be put on (Colossians 3:12).

3.) Jesus was filled with it and demonstrated it continually, especially with the sick (Matthew 15:32, 14:14, 20:34, Mark 1:41).Typical passage: "Filled with compassion, Jesus reached out his hand and touched the man. 'I am willing,' he said. 'Be clean!'" (Mark 1:41).

4.) We are not ready to counsel the sick if we are not *filled with* compassion.

B. Wisdom and judgment are essential.

1.) 1 Thessalonians 5:14 teaches "different strokes for different folks." (Some need support and affirmation; others need a challenge; many need a combination.)

2.) We should go in with compassion and a listening ear (James 1:19, Proverbs 18:13).

a.) This gives us the opportunity to get in touch with where people really are.

b.) It gives them the opportunity to feel really understood.

(1) Nothing is more important in working with people than causing them to feel you hear them and understand them.

(2) Brings *emotional clearance.* Until this happens they cannot hear you. All your won-

derful insight and excellent direction will fall on deaf ears. My approach: Assume the best with people. Operate on that assumption *until proven wrong*.

3.) Once you have heard people and helped them feel understood, there is more you can do. There is truth you can speak. Two things will be true:

a.) You will know much better *WHAT* truth they need to hear.

b.) They will be much more likely to hear you…because you will have built trust.

III. What Do We Need to Teach the PC Person?

A. Realize that circumstances alter your life (*bios*), but they don't end your life (*zoë*).

B. The principles of 2 Corinthians 1, 4, and 12 and Philippians 4.

C. Your illness can become a vehicle through which God works in most unexpected ways.

D. It is great when people understand and are supportive. But realize two things:

1.) No one ever can fully understand.

2.) You can still live well even if you are misunderstood. (Disciples are always misunderstood people.)

E. Sin is still your greatest challenge. Deal with sin biblically.

F. Whatever the challenge, God is always greater.

G. Whatever happens, don't lose your sense of humor. Proverbs 17:22 says that it is a gift from God. If you don't have one, buy one; get trained to have one; do whatever it takes!

H. Reading: *Mind Change*, *This Doesn't Feel Like Love*, and *Mind Change Moments*.

IV. Seven Great Temptations of Physically Challenged People (inspired by material from Linda Haney)

A. Self-pity—poor me, poor me, poor me

B. Resentment—especially toward God

C. Deceitfulness—using your challenge to excuse yourself from things you really don't want to do anyway

D. Faithlessness—"God can't use me any more."

E. Using your challenge as a license to sin—"I just can't help being angry or bitter."

F. Self-righteousness/pride—"I'm more spiritual than others because of what I've gone through. Others just couldn't possibly understand what I now understand."

G. Bitterness/an unforgiving spirit—especially of those who don't understand or are not sensitive enough.

No temptation has seized you except what is common to man. And God is faithful; he will not let you be tempted beyond what you can bear. But when you are tempted, he will also provide a way out so that you can stand up under it.

1 Corinthians 10:13

Tom A. Jones
Nashville, Tennessee

The Fine Art of Hospitality

Edited selections from *The Fine Art of Hospitality*

Practicing Hospitality
Restorers of the Lost Art
Sheila Jones
Nashville, Tennessee

Many people have a difficult time relating to the word "hospitality." To Generation Xers it conjures up pictures of prim and proper fifty-something ladies in white gloves eating finger sandwiches and petits fours—accompanied by classical music and inane conversation. Many, if not most, have a skewed view of hospitality and feel awkward in their attempts to practice it. Some grew up in homes where their parents rarely, if ever, invited non-relatives to eat a meal. Others watched from a safe distance as their mothers fretted and fumed over a meal as if their total worth as a person depended upon the impression made on the guests that evening. Still others remember fathers who were anything but enthusiastic that they would be required to leave the TV set, and accompanying TV tray, to sit at the table and talk to people they didn't know and didn't care to know.

The Scriptures are clear. We are commanded to "practice hospitality" (Romans 12:13). For those of us who are followers of Jesus and of his word, we must know what hospitality is so we can be obedient and practice it. The Jewish people in biblical times placed the highest priority upon being hospitable to others—especially strangers. During feast time, homes in Jerusalem and surrounding towns were opened to pilgrims coming to the Holy City to worship at the temple. There were no Holiday Inns, no McDonald's, no RV camps with electricity hookups and hot showers. They relied upon each other for food and shelter when they were away from home.

Hospitality: A Definition

Hospitality, simply defined, is sharing your heart and your home with others. A truly hospitable person is a giver, a person with a servant heart. He or she is sensitive to the needs of others and is willing and eager to expend energy, time and money to meet those needs. With this heart, they welcome others into a home in which they already show hospitality to their own family. Hospitality is not necessarily elegant entertaining; it is not rising to the occasion to put on a good show; it is not a cloak to dress up in and take off after guests leave. It is a reflection of the very heart of God to others.

Practicing Hospitality

In order to be encouraging and effective in our hospitality, we must first be content in the situations (houses or apartments) God has given us. We must have order and consistency in cleaning and decorating our houses, so we can reflect the nature and beauty of God's character.

We have to realize, though, that we can have a beautiful house and well-organized approaches to maintaining it, yet miss the whole meaning of "home" as God intended it. Home is the heart of hospitality. Building warmth and trust within your own family is essential to inviting others to join you as family. Home should be a safe harbor for children and guests alike. Even if you live in a singles' household (or by yourself), you can and must foster a sense of home and family.

After setting your house in order and establishing family in your home, you are ready to learn more about the meaning and practice of hospitality itself. Sharing your food and home with those who are not disciples is one of the best ways to show them your heart and life; it is also one of the best ways to encourage those who are already disciples. Peter says to disciples, "Offer hospitality to one another without grumbling" (1 Peter 4:9). There is something disarming and vulnerable about inviting others into your home. As you show hospitality, they will see the love of God.

God's Word in the Matter

Kay McKean
Orlando

"In the beginning God created the heavens and the earth." The first words of the Bible describe for us how God took nothing, and out of that nothing he created something: a home for mankind. Our home, planet Earth, was created by God to become an environment that would be beautiful for his people, that would sustain them so that they could live and work and raise families, and so that they could glorify and worship God.

The first ones to be given this home were Adam and Eve. God commanded them to live in their home, the Garden of Eden, and also to do the work that God gave them to do: to give names to all the creatures that God had created. Other players in God's drama were also given homes. Noah's home was the ark, where he was to be host, not only to human beings, but also to animals so that they would be protected from the flood. Abraham's traveling home was a tent, from which he entertained heavenly visitors. The Israelites were given a home, a land of their own, where centuries later, the Messiah would be born. Whatever the location or type of dwelling, homes were always intended to be a place from which the work of God would be accomplished.

God Blesses Hospitality

The home was also a means through which God could bless his people. After Abraham's hospitality toward his three visitors, he was promised a son. Lot's home was opened to angels who ultimately secured his escape from the destruction of Sodom and Gomorrah. Rebekah invited Abraham's servant to her family's home, and got a husband in the bargain! The widow of Zaraphath provided housing for Elijah, and survived a famine because of it. A Shunammite woman built a room onto her house for Elisha, and was blessed with a son. Esther prepared a palace feast, and saved her people from destruction.

As history marched forward to the time of Christ, we see that God was still using homes to bring him glory, regardless of the type of dwelling they might have been. God took a shelter for animals, and made it into the birthplace of the Savior of the world. The homes of "sinners" and "tax collectors" became catalysts for repentance and beacons of hope. God used the homes of Jews and Gentiles, men and women, jailers and prominent citizens to advance his kingdom following the days of Pentecost.

Our Father continues to use homes as places where the saved can be refreshed and the good news can be preached to the lost. Bible studies, church services and reviving devotionals have been presented in living rooms, dormitory rooms and kitchens across the world. Whatever the dwelling may be (a boat, a cave, a hut, a tent, a cottage, a palace or a suburban ranch with two-car garage) God can use it to further his cause, if the inhabitants are surrendered to doing his will.

Drawing Close to God

Jesus and his followers demonstrate the incredible blessings that can occur when the home is used as a place to draw closer to God. Jesus himself did not have a home to call his own, as he reminds us in Matthew 8:20, "Foxes have holes and birds of the air have nests, but the Son of Man has no place to lay his head." However, this did not stop him from showing the blessings of hospitality, even if it was in another person's home! Each time Jesus was invited, or invited himself, into someone's home, the residents were able to either receive or to witness healing, salvation, and the very words of life.

Think on the numerous examples of this: Zaccheus the tax collector radically repented following a meal in his home with Jesus (Luke 19:5–8); a lesson on love and forgiveness was delivered and exhibited in a Pharisee's home (Luke 7:36–50); a visit to Martha's home led to a reminder of what was truly best and most important (Luke 10:38–42); Jesus' anointing and his commendation of a woman's love took place during a meal at Simon's home (Mark 14:3–9); a paralytic was forgiven and healed after he and his friends "crashed" a gathering in Capernaum (Mark 2:1–12); Jesus sent out the mission team of seventy-two, telling them to enter homes and to eat and drink what they were given (Matthew 10:7). These are only a few of the instances where the home is mentioned as the venue for the work of God. Surely God is deliberately showing us the incredible ways that he can be glorified through the opening of homes.

The Early Church

In the infancy of the church, it is not surprising to see the early disciples walking the same path of hospitality and thereby advancing the kingdom in so many ways. The church was meeting together daily as they "broke bread in their homes and ate together with glad and sincere hearts" (Acts 2:46). The ministry to the Gentiles began in Cornelius' home (Acts 10:25ff). A prayer group meeting at Mary's house received Peter after his miraculous escape from prison (Acts 12:12). Paul's ministry in Philippi was headquartered in the home of Lydia, his first convert there (Acts 13–15). The Philippian jailer prepared a meal for Paul and Silas in his home following his baptism (Acts 16:31–34). Priscilla and Aquila were hosts to Paul in Corinth, and later to Apollos in Ephesus (Acts 18:3, 26). The recorded Acts of the Apostles closes out with the message of hospitality: "For two whole years Paul stayed there *in his own rented house* and welcomed all who came to see him. Boldly and without hindrance he preached the kingdom of God and taught about the Lord Jesus Christ" (Acts 18:30–31, emphasis added).

The letters to the early Christians show the importance and necessity of homes being used to serve God. The church met at the home of Priscilla and Aquila in Rome (Romans 16:5) and in the home of Nympha in Colosse (Colossians 4:15). Paul and the whole church enjoyed the hospitality of Gaius (Romans 16:23). Paul asked Philemon to welcome Onesimus, and also to prepare a guest room for himself (Philemon 17:22). The Bible makes it clear that Christian hospitality was vital to the spread of the gospel and the growth of the church!

Commands and Examples

The term "cocooning" has been used recently to indicate the isolating of a person or family in order to survive these uncertain and tumultuous times. It is understandable to want to lock our doors, pull down the shades and keep to ourselves for safety and security. But when we have an "us four no more" mentality, not only do we deny others a chance to have their needs met, we also deny ourselves the opportunity to enjoy the blessings of sharing with others. Romans 12:13 is not just a suggestion, but a command from God for us to fulfill his purpose for our lives: "Share with God's people who are in need. Practice hospitality."

Unconditional. Hospitality is not limited to inviting into our homes people who are just like us. Jesus condemned this action in Luke 14:13:"When you give a banquet, invite the poor, the crippled, the lame, the blind, and you will be blessed." Many people open their homes only to people with whom they feel naturally comfortable. Clearly the directive is to open our homes to all types of people in order to serve and share with them all. In this way, we have the added benefit of learning about people from all walks of life: We are able to learn from people of different races, cultures and backgrounds.

Unselfish. Hospitality is not a means to popularity or selfish gain, as Jesus goes on to say in Luke 14:14: "Although they cannot repay you, you will be repaid at the resurrection of the righteous." We see that Jesus' idea of hospitality is not simply to entertain, to impress, to get a promotion or to get ahead, but to give. Any other attitude will not bring about the blessings that God has promised.

Compassionate. One of the greatest aspects of hospitality is having the opportunity to meet the needs of others. In Matthew 25:31–45, we learn that as we feed, clothe, visit, look after and invite in others, it is as if we are doing so for Jesus himself! Our hospitality cannot be a self-serving agenda, designed to make ourselves feel good, but rather, a way to learn how to understand, serve and love other people.

Joyful. A very specific reminder is given to us in 1 Peter 4:9: "Offer hospitality to one another without grumbling." It is ludicrous to consider the possibility of having someone into your home and expecting them to feel comfortable if you are muttering and scowling, reminding them of how much trouble it is! While few would actually go that far, guests can sense tension, anxiety and exasperation, even if we are trying to hide it. On the contrary, our visitors should sense our thankfulness and joy that they have come to visit us!

Quality. The wedding at Cana gave Jesus the opportunity to serve by turning water into wine. This wasn't just watery wine, but was, as we see in John 2:10, "the best wine." God's habit of always giving the best is the example we must follow as we are serving others in our homes. Throughout Scripture we see that hospitality was not displayed in a sloppy, uncaring way, but with great attention and care. What a wonderful opportunity for us to deny ourselves and give the best we have for the benefit of others.

Prepared. Perhaps one of the most encouraging passages in the Bible is Jesus' statement, found in John 14:2, that he would go and "prepare a place" for us in his Father's house. To be hospitable does require some planning and effort. Although our homes should be open at all times to others, there is a need for disciples to work and prepare for guests who are expected. Waiting until the last moment to receive people into our homes indicates a lack of concern and respect. When we know guests are coming, we should do all we can to let them know we have looked forward to their arrival and have done all we can do to make them feel welcome.

Following the Example

God's kingdom must advance, and we as 21st-century disciples will have a great hand in that advancement as we obey the command to be hospitable. As I read in the Bible of souls being saved through hospitality, I am reminded of so many stories of conversions in recent years that began with the question, "Would you like to come to my home?" As those in our modern world become more and more isolated from one another, we are exhorted to be different and to open our homes to the lost and to the saved.

Hospitality may come naturally to some people, while others have to work at it more. We can all be encouraged and challenged by men and women who have left their own familiar culture and country and have learned how to be hospitable in a foreign land, often in a foreign language. Missionaries around the world must learn how to make a home in an unfamiliar environment and use that home to further the kingdom of God. I am personally inspired by the women who have learned new ways to shop, cook, serve and speak so that that they can help others know God. These are great examples to us of modern day hospitality, and we must strive to imitate their hearts and their actions.

The Host with the Most

God is our ultimate example of hospitality. He has provided a home for us on this earth, a place to live and work and do his will. He has welcomed us into his kingdom and provided us with a sustaining environment, the church. The church, the people of God, is like a home. It provides security; it is a haven, a safe place. It is not a place to hide, but rather, supplies the courage to go out into the world and help others. The head of this "home" is Jesus himself, and he leads his family to incredible blessings.

Finally, God protects us in the church until we go to be with him forever in our eternal home. The scriptures that describe heaven for us speak of feasts and banquets, of weddings, of beautiful places, of joy, of celebration—all the things that are considered lovely in this world. I believe that God knows we can't fathom how wonderful heaven will be, but he gives us enough clues to know that it will be awesome! What is even better is that God will be there to welcome us! To give us the privilege to go to heaven is the greatest act of hospitality we will ever experience!

Real Men Are Hospitable

Ron Brumley
San Diego, California

The majority of men tend to leave hospitality up to the women. These are some of the same men who believe in 1 Timothy 3:2 and in Titus 1:8 that says "...the overseer must be...hospitable...." This quality of character that elders are to exhibit, is addressed to the elder—not the wives of elders. This truth must attract our attention, men, and elicit our obedience.

Certainly, some men are more blessed with the gift of serving, which includes being hospitable. But as with most gifts from God, the exercise of them brings about growth and maturity. It is my firm conviction that all male disciples can and need to grow in the gift of serving—of being hospitable as we reach out and influence the disparate world in which we live. For elders, and those who have their hearts set on being an elder, God says we must be hospitable. So men, let's read and study and grow in our hospitality. It's definitely a subject *not for women only*.

To start with, a good working definition of hospitality is having the heart and making the effort to meet the needs of other people, both family and strangers. Our focus here is the expression of hospitality as practiced in our homes. All people have the need to feel warmly loved and included. All of us have the need to feel enjoyed, appreciated and included into a family. Our homes, apartments, town houses, condos and all our belongings are gifts to us from our generous and loving heavenly Father, who intends for us to use them to further his purposes. All the wonderful blessings and gifts we receive from God can be either a tremendous asset in our expression of hospitality or a huge stumbling block as we consume ourselves in fulfilling our own pleasures and comforts.

Hospitality goes beyond the courtesy of rising and greeting people as they enter our home (though important). It goes beyond preparing and sharing a meal with others (though important). Hospitality is about communicating in a variety of ways the great lengths we have gone to in order to make the time with our guests special for them—that we've organized everything and set the tone and atmosphere with them in mind. By our interest in them and our conversation that draws them out, they clearly sense that they are our focus for the evening.

NOTE: For a more thorough treatment of the subject of hospitality see *The Fine Art of Hospitality: Sharing Your Heart and Your Home with Others*, (published by Illumination Publishers).

Religious or Righteous?

Fred Faller, Boston, Massachusetts

> *"For I tell you that unless your righteousness surpasses that of the Pharisees and teachers of the law, you will certainly not enter the kingdom of heaven."*
>
> Matthew 5:20

What do you think of when you hear the word "righteousness"? About a year ago I was challenged about my understanding of the nature of righteousness in the Bible and in my daily living. J. P. Tynes introduced the idea in a class that the word I used for "righteousness" in the Old Testament carries a deeply embedded cultural concept. The challenge was that this concept was more tied to the fulfillment of the relationship between two persons than to the fulfillment of a legalistic code. Thinking like an Old Testament Jew, even two thieves could be considered "righteous" in their relationship to one another if it were characterized by sharing, fairness, camaraderie and loyalty.

This was an intriguing thought that shook the foundation of the absolute righteousness that I had always cast upon God's nature and law. Furthermore, it occurred to me that understanding this concept fully could transform the way we see ourselves as Christians and the importance of relationships in our daily lives.

I set about to investigate this curiosity for myself, and what I found has done more to revolutionize my own concept of God and the church than any other single understanding about the Bible.

Righteousness in the Old Testament

As I more carefully researched this idea to see if it had validity, the results were startling. Of the theological dictionaries of the Old Testament all six contained a discussion of "righteousness" in the terms I described earlier. I have included here an excerpt from one of these references because it states the case more succinctly than I could in my own words:

> "Righteousness," as it is understood in the OT, is a thoroughly Hebraic concept, foreign to the Western mind and at variance with the common understanding of the term. The failure to comprehend its meaning is perhaps most responsible for the view of the OT religion as 'legalistic' and as far removed from the graciousness of the NT.
>
> Rather, "righteousness" is, in the Old Testament, the fulfillment of the demands of a relationship, whether that relationship be with men or with God. Each man is set within a multitude of relationships: king with people, judge with complainants, priests with worshipers, common man with family, tribesman with community, community with resident alien and poor, all with God. And each of these relationships brings with it specific demands, the fulfillment of which constitutes righteousness. ("Righteousness" by E. R. Achtemeier in *Interpreter's Dictionary of the Bible*, Abingdon Press 1962, volume 4, pp. 80–85).

This idea can be seen in passages like Psalm 40:10 where David says, "I do not hide your righteousness in my heart; I speak of your faithfulness and salvation." God's righteousness is equated with his faithfulness in relationships and his saving or rescuing of those he loves. In Psalm 65 we see that God answers "with awesome deeds of righteousness" by forgiving those overwhelmed with sins and filling them with the good things from his house. In Psalm 103:6 God's righteousness means his commitment to the oppressed. Righteousness is clearly not being used to mean that God obeys some abstract moral code but that he is faithful in relationships.

Isaiah 32:1–2 envisions the coming kingdom of God as one in which "a king will reign in righteousness and rulers will rule with justice," and where

> *"each man will be like a shelter*
> *from the wind*
> *and a refuge from the storm,*
> *like streams of water in the desert*
> *and the shadow of a great*
> *rock in a thirsty land."*

The kingdom of Righteousness is one where the king will be committed to his relationships with his people, where leaders under him will have this same heart, and where all the people will be faithful to the care and protection of one another.

Jesus and Righteousness

Jesus lived out this kind of righteousness with a passion that confounded many of the people around him. While the Pharisees were muttering about the character of the woman who was washing Jesus' feet with perfume, Jesus was caring about her—thus meeting the simple demands of the relationship. When Zaccheus climbed the tree just to get a glimpse of Jesus, Jesus met that anticipation by having lunch with the man and his family while the Jews stood outside and pondered Jesus' poor choice of friends. He initiated with the woman at the well, while the disciples could not figure out why he would be talking to a woman. Jesus stopped amid the throngs to meet the need of the bleeding woman when she cried out for attention by simply touching his garment. Jesus saw that right relationships were the key to righteousness, rather than legalistically and dutifully acting out some prescribed behavior.

Relationship with God

Throughout eternity, it has been God's plan to establish and keep a relationship with man. God has expectations of us to fulfill the other side of that relationship. Isaiah 59:1–2 simply states that God has always done his part and that it is our sin, our failing, that severs the relationship. Our righteousness before God is simply based on fulfilling the demands of the relationship that he desires to have with us. This righteousness demonstrates so clearly the failure of a "works" mentality in Christianity. Prayer is not a time to accomplish your list of things to get done with God's help, but it is time with God, fulfilling the relationship he desires to have with you. The righteousness of prayer is not a daily duty or task before God or because God will not work if we do not pray; it is part of our relationship. If we do not communicate, we cannot work together. All the good works we could list that are void of relationship can no longer be considered righteous. It is the relationship that will ultimately be the test on Judgment Day.

Many people who appeared to work hard in serving God, people who may have even done miracles and exorcisms, will stand before Jesus describing their lives of service but Jesus will say to them, "I never knew you. Away from me, you evildoers" (Matthew

7:21–23). This is reflected in Matthew 25 when the sheep and the goats are separated for eternity. The concluding judgment is that "they will go away to eternal punishment, but the righteous to eternal life" (Matthew 25:46).

The Apostle Paul, in struggling to advance his relationship with God, compares his legalistic tradition in Judaism with the surpassing value of knowing Christ. He continues,

> *I consider them rubbish that I may gain Christ, and be found in him, not having a righteousness of my own, that comes from the law, but that which is through faith in Christ—the righteousness that comes from God and is by faith.*
> Philippians 3:8–9

This statement about righteousness is not just sandwiched between two very pointed statements of Paul's desire to know Christ; it is in fact all one thought: that Paul's greatest pursuit was to have a right relationship with God, the essence of righteousness before God. That righteousness is something that God has initiated in spite of us (1 John 4:9–11). Our response and only hope is faith in God's promise and way of making us righteous through the cross (2 Corinthians 5:18–19; Ephesians 2:17–18).

Righteousness of Christian Relationships

The sin that stands between brothers who are striving to be righteous is an affront to God that is heartily condemned throughout the Bible. Think of all the passages about sin in the New Testament, and see how many of them are set in the context of the failure to meet the needs of a relationship. These relationships are always cast in the presence of God and are associated with our fulfillment of that relationship as well. The "one another" passages do not constitute a "list of scriptures" that tell us how we ought to be. They represent the struggle of God through his word to accurately represent the nature of righteousness. Whatever action or thought that breaks down a relationship or destroys unity is simply unrighteous. That which builds up and promotes unity is righteous.

Whether we are righteous as we eat meat previously sacrificed to idols, drink wine with dinner, talk with a third person about conflict with another, etc., has little to do with the action itself, but with *whether relationships are built or destroyed as a result of our action.* Even the absolutes of sexual immorality, lying, stealing, murder and the like, are not isolated activities that God has capriciously defined as sins. They are actions that destroy relationships with others and with God himself. They are simply unrighteous in the purest sense. "Those who live like this will not inherit the kingdom of God" (Galatians 5:21). God is opposed to adultery, homosexuality, pornography and premarital sex, not because he dislikes us or is trying to deprive us, but because sin destroys relationships, and we can have a fatal attraction to it.

Priorities in Relationships

There will be times when the demands of one relationship come in conflict with the demands of another. Certainly, there is one relationship that always must have the priority: our relationship with God. The righteous choice is always the one which puts our relationship with God first. We cannot interact righteously with another person if we put that person before God, even though they may want to make that demand on us

(Matthew 10:37–38). "Seek first the kingdom of heaven and *his righteousness*" (Matthew 6:33, emphasis added). Our unity with God is always the first priority, even if it means sacrificing another relationship. Do not be fooled; we are never righteous in our relationship with someone if we love them more than God, or sin with them to keep the relationship.

Impossibility of 'Self-Righteousness'

True righteousness can never be self-generated or self-perpetuated. The man who strives with all his might to be "righteous," i.e. doing all the right things, while ignoring or looking down on others cannot be righteous. Just as our righteousness with God is totally dependent on his gracious forgiveness of the sins that separate us from him, so is our righteousness with other people. For example, Paul, as we saw earlier in Philippians 3:9, earnestly desired that it not be "a righteousness of my own that comes from law, but that which is through faith in Christ Jesus—the righteousness that comes from God and is by faith." In Romans 3:20, Paul further states that "no one will be declared righteous in his sight by observing the law." We must understand that whatever righteousness we have is only because we are forgiven sons and daughters, by faith, and this is a gift of God, so that no one can boast (Ephesians 2:8–9). Our righteousness with others requires the same forgiveness and grace and faith. We must "settle matters quickly" and "not let the sun go down on our anger." We must have the righteousness of God by being more interested in sustaining the relationship than executing justice due. Thus, "self-righteousness" is really a contradiction in terms.

Righteousness of the Church

In Isaiah 9:7, the prophecy of Jesus states that he will establish and uphold his kingdom with justice and righteousness. Right relationships are the building blocks of a great church. This is perhaps one of the greatest discoveries of the "multiplying ministries" and their worldwide impact. It also divulges the greatest failure of many churches that have taught the right doctrine but were not serious about the relationships that establish and uphold the kingdom. We are not and cannot be autonomous or independent as part of the kingdom of God. The demands of true righteousness form the "joints and ligaments," the relationships, that hold the various parts of the church together. Righteousness sustains the very purpose and meaning of the church as the community of saved people who serve as the light to the world and the salt of the earth.

Righteousness of Evangelism

In light of the true definition of righteousness, evangelism can no longer be "one of the things that God expects me to do." It actually is fulfilling the demands of the relationships that surround us every day. God's eternal plan has been to reconcile people to himself and unite people where sin has divided them. (Read Ephesians and 2 Corinthians 5.) The encounters we have daily with many people, no matter how prolonged or how brief, are relationships that set demands on us for our example, our patience, love, consideration, kindness, etc. When we meet these demands, we are righteous. When we fail, we are unrighteous.

Also, when sin is not forgiven, there is always a barrier to a relationship. We know that no relationship can be complete and unified while sin remains on either side.

Thus, the fulfillment of the demands of every relationship we have is eventually the repentance that leads to forgiveness from God and from each other. Only then can the unity and harmony between two people be complete. *Attempting to fulfill this need in the relationships that surround us is evangelism in its purest form.* It cannot be relegated only to a scheduled activity but must rather be a comprehensive passion to see all relationships restored completely according to God's plan. The righteousness of God manifested itself in his striving to do all he could to bring us back to him without compromising truth and the nature of God. Righteousness for us must have his one focus: striving to do everything we can to bring others to a right relationship with God without compromising.

Call to Righteousness

Each of us must seriously reflect on the depths and importance of biblical righteousness in our lives. We must begin to live out this concept with the passion of Jesus, never compromising its purity for our own selfish ambitions or pride. When the objective of our lives is right relationships with God and with all men with all the force that God has given in the Bible, we, as a movement, will continue to see growth, not only in the number of people who are brought into the kingdom, but in the quality of the fabric of the kingdom itself.

Fred Faller is an MIT graduate and works as a principal mechanical engineer in Burlington, Mass. He is also a teacher in the Boston Church of Christ and the author of The Portals of Tessalindria *series of visionary fiction.*

Power Thoughts from Mind Change

Tom A. Jones, Nashville, Tennessee

The following selection is from *Mind Change: The Overcomer's Handbook*

At the end of Tom Jones' book he listed fifty thoughts that he has found helpful in turning his mind in a spiritual direction. These thoughts were introduced with a chapter in which he advises readers how to use and how not to use these thoughts. We have included that chapter and the fifty "power thoughts" here, but even greater benefit would come from reading these ideas in the context of the book.

The following thoughts were written down in the midst of my own struggle to overcome. I would describe myself as a person who naturally thinks negatively. I am one of those people who looks at the glass that is half-full and sees it as half-empty. In my purely natural state, negative thoughts steadily trickle into my mind when I'm at my best and cascade like a waterfall when I'm at my worst. Take that natural man and combine him with a frustrating, unpredictable, debilitating illness like M.S. and you can guess what you would get. But thank God the man who got M.S. also had a Bible, and as he used that Bible he found (and is still finding) keys to overcoming.

Knowing God has not stopped negative or unspiritual thoughts from appearing on the screen of my mind, but knowing God has given me some very important say about whether they stay there or whether something else replaces them. What you will find in the following pages is the right kind of thoughts I wrote down to replace the wrong ones. These are the thoughts I go back to again and again, and it is on these thoughts that I seek to lock my focus.

In some cases, I have focused on these truths so much that I feel they have finally become part of me. But I think I know better than to be prideful about that. A new and harder hit from life may very well have me reaching again to grasp what I thought I already had. In other cases, I'm still working to get these truths deep in my heart. But in all cases, I find I am worlds better off meditating on these thoughts than on the negative ones that so naturally come my way. After writing many of these down and using them over a period of months, one day I wrote at the end of them, "Thank God for these thoughts." I knew they had made a powerful difference in my life. I knew God had used them to help me keep giving and serving and believing. I knew that, for me, they were gifts from God to meet various needs in my life. And so I share them with you, with a prayer that they will help you, too, to be an overcomer.

How to Use These Thoughts

1. As you read these thoughts, keep in mind that most were written in response to some negative thought I had and was tempted to cultivate. I have not written those negative thoughts out (1) because I didn't write them down at the time and cannot remember them all and (2) you will be most impacted if you think of what thoughts in your life most need to be replaced.

2. I would encourage you to make this something of a workbook. You may eventually find that your personal notes will come to mean even more to you than the original thoughts I have written.

3. If you don't seem to relate to one of the thoughts, move on to another. The one

you skipped may mean more another day.

4. I would advise you not to skim through these. I came to them one at a time and found the most force came from mediating on them carefully one at a time. In going back to them, I often pick two or three that seem most appropriate for what I am facing.

5. Do look up the scriptures on each page. Seeing the biblical authority for such thoughts can only strengthen your faith in their validity and power.

6. Warning: Never think that the short thoughts found here are designed to replace serious in-depth Bible study. These thoughts should not be seen as easy-to-swallow pills that do away with the need for spiritual meals. You will become an overcomer as you wrestle with circumstances and with the Scriptures and emerge with God's truth that speaks powerfully to your situation. Let these thoughts just be examples of how to do that.

7. Understand that the decision to put these in print did not come because of any feeling that they are complete. Even as this book goes to press, I will be adding to my list. My hope is that this book will encourage you to develop your personal list of thoughts you most need.

8. This book, I am confident, will be of more help to some people than to others. If any one thing has become clear to me after 25 years of working with people, it is that we are as different as we are alike. What helps some people sometimes does not connect with others. If the approach taken here is not helpful to you, move on to something that is (because we all need help).

9. Finally, understand that the promises included in these thoughts are the privileges of those in the kingdom of God. Not just anyone, for example, can be sure that God is at work for good in all things in his life. The Bible says that promise is only for those who love God and are called according to his purpose (Romans 8:28). These assurances can only be claimed by those who have died with Christ to an old life and have been raised with him to a new one (Romans 6:1–4). If that has happened to you, rejoice and read on! If it has not, seek, and you, too, can find.

> *"To him who overcomes, I will give the right to sit with me on my throne, just as I overcame and sat down with my Father on his throne."*
>
> Revelation 3:21

In every situation there is a right and spiritual way to think.

It may take me some time to find it.
It may take some discipline to embrace it.
But it is always there, and it is always best.
It is always the key to overcoming any challenge.

Philippians 1:27
Ephesians 5:20
1 Thessalonians 5:16-18

God is in control.

Today...tomorrow...forever.
God is God.
Nothing is outside his sovereignty.
He cannot lose control.
He is never surprised or found unprepared.
God never asks, "What are we going to do now?"

Psalm 2:2-6
Psalm 90:2
Isaiah 52:17

God will provide.

No matter what the need.
He cares.
He allows us to have needs.
He sees our needs.
He meets them all.

Isaiah 58:11
Matthew 6:28-34
Philippians 4:19

Accept whatever comes...with faith.

Disappointment? Faith.
Unfairness? Faith.
Fear? Faith.
Temptation? Faith.
Opportunity? Faith.
Victory? Faith.

Philippians 1:27
Hebrews 11:13-16
1 John 5:4

Wastes: regret, wishing, worry.

Be smart. Don't use time for any of these.
No regret—accept forgiveness.
No wishing—bloom where you are planted.
No worry—trust God who is not perplexed at all.

Matthew 6:27

Helps: faith, thanksgiving, determination.

Faith inspires you.
Thanksgiving gives perspective.
Determination keeps you moving.

Ephesians 5:4
Philippians 4:6

There is much more to life than your problem.

It may be loud.
It may shout for attention.
It may seem unbearable.
But God is greater.

2 Corinthians 4:16-18
Romans 8:18
Philippians 2:4

Be Thankful.
Laugh.
Sing.
Trust God.

Apply this today.
Apply it every day.
Yes, even with what is happening today.
Don't let any new development stop you.

1 Thessalonians 5:16-18
Proverbs 31:25
Psalm 146:7
John 14:1

Joy, not suffering will be eternal.

Pain is bearable
when it leads to something.
We are on our way to everlasting joy .
"The toils of the road will seem nothing
when we get to the end of the way."

Isaiah 51:11
Isaiah 61:7
Romans 8:18-21
James 1:2-4

Humility is the most powerful force in the world.

God loves it.
God honors it.
God blesses it.
With it, you cannot lose.
You can have it in all circumstances

Luke 14:11
James 3:13-18
James 4:6
1 Peter 5:5

Spiritual truth is greater than physical circumstances.

The physical is temporary;
the spiritual is eternal.
More obvious does not mean more real.
That which is tied to eternity is superior
to that tied to the temporary.

Romans 8:17
2 Corinthians 4:7-8
2 Corinthians 4:16-18
2 Corinthians 12:7-10
Hebrews 10:32-34

In all things God works for your good.

No exceptions and no lapses.
Even in what happened yesterday.
Even in something that caused great pain.
Even in something that dashed your hopes.
All things means all things.

Isaiah 49:15-16
Jeremiah 29:11
Romans 8:28
1Peter 4:12ff

In Christ you are: Gifted. Forgiven. Assigned. Valuable. Secure.

You may hear other voices.
But this is the truth.
It is true after a bad day as much as after a good day.

1Peter 4:10
Romans 8:1
1 Corinthians 7:17
Luke 12:24
John 10:28

Thank God for problems.

Go ahead. Do it now.
In his hands they are tools to shape character.
They will become some of your most important teachers.

Romans 5:1-5
1 Thessalonians 5:16-18
James 1:2-4

No complaining!

None!
Not about anyone.
Not about anything.
Address problems, and find solutions but don't complain.

Philippians 2:13
Philippians 4:8-9
1 Peter 4:9

Be "unreasonably," "illogically" joyful because your name is written in heaven.

It seems you have more to do
that you can get done...but
your name is written in heaven.
Your prayers didn't get answered the
way you thought they would...but
your name is written in heaven.
You are having "one of those days"...but
your name is written in heaven.
You didn't do everything right...but
your name is written in heaven."

Luke 10:18-20

Decide to enjoy the challenge.

If it is going to be there, you might as well
enjoy it.
God is allowing it for some good purpose.
Like Jacob, don't let go of it
until it blesses you.

Genesis 32:22-28
James 1:2-4

Choose your mood.

If the one you have right now is not right,
you can exchange it.
Don't allow the "wrong side of the
bed" to control your life.

Deuteronomy 30:19-20
Joshua 24:15
Proverbs 8:10-11
Psalm 119:30

Every frustration is an opportunity for faith.

Don't whine. Don't explode.
Pray.
Look for God.
Be sure that he is near and ready to work.

Acts 16:6-10
Philippians 4:4-7

Morning breath of the soul? Rinse it!

Waking up with the blahs?
Feeling unmotivated,
uninspired or discouraged?
Dreading some things you have to do?
Take prayer and the Word and deal with it!
Say "This is not of God,
I won't stand for it."

He arose!

That changes everything!
How different does your problem look
when placed
at the mouth of the empty tomb?

Romans 8:11
1 Corinthians 15:12-20
1 Peter 3:21-22

Don't resent the spiritual battle.

Be thankful you have the weapons
to fight it.
Be glad you are on the winning side.

2 Corinthians 10:3-5
Ephesians 6: 10-18
Revelation 22:1-5

Make someone feel loved today.

There is nothing better than
getting out of yourself.
There is no better way to put
your problems in perspective
than by meeting another's need.
There is nothing so powerful as giving to
another person.

1 Corinthians 13
Philippians 2:3-4
1 John 3:16-20

Make a list of 100 things for which you are thankful.

Count your many blessings,
name them one by one.
You'll be surprised at how many you have.

Colossians 2:6-7
Hebrews 12:28-29

Know what most threatens your dedication to Christ... then nail it!

Identify it.
Confess it.
Ask others to pray about it.
But whatever you do, overcome it.

1 Timothy 5:11
Hebrews 12:1-2

God has not given you too much.

If there is something you have to
face, you can face it.
If there is something you must
overcome, you can overcome it.

"When something must be done, there is
no use talking
about whether or not it can be done."
(C. S. Lewis)

1 Corinthians 10:13

"Praise be to the Lord, to God our Savior, who daily bears our burdens."

Psalm 68:19

There is no condemnation for you who are in Christ Jesus.

Are you perfect? No.
Are you in Christ? Yes.
Is he your Lord? Yes.
Are you totally forgiven?
Absolutely.

Romans 8:1

Nothing on earth (or in the heavens) can separate you from the love of Christ.

Not pain.
Not loss. Not grief.
Not abuse. Not rejection.
Not disappointment. Not failure.
Nothing.

Romans 8:35–39

You are shielded by God's power.

Anything that hits you, you can handle with God's power.
Anything too much for you,
God keeps out.

1 Peter 1:3–5

Find out what pleases the Lord.

Seek it.
Desire it.
What pleases him
will be best for you.

Ephesians 5:10

God is awesome... in control... at work in everything for the good of those who love him.

Believe it on days when you feel it.
Believe on days when you don't feel it.
It is true every day.

Romans 8:28

When you suffer, never ask: "Why Me?" Instead ask: "How can I show faith, hope and love in this situation?"

There will always be a good answer.
Righteousness in the midst of suffering
shines all the more brightly.

Enlarge your view of God.

If he doesn't look big enough to
overcome your problem, you don't
see him clearly.

Whoever gives up on God always gives up too soon.

He doesn't wear your watch.
He doesn't use your datebook.
He doesn't always follow your script.
But he always comes through.

Don't ever lose your sense of humor.

"A cheerful heart is good medicine,
but a crushed spirit dries up the bones."

Proverbs 17:22

It is God's will for you to totally trust him and to be completely at peace in every situation.

You will have to learn this.
It took Paul some time to learn this
(compare 2 Corinthians 1
with Philippians 4).
It will take you time to learn it.
Just decide that you will learn it.

Philippians 4:4-7

Whatever God wants you to change, you can change.

Some things will take longer,
but God's will can always
be found and be done.

Romans 12:1-2

Celebrate every victory.

Small victories? Celebrate!
Big victories? Celebrate!
Celebrating is God's plan
and a way of building for more victories.

2 Chronicles 30

Just live the next thirty minutes by faith.

This is one you will need for the extra-challenging days.

But it is amazing what thirty minutes of faith can lead to and how this can turn a day around.

Look at a favorite promise of God. Read it several times and say "Amen!" so loudly the devils in hell can't miss it.

2 Corinthians 1:20

Forgive as God has forgiven you—quickly and completely.

Nothing will overcome you like an unforgiving spirit.

Nothing will separate you from the Overcomer like an unforgiving heart.

Matthew 6, Ephesians 4

Give praise to the God who daily bears our burdens.

Psalm 68:19

If you want to learn more about overcoming, read *Mind Change Moments,* by Tom A. Jones. Available at www.ipibooks.com.

Classic Expressions of Pride

1. Not wanting to talk with someone or spend time with someone because they just don't quite measure up.
2. Thinking: "They should have asked me to do that. I would have done it better."
3. Wanting to turn the conversation to highlight something you have done.
4. Getting most of your sense of worth from having a group of people who are loyal to you.
5. Feeling a good report of someone else lessens your worth.
6. Having as your deepest conviction about advice that, "After all, advice is just advice. You don't have to take it."
7. Lack of openness about important areas of your life like your times with God, your marriage, your dating, your other relationships.
8. Asking your spouse not to discuss your marriage with others or to call for help.
9. Not asking for counsel, advice or perspective about dating, marriage, parenting, finances, evangelism and other vital areas.
10. Knowing that you are wrong, but resisting admitting it to yourself and then to others.
11. For men only: being particularly defensive about something pointed out to you by a woman.
12. For leaders: preaching what others ought to be doing, but not being open about the fact that you are not doing those things.
13. Believing your approach to ministry is much better than that of others. Thinking you have a right balance or emphasis that others don't have.
14. Hearing about some leader's problems and feeling better about yourself because that has not happened to you.
15. Hearing a speaker giving out praise and waiting for your name to be spoken.
16. Feeling cheated because you did not get to work with someone or did not get to be involved with a project for which you thought you were well-suited.
17. Only half listening to what someone is telling you because they are not that important a person.
18. Resenting the input of a much younger Christian. Feeling that they should not give such to someone who has been around as long as you. (Thinking longevity gives you some exemptions.)
19. Being given a lot to do and then going after it, without much prayer.
20. Seldom asking others seriously to pray for you because you don't believe something will go well without it.
21. Not volunteering for something because you fear making mistakes or failing, and don't want to look bad.

22. Not being supportive and encouraging of peers. Not celebrating their victories because you are highly competitive.

23. Interrupting and finishing people's sentences.

24. Having a strong desire to guard your territory and letting that rob you of a greater "good of the kingdom" outlook.

25. Filtering out things that you don't like to hear from the advice and counsel you are given. Doing only those elements that you already felt good about.

26. Avoiding situations where you might have to do something that looks menial or servile. Coming up with great spiritual excuses about it.

27. Consistently thinking that the assignments given you or the ministry arrangements made for you don't show appreciation for who you are and what you have to offer.

28. Not planning special times to just go be with God.

29. Thinking pride is not that big a problem for you.

30. Not confessing sin unless you are backed into a corner and confronted.

NOTE: For a more thorough treatment of pride and humility, see *The Prideful Soul's Guide to Humility* by Thomas Jones and Michael Fontenot (published by Illumination Publsihers, www.ipibooks.com).

Short Thoughts on Humility

1. The deepest humility comes from contemplating the greatness of God. Humility from any other source is shallow and vulnerable.

2. Jesus was humble even before he entered into this world. Without humility he would not have come.

3. Jesus coming means that the powerful God of the universe is, in his essence, humble.

4. If there is not much that awes you, pride rules in your heart.

5. The humble man will be an approachable man. When people are afraid of others, pride is usually involved. Jesus was the perfect Son of God. But he was famously approachable.

6. We need to confess our sin not because we are humble but to keep us humble.

7. Humility is not low self-esteem. You can have low self-esteem and also be extremely prideful.

8. The humble person sees his weaknesses. He can tell you what they are because he has asked others to help him see them.

9. Humility means having a willingness to associate with (have friendships with) those of low position (in the world's eyes). It further means not viewing people of lower position as lower at all.

10. The humble man puts his confidence in God, not in his ability or talent.

11. The humble man considers the words of his critics. He knows they may be wrong. But he recognizes that they can be right.

12. The humble man is not afraid to look needy. (In other words, he is not afraid to admit the truth!)

13. The humble man sees the impact of others on his life, and he is grateful and appreciative.

14. The humble man is not just *willing* to confess his sin; he is *known* for confessing his sin.

15. The humble man is not completely free of pride. He is one who quickly sees his pride and repents.

16. Humility is like perfection: It is a goal to be pursued, even as we confess freely that we have not arrived.

17. The power of humility does not lie in the attaining of it but in the pursuit of it.

18. The humble man listens well when others speak. The prideful man does not think he needs to.

19. The humble man listens well to all people. The prideful man selects those who deserve his attention.

20. The humble man is willing to be embarrassed if it might advance the gospel. The prideful man must protect his image.

21. The humble man will often see the need for prayer. He will be known for his prayer life.

22. The humble person is always a grateful person. Ingratitude springs from pride and self-absorption—from a view that says, "I deserve better."

23. "I deserve" is not in the vocabulary of the humble. "I am blessed" is what comes out of his mouth, for that is what is in his heart.

24. The humble person freely, joyfully and thankfully accepts forgiveness. Pride is what causes him to say, "Oh, no, I couldn't."

25. Nothing should humble us more than the cross of Christ. If we can stand in the presence of such unconditional love and not be brought to our knees, our hearts have grown rock hard.

26. How can we stand at the foot of the cross and look down on anyone? Are we forgetting that we put Jesus there and that he was dying for us?

27. Humility is not about being a nice person. It is about unleashing the power of God.

28. The prideful man is wise in his own eyes and clever in his own sight. The Bible says "woe" to such a man (Isaiah 5:21).

29. Want to see a man humbled because he has seen God? Read Isaiah 6 and Revelation 1:9–17.

30. Isaiah went on to be a powerful prophet. John wrote a powerful book. It all started in complete humility. It always does.

31. "To keep me from becoming conceited…" (2 Corinthians 12:7): God is concerned about keeping his people from becoming conceited and prideful. He will do whatever it takes.

32. People who have not stood in awe of God are not ready to serve God. A man who goes forth to serve God or to lead the people of God is a dangerous man if he has not and does not regularly stand in awe of God.

33. Pride wants credit. Humility wants to give it.

Explore the nature of humility and read *The Prideful Soul's Guide to Humility,* by Tom A. Jones

Who You Are

Thirty-Three Affirmations from Ephesians

In the first three chapters of Ephesians, Paul makes at least thirty-three affirmations about who you are and what you have received if you are in Christ.

These affirmations can be used privately, as you read each one and put in your name, as in "You, John, have been blessed with every spiritual blessing in Christ," and "You, John, have been chosen before the creation of the world to be holy and blameless in his sight."

It is also a powerful exercise to read these in a group with each person in the group reading one of these affirmations to the person on his or her right.

By sight we may seem to be very ordinary people with ordinary problems, but by faith we can claim who we have become in Christ and then marvel at the amazing grace that has made all these true.

Ephesians 1

1. You are saints (v1).
2. You are faithful in Christ Jesus (v1).
3. You have been blessed with every spiritual blessing in Christ (v3).
4. You were chosen before the creation of the world to be holy and blameless in his sight (v4).
5. In love you were predestined to be adopted as his sons through Christ...for his pleasure. (You bring God pleasure!) (v5)
6. You have been freely given his glorious grace (v6).
7. You have redemption through his blood, the forgiveness of sins, in accordance with riches of God's grace (v7).
8. You were let in on the mystery of God's will (v8).
9. You were chosen by him who works everything out (v11).
10. You are for the praise of his glory (v12).
11. You were included in Christ when you heard the gospel of your salvation (v13).
12. Having believed (that is, because of your faith), you were marked with the seal, the promised Holy Spirit (v13).
13. You have the Spirit as a guarantee of your inheritance (v14).
14. You are going to experience an ultimate redemption—to the praise of God's glory (v14).

Ephesians 2

15. Because of his great love and his rich mercy, you were made alive in Christ (v4).
16. You were saved by grace (v5).
17. God raised you up and seated you with Christ in the heavenly realms (v6).
18. In the coming ages he is going to show the incomparable riches of his grace and kindness to you in Christ (v7).
19. You have been saved by grace through faith (v8).
20. You are God's workmanship, created in Christ Jesus to do good works that God prepared (v10).
21. You have been brought near to God through the blood of Christ (v13).
22. You are part of the "one new man"—the peaceable kingdom (vv15–16).
23. You and your brothers and sisters in Christ all have access to the Father by the one Spirit (v18).
24. You are no longer foreigners and aliens, but you are fellow citizens and members of God's household (v19).
25. You are part of great holy temple that is a dwelling in which God lives by his Spirit (v22).

Ephesians 3

26. You are heirs, members of one body and sharers together in the promise in Christ Jesus (v6).
27. You are the church through which God is making his manifold wisdom known even to the forces of darkness (v10).
28. Through your faith in Christ, you are able to approach God with freedom and confidence (even boldness) (v12).
29. You can be strengthened with power through his Spirit in your inner being (v16).
30. Christ can dwell in your hearts through faith (v17).
31. Together with others, you can know the love of Christ which surpasses knowledge (vv18–19).
32. You can be filled to the measure of all the fullness of God (v19).
33. There is a power at work within you that is able to do abundantly more than all you ask or imagine (v20).

Ministering to the Dying and Their Families

I. **Ministering to the Dying**

A. **Reach out to them**
Matthew 25:34–40

1. Do not pull away from the dying.
2. Visit the hospital, nursing home or their home. Do not be a stranger.

B. **Seek to understand** James 1:19

1. Ask about their situation.
2. Be sincere.

C. **Educate yourself about loss and grief** Ecclesiastes 7:2–4

1. Know that this is a difficult area to listen to and talk about.
2. Read a book. (Recommendations: *How to Go on Living When Someone You Loved Dies* by Therese A. Rando or *Caring and Coping When Your Loved One Is Seriously Ill* by Earl A. Grollman.)
3. Realize this is about them, not you. You cannot "fix" them or take away their pain.

D. **Realize your limitations** Proverbs 14:10

1. You may not be the one to help them face reality.
2. Grief is unique to every person. What you may think was helpful for one person may not be helpful for another.

E. **Understand the gift of listening and presence** Proverbs 18:13

1. Learn how to listen, it can guide your helping.
2. Being with someone and caring is one of the greatest helps you can provide.

F. **What to say** Proverbs 24:26

1. Nothing, if you are not sure. Do not fabricate conversation or ask or say things out of your need to feel comfortable. Your presence is as great as anything you could say.
2. "I love you," "I care about you," "Tell me about how things are going for you."

G. **Help with needs** Proverbs 17:17

1. Help them with cleaning, shopping, laundry, rides and company. Be a volunteer.
2. Find resources—medical, financial, informational.
3. Be as consistent as possible.
4. Don't make promises you can't keep.

H. **Spiritual help** Matthew 7:12

1. Read and pray with them.
2. Take communion to them.
3. Encourage with how they have helped others and what they mean to you and others.
4. Honor them in special ways but be sensitive. Suggestions: a time of honoring and celebration with close friends and family before they die, the prayers of children (a particular children's class at church) are a way of honoring, a collection of cards or letters from friends and family that tell them the difference the dying person has made in their lives.
5. Help them recognize opportunities even in the midst of challenges. (e.g., finishing any "unfinished" business such as resolving or renewing relationships, accomplishing something they've dreamed of doing, setting their children up for future spiritual success, coming to terms with who they are and what they have

accomplished in life, leaving a legacy such as a video, letters, writings, etc.).

II. Ministering to Their Families

A. Reach out to Genesis 24:67

1. Know that the whole family suffers.
2. Understand that they will grieve even before the death.

B. Communication Proverbs 1:5

1. Listen to the family—their challenges will each be different—then respond.
2. Be a sounding board; sometimes people need help with decisions.
3. Be wise; what you say may be communicated to other family members.

C. Helping with needs Proverbs 11:25

1. Know your role—you may be one of many helpers.
2. Family members will usually need respite from the day-to-day challenges.
3. Do specific things. Do not leave a message saying, "Let me know if I can help."

D. Spiritual Help 2 Corinthians 1:10–11

1. Ask them what you can pray for.
2. Ask God about the right scripture to share; meditate on their needs.
3. Remember each member's needs will be different.
4. Encourage them to finish any "unfinished" business with the dying person and saying anything they need to say (e.g., I forgive you, forgive me, thank you, I love you, goodbye). Remember, the family goes on living.
5. Support hope realistically, never take it away—medically or spiritually. Remember that the family may live with the dying a long or short time, which is much harder if they have no hope. In assisting the family we should err on the side of hope, keeping a hopeful perspective rather than jumping back and forth over each diagnosis or being the bearer of somber, "educated" opinions.

III. Ministering to the Bereaved

A. Reach out to Job 2:11–13; Romans 12:15

1. Go to the wake, the funeral and to their home.
2. Know that three to four weeks after the death they will need you as well.

B. The gift of listening and presence Proverbs 12:25

1. Know this—you do not know how they feel.
2. If you are humorous it can help. Be wise and discerning about when and where to lighten the topic.
3. Stories about the deceased can help.
4. Being there and holding a hand is powerful.

C. Helping with needs Proverbs 18:16

1. Assist with any arrangements that you can, e.g., funeral, food, chores, phone calls.
2. Call them and simply say, "I love you."

D. Educate yourself about loss and grief Proverbs 14:10, 13; 19:11

1. Understand that working through grief is their responsibility, you can only help.
2. For the bereaved, going home after the death is tough.

3. Avoid cliches like "At least they are not suffering anymore," and sparingly use "How are you?"
4. Remember challenging days like Mother's Day, birthday of the person, family holidays, anniversaries, major holidays like Christmas, etc.

E. Be an advocate Proverbs 20:6, 27:9

1. Speak up for those in grief.
2. Remind others about the bereaved.
3. Your life goes on as normal—just remember that theirs does not.

F. Spiritual Help Hebrews 13:3

1. Pray for them.
2. Send cards and notes.
3. Be sensitive; do not draw conclusions too early.
4. Over time help them find spiritual meaning in the loss.
5. Remember you also will experience loss at some point.

My appeal to all of us in this area of life is to be a learner. Death and dying is different for everyone. We need to take the counsel, "Be quick to listen, slow to speak..." as a guide in helping others through these challenging times. Let God, the Scriptures and those who work with the dying and bereaved teach us how to do a great job for others in this area of life.

Dennis Young

To understand more about the grieving process read *Grief Journey: Finding Peace in All of Life's Losses* by Tim Sumerlin

Evangelism: The Heart of God

Frank Kim, Denver, Colorado

The Father

The man wipes his brow with a grizzled hand. He sits on the porch, watching as he has done every day for years. Eyes strain to search the horizon, picking out the road trailing into a ribbon as it lazily bends out of sight. Yet, the eyes reflect neither fatigue nor weariness. There is, rather, a curious mixture of concern, longing and anticipation. One last time his view lingers on the bluff, about to call it another day, when suddenly...a figure appears.

Immediately, he leaps to his feet. His heart races. His lips tremble. His eyes shine. It's him. Absolutely, it's him.

Leaping the weathered stairs, calling out to the servants, he begins to run.

The Son

It had been years, such a long time. The innumerable failures dragged at him, seemingly heavier with every step that took him home. Actually, the guilt seemed to have intensified since the day he decided to come back, for now he thought of almost nothing other than his father. The disappointment. The betrayal. How he had completely destroyed the special relationship they had shared—almost.

For somewhere deep within had remained the gnawing, inexplicable feeling that his father still waited for him—that he had not been forgotten. Often, this had annoyed him, for he had wished to close the door on his youth, wanting to escape the guilt of what he had done. Yet in the end, like a magnet reaching through the years and over the miles, that feeling is what brought him back. His father was waiting.

The bluff. The last curve. His legs become wooden; his pace slackens; he stops. Suddenly, his mouth is dry. Suppose he's still angry? What right do I have to come back? What if he chases me away? What if he rejects me? How can he ever forgive me? But...I have nowhere else to go. I can't go back.

His feet move forward; he rounds the bend. He looks up. The house, just as he remembered. The father, waiting, just as he had dreamed. Then...

His father rushing toward him, waving, laughing, crying—full of compassion and love. Welcome home!

The Celebration

On a cold November night many years ago, that was me. Do you remember when that was you? At a time when we knew that there was no other way, no other choice—wasn't it good to know that God had never given up? That he not only waited for us, but that he welcomed us with forgiveness, compassion and joy? As Kip McKean pulled me out of the cold baptistery waters, as I looked into the jubilant faces of the five or six friends who had come to witness a modern-day miracle (if Frank can make it, anyone can!), and as I felt the deep conviction of having been reunited with my God, I understood in that moment the greatest joy available on earth. The joy of coming home. At that same moment, what did God feel?

The heart of God. Isn't this where the Bible story begins? In the beginning, God longed for relationship and out of that desire created order out of chaos, man out of clay. Throughout the sacred pages—a history packed with adventure, heroism, betrayal, mystery and passion—the heart of God fairly pulses and throbs off the page, as time after time we are confronted by God's indomitable desire to have a relationship with man.

This true story reaches its pinnacle as God's incredible love is made manifest in the person of Jesus Christ who came to seek and to save the lost. He is the perfect reflection of how God feels about us. A shepherd who refuses to give up, a vine who will bear much fruit, an unquenchable light shining to lead lost souls out of darkness. From beginning to end, the message is vibrant with God's heart—God's passionate desire for each of us to come home.

God wants all men to be saved. We obscure the focus; we neglect its intensity; we lose ourselves in triviality. And yet, everything God has done has been directed toward that singular purpose. In Luke 15, the older son spent years with the father, but never grasped his deepest desire. Ultimately, his lack of understanding led to empty servitude and destructive bitterness. Serving time, but not serving his father.

Evangelism is not about earning your way to heaven. It's not about making your name. It's not about numbers. Evangelism is nothing to be ashamed of, it's not religious, and no, it's not optional.

Evangelism is our outward reflection of having internalized the heart and the deepest desires of God. Evangelism is God's eyes roaming back and forth throughout the world, searching for those who are ready to come home. Evangelism is God's unbounded joy and heavenly celebration as the dead are raised back to life. Evangelism is clearly the heart of God.

No man or woman can claim to truly love God who does not share his most obvious and profound desire. We can and must grow consistently in our holiness, our knowledge, our humility and our love. We must daily fight the battle of emulating the character of Christ in all its perfection. But all of our spiritual growth will eventually find its fulfillment in the heart of God, the mission of Christ: to seek and to save what is lost. Without this enthusiasm, this fire burning within, all of our deeds and words threaten to become empty role-play, missing the eternal point. Serving time, but certainly not serving God.

What is evangelism to you? In your answer you will find a spiritual mirror in which you can see the sum of your faith. The one who loves God, loves what God loves. The one who pleases God, enjoys what God enjoys. The one who earnestly seeks God will celebrate much more than his own personal blessing. The true disciple's greatest ardor, greatest passion, greatest sacrifice and most unrestrained joy will be spent in the pursuit of God's greatest dream—to see his children come home. That is what sharing your faith is all about.

Learn more about the Bible by reading Douglas Jacoby's *A Quick Overview of the Bible*. www.ipibooks.com.

Some Tools for Bible Study

Translations

Holy Bible: New Living Translation (1996)—a very readable English translation
New American Standard Bible (1962)—a more readable revision of the ASV
Revised Standard Version (1952)—a great thought-for-thought translation
New Revised Standard Version (1989)—a more readable revision of the RSV
New International Version (2011)—a most readable English translation
The Jerusalem Bible—a great comparative translation
The Poet's Bible by David Rosenberg—a wonderful translation of many of the OT poetic texts
The English Standard Bible (2001)
The Message—a paraphrase, uses common, everyday language
Many translations can be accessed on the Internet.

Study Bibles

The Harper's Study Bible
The Thompson Chain Reference Bible
The NIV Study Bible

Concordances

NIV Exhaustive Concordance published by Zondervan
Software versions—"QuickVerse" from Parsons Technology and "WordSearch" from NavPress

History of the Biblical Text

The Text of the New Testament—Bruce Metzger*
How We Got the Bible—Neil Lightfoot #

Bible Handbooks

Eerdman's Handbook to the Bible
Abingdon's Bible Study Handbook

Bible Dictionaries

New Bible Dictionary—ed. by J. D. Douglas *The International Standard Bible Encyclopedia*, 5 Vols. *
Harper's Bible Dictionary—ed. by Achtemeier

Word Studies

New International Dictionary of New Testament Theology, 3 Vols. *
Theological Wordbook of the Old Testament, 2 Vols. *
New Testament Words—William Barclay. #

= "for the beginner"
* = "for deeper study"

Atlases

Oxford Bible Atlas / Rand McNally Bible Atlas
The Harper Atlas of the Bible

Old Testament Background

The History of Israel—John Bright *
Old Testament History—Charles Pfeiffer *
A Survey of the Old Testament Introduction—Gleason Archer
Introduction to the Old Testament—R. K. Harrison

Old Testament Commentaries

The New Bible Commentary: Revised, 1 Vol.
Tyndale Old Testament Commentaries
The Daily Bible Study Series
The Living Word Commentaries
Word Biblical Commentaries

New Testament Background

New Testament Times—Merrill C. Tenney
The New Testament Era—Bo Reicke
The New Testament Environment—Eduard Lohse
Introduction to the New Testament—H. C. Thiessen *
New Testament Introduction—Donald Guthrie *
Between the Testaments—D. S. Russell *
New Testament Survey—Merrill C. Tenny

New Testament Commentaries

Tyndale New Testament Commentaries
The New International Commentaries
The Living Word Commentaries
The Daily Bible Study Series—William Barclay
The New International Greek Commentaries *

Church History

Eerdman's Handbook to the History of Christianity—ed. by Tim Dowley
Church History in Plain Language—Bruce Shelley
The Christian Story, Volume 1—John M. Oakes
The Christian Story, Volume 2—John M. Oakes
Nelson's Quick Reference Introduction to Church History—ed. by Howard F. Vos

Christian Evidences

Compelling Evidence for God—Douglas Jacoby
How Should We Then Live?—Francis A. Schaeffer
The God Who Is There—Francis A. Schaeffer *He Is There and He Is Not Silent*—Francis A. Schaeffer
Evidence That Demands a Verdict—Josh McDowell

Recommended Books for Deeper Study

Bible Basics

A Quick Overview of the Bible, by Douglas Jacoby

Be Still My Soul—A Practical Guide to a Deepr Relationship with God, by Sam Laing

Deep Convictions, by Tom A. Jaones

First Principles, edited by John Markowski

Foundations of Discipling, by Dave Pocta

Getting the Most from the Bible (Second Edition), by Dr. G. Steve Kinnard

Letters to New Disciples, by Tom A. Jones

Study It, Grasp It, Live It!, by Jon Sherwood

The Baptized Life, by Tom A. Jones

The Lion Never Sleeps, by Mike Taliaferro

The Power of Discipling, by Gordon Ferugson

Apologetics

Answering Skeptics, by Douglas Jacoby

Compelling Evidence for God and the Bible, by Douglas Jacoby

Field Manual for Christian Apologetics, by Dr. John M. Oakes

Is There A God?, by Dr. John M. Oakes

Jesus and Islam, by Douglas Jacoby

Mormonism: What Does the Evidence and Testimony Reveal?, by Dr. John Oakes

Origins: The Ancient Impact and Modern Implications of Genesis 1-11, by Douglas Jacoby

Reasons For Belief—A Handbook of Christian Evidence, by Dr. John M. Oakes

The Resurrection: A Historical Analysis, by C. Foster Stanback

That You May Believe—Reflections on Science and the Miracles of Jesus, by David Eastman and Dr. John M. Oakes

Bible Exposition

Exodus: Night of Redemption, by Douglas Jacoby

God's Perfect Plan for Imperfect People: The Message of Ephesians, by Tom A. Jones

Jesus Unequaled: An Expostion of Colossians, by G. Steve Kinnard

Life to the Full: The Letters of James, Peter, John, Jude, by Douglas Jacoby

Revelation Revealed, by Gordon Ferguson

Romans, by Gordon Ferguson

The Gospel fo Matthew, by G. Steve Kinnard

The Call of the Wise: An Introduction and Topical Index to the book of Proverbs, by G. Steve Kinnard

Thrive—Using Psalms to Help You Flourish, by Douglas Jacoby

Christian Living

An Aging Grace, edited by Jeanie Shaw

But What About Your Anger?, by Lee Bogers

Crossing the Line—Culture, Race, and Kingdom, by Michael Burns

Grief Jouney—Finding Peace in All of Life's Losses, by Dr. Tim Sumerlin

The Prayer of the Righteous, by Mark Templer

The Prideful Soul's Guide to Humility, by Tom A. Jones and Steve Brown

The Victory of Surrender, by Gordon Ferguson

Golden Rule Membership—What God Expects of Every Disciple, by Dr. John M. Oakes

Marriage and Family

As For Me and My House—50 Devotionals for Families, by Tom and Lori Ziegler

Fairy Tales Do Come True!, by Gordon Ferguson

Building Emotional Intimacy in Your Marriage, by Jeff and Florence Schachinger

Hot and Holy—The Five Senses of Romantic Love, by Sam Laing

The Wonder Years: Parenting Preteens & Teens, by Sam and Geri Laing

Raising Awesome Kids by Sam and Geri Laing

The Tender Years—Parenting Preschoolers, by Geri Laing and Elizabeth Laing Thompson

The Essential 8: Principles of a Growing Marriage, by Sam and Geri Laing

The Essential 8: Principles of a Strong Christian Family, by Sam and Geri Laing

(All available at www.ipibooks.com)

Part Three

Ideas

Twenty-Five Ways to Encourage Children

The encouragement of children is a key to the solving of discipline problems.

How to Encourage

1. Emphasize the deed, not the doer.
2. Emphasize the doing, and the joy of doing.
3. Emphasize the good part of what they did.
4. Avoid saying "don't." Stress the positive.

Phrases That Encourage

1. You are so good at... (You did good!)
2. Would you help plan this?
3. What would you think about...?
4. Some beginnings are difficult.
5. You are fun to be with.(I had a good time with you.)
6. Everyone makes mistakes.
7. I missed you...
8. I think ____ , but what do you think?
9. Please,...
10. That's a hard job.
11. I'm so glad that you had a good time in class today!
12. Let's see why it didn't work.
13. Don't ever let the things you can't do keep you from doing the things you can.
14. You did a great job on...(That's a great job!)
15. Thank you for all your help today. Thank you for saying that, doing that, etc.
16. You're a hard worker! (You're a good helper!)
17. I'm sorry for...
18. That's great news!
19. You're special.
20. I love you—I will always love you!
21. I believe in you.

Larry and Lea Wood
Durham, North Carolina

To learn more about teaching children read *A Heart to Teach*. Get it at www.ipibooks.com.

Great Family Devotionals

Edited by Tom and Lori Ziegler

The following material is taken from *As for Me and My House: 50 Easy-to-Use Devotionals for Families* ©Discipleship Publications International.

Tips for Great Family Devotionals

1. Have fun! Family devotionals should be happy, joyful times together. They should not be consistently serious so that the Bible becomes boring or scary to your children.
2. Be consistent. Family devotionals should be held at the same time every week, if at all possible. That does not mean that you cannot change the schedule at times, but children have a keen sense of timing, even before they can read or tell time. Children instinctively know when it is time to eat, when a favorite television program is on or if it is a church day. Make family devotionals part of your regular schedule.
3. For small children, use a children's Bible if possible. If that is not possible, select one or two verses to read from a story. Then paraphrase the rest in your own, animated words. If you read straight from an adult Bible, you will lose your children's attention. Instead, show them the Bible and open to the intended story. That way they will know it is in the Bible, and that it is not just a made-up story like a fairy tale.
4. Use every sense when teaching the Bible to children. Children learn more quickly if they can involve their senses of hearing, seeing, tasting, touching and smelling. You will bring the Bible alive to your children when you stimulate their senses.
5. Act Bible stories out with children ages two through eight. All of our children are actors at heart. You will build a great sense of confidence in them if you encourage this.
6. Remember, these are family devotionals. Every member of the family should participate regularly. Teach a spirit of unity and teamwork in your family. There is no better teacher than your example. Parents and children alike should sing, pray and act stories out with all their hearts.
7. If you have children whose ages fall into a broad range, be sure to adapt your material to meet the various needs. Don't just go for the lowest common denominator. You may be surprised at how quickly the younger ones learn lessons that are aimed at the older children. Read Bible stories daily with your younger children to make sure their needs are met, and that they are gaining a well-rounded knowledge of the Bible.
8. Leave every devotional on a positive note. Even if the topic is a serious one like lying, leave your family with a sense of hope and excitement about changing. God is a gracious and forgiving God, and we must make sure our children learn not only how serious God is about hating sin, but also how serious he is about forgiveness: He keeps absolutely no record of wrongs.
9. Follow the same theme all week long. Even if you have one longer devotional a week, do something every day to help your family remember what everyone is working on. This is how you "train" your child in the way he should go.
10. Keep the length of your devotional age-appropriate. The attention span of children is not very long. For children ages

two and three, about ten minutes is all they can handle.

Bible Stories References

To further help you develop your children's love for God's word, two lists of basic Bible stories to teach at home have been provided for you. You can read them as part of daily quiet times with your children, or you can imitate the format used for the family devotionals to develop your own devotionals from these stories. Or you could do both! We hope this helps you build a strong, spiritual family that loves the word of God.

Old Testament Stories

1. Creation (Genesis 1)
2. Adam and Eve (Genesis 2–3)
3. Cain and Abel (Genesis 4)
4. Noah and the Ark (Genesis 6–8)
5. The Tower of Babel (Genesis 11)
6. Sodom and Gomorrah (Genesis 18:16–19:29)
7. Abraham Sacrifices Isaac (Genesis 22)
8. Joseph and His Coat of Many Colors (Genesis 37:1–11)
9. Joseph in Jail and His Vision (Genesis 40–41)
10. Moses' Birth (Exodus 2)
11. Moses and the Burning Bush (Exodus 3)
12. Moses and the Plagues (Exodus 7–11)
13. Moses Parts the Red Sea (Exodus 13:17–14:31)
14. Manna from Heaven (Exodus 16)
15. The Golden Calf (Exodus 32)
16. The Rewards for Obedience (Leviticus 26)
17. Miriam and Aaron Oppose Moses (Numbers 12)
18. The Twelve Spies Sent into Canaan (Numbers 13; Deuteronomy 1:19–46)
19. The Bronze Snake (Numbers 21:4–9)
20. Balaam's Donkey (Numbers 22:21–41)
21. Be Strong and Courageous (Joshua 1)
22. Joshua and the Battle of Jericho (Joshua 5:13–6:27)
23. Achan's Sin (Joshua 7)
24. Sun Stands Still (Joshua 10:1–15)
25. Ehud and Eglon (Judges 3:12–30)
26. Deborah (Judges 4)
27. Gideon (Judges 6–7)
28. Samson (Judges 13–16)
29. Ruth and Naomi (Ruth)
30. David and Goliath (1 Samuel 17)
31. Jonathan and David (1 Samuel 18–20)
32. Abigail (1 Samuel 25)
33. David's Mighty Men (2 Samuel 23:8–39; 1 Chronicles 11:10–47)
34. Solomon and the Women with the Baby (1 Kings 3:16–28)
35. Elijah on Mount Carmel (1 Kings 18:16–46)
36. Elijah Carried up to Heaven (2 Kings 2)
37. Naaman (2 Kings 5)
38. Jezebel Eaten by Dogs (2 Kings 9:30–37)
39. Hezekiah (2 Kings 18–20)
40. Josiah (2 Kings 22–23)
41. Solomon and the Queen of Sheba (2 Chronicles 9)
42. Esther
43. Job
44. Shadrach, Meshach and Abednego (Daniel 3)
45. Daniel and the Lions' Den (Daniel 6)
46. Jonah and the Fish (Jonah 1–4)

New Testament Stories

1. The Birth of Jesus (Luke 1)
2. The Birth of John the Baptist (Luke 1)
3. Gabriel's Appearance to Mary (Luke 1:26–38)
4. Jesus As a Boy in the Temple (Luke 2:41–52)
5. Jesus Heals a Leper (Mark 1:40–45;

Luke 5:12–16)

6. The Temptation of Jesus (Matthew 4:1–11)
7. The Crucifixion (Matthew 26–28)
8. The Samaritan Woman at the Well (John 4)
9. The Prodigal Son (Luke 15:11–32)
10. The Parable of the Sower (Matthew 13:1–23)
11. The Feeding the Five Thousand (Matthew 14:13–21; Mark 6:30–44)
12. The Rich Young Man (Matthew 19:16–30)
13. The Parable of the Two Sons (Matthew 21:28–32)
14. The Parable of the Wedding Banquet (Matthew 22:1–14)
15. The Parable of the Talents (Matthew 25:14–30)
16. Jesus Walking on the Water (Matthew 14:22–36; Mark 6:45–56)
17. Widow's Offering (Mark 12:41–44; Luke 21:1–4)
18. The Sheep and Goats (Matthew 25:31–46)
19. Driving Demons into the Pigs (Mark 5:1–20)
20. Healing the Paralytic (Mark 2)
21. Good Samaritan (Luke 10:25–37)
22. The Persistent Widow (Luke 18:1–8)
23. The Pharisee and Tax Collector (Luke 18:9–14)
24. The Good Shepherd (John 10:1–21)
25. Lazarus (John 11:1–44)
26. Pentecost (Acts 2)
27. Saul on the Road to Damascus (Acts 9:1–19)
28. Saul in a Basket over the Wall (Acts 9:19b–31)
29. Ethiopian Eunuch (Acts 8:26–40)
30. Peter's Miraculous Escape (Acts 12:1–19)
31. Lydia (Acts 16:11–15)
32. Jailer (Acts 16:16–40)
33. Paul's Shipwreck (Acts 27:1–28:10)

For more family devotionals get *As For Me and by House* by Tom and Lori Ziegler

1

Birth Order

—Ben and Beth Weast

Scripture: Exodus 2:1–11;
Numbers 12:1–15

Objective

Each child will learn that God decides when he or she is born into the family. In God's eyes each child has a special role in the family. Because of that specialness to God, they must learn what God expects of them, and then obey. God determines the birth order. Siblings helping each other is special in God's eyes! The older sister, Miriam was there to protect her baby brother Moses when his mother had to place him in the river. Years later, Moses begged God to have mercy on Miriam after she had sinned against him and God.

Activity

Prior to the devotional, study the text. Do you remember the petty fights you had with your siblings when you were growing up? Why did you fight? When you call everyone together for the devotional, have the children sit in the order in which they were born.

Some song suggestions for this devotional include: "Blue Skies," "Lord, God Almighty," "Whose Side Are You Living On?" "All to Jesus I Surrender," or "Trust and Obey." These songs all emphasize the greatness of God's plans, obedience to and trust in him, and loving each other. Tell the story of Moses and Miriam from Exodus and Numbers. Ask some very simple questions. The questions could include:

1. What would have happened to Moses had Miriam not been watching over him?
2. What would have happened to Miriam had Moses not begged God to have mercy on her?
3. Who gave Moses an older sister to watch out for him?
4. Who gave Miriam a younger brother to help her?

Point to the order in which the children are sitting, and ask:

1. Who decided that you would be born in this order?
2. What did you learn from Miriam about how the older should treat the younger?
3. What did you learn from Moses about how the younger should treat the older?

Have the family perform "thumbs up, thumbs down" skits. Dad and Mom can do two or three short skits in which they show an older sibling leaving the younger behind at school, the younger sibling refusing to learn from the older, etc. Create topics that fit the struggles your children are having with their roles in the family. Perform the skits, and then have the children rate the behavior as "thumbs up" if that's how they think Jesus would act or "thumbs down" if not.

Application

In our family we teach the older that, like Miriam, she is her sister's keeper, her protector and her example of righteousness. We teach the younger that she has the role of being a grateful follower, ready to help her older sister be righteous. We have used this devotional specifically to teach the older that it is a special treat from God for her to teach her younger sister how to read, to use the computer, to make her bed, etc.—and to teach the younger that God has provided her with someone to guide and help her. (Children whose birth order falls in the middle will get to experience both roles. Help them to see that this is a privilege.)

Plans, Commitments or Follow-Up

Create a reward chart for preschool, kindergarten and school-age children. List three to four items regarding being a "brother's keeper" or "follower."

Set specific goals for preteens and teens. Give them five goals regarding how the older can be a "Miriam" to the younger and how the younger can be a "Moses" to the older.

Scripture Memory or Additional Study

Deuteronomy 22:4

If you see your brother's donkey or his ox fallen on the road, do not ignore it. Help him get it to its feet. (Have some fun with this one!)

2
Creation

—Kevin and Debbie McDaniel

Scripture: Genesis 1:1–31

Objective

We want our children to be impressed with God, and to be fired up about how incredible, powerful, fun and creative God is!

Activity

In this devotional we play a thirty-minute video about animals in Africa. (You could chose any wildlife videos.) Typically, you should be able to find something like this at your local library or at a nearby video store. If you do not have a video player, then a book on Africa would be great. While we watch the awesome scenes of the African plains, we eat popcorn and have brownies and ice cream with hot fudge. It's a good time!

We have an engaging discussion about wildebeests, zebras, lions, giraffes, etc. Ask:

1. Which of these animals are the coolest, strongest, toughest, biggest or fastest?
2. Why is the giraffe's neck so long?
3. Why is the cheetah so fast?
4. Why is the elephant's trunk so big?
5. Are any of these animals goofy-looking? (You will most likely see some funny-looking and some funny-acting animals on the video. Creation is proof that God has a great sense of humor!)

Application

Read Genesis 1:1–31. Our children really want to learn about the animals they see on the video. They want to learn how God made them. The text has some great "stuff" in it about God that we should point out:

1. God created the heavens and the earth!!
2. How did God do this? He just said the word. God is powerful!
3. He made light, the sky, the oceans, the trees, the stars, all the fish and all the animals. Guess who else he made? He made us!
4. Did God make any mistakes in making us? No way! In fact the Bible says, "God saw all that he had made, and it was very good." Ask: "How did God

make you?" The answer is "very good"!

Plans, Commitments or Follow-Up

After this devotional we again make a point of emphasizing how awesome and powerful God is. We talk a lot around our house about how awesome we are because God made us just the way he wanted us. You can ask our children, "Why are you so awesome?" They usually answer, "'Cause God made me that way."

We believe it gives our children great confidence and security to know that even when they make mistakes, they are still awesome! Why? Because God did not make a mistake when he made them! He created them just the way he wanted them. This is a conversation that will put a smile on your children's faces.

Scripture Memory or Additional Study

Psalm 139:14

I praise you because I am fearfully and
wonderfully made;
your works are wonderful,
I know that full well.

3
Family

—Tom and Lori Ziegler

Scripture: Psalm 133:1; Hebrews 12:14

Objective

The purpose of this devotional is building unity and family pride.

Activity

Bring out pictures of your family. Talk about what was happening when the photos were taken. Have each family member tell which family activity they thought was the most fun and why. Use this time to laugh and to remember the fun times you have had together. Have each family member elaborate on one of their favorite times together as a family. Talk about what made it special. Have each person share what they remember most about the event. This will help to show what is important to each person in your family.

Have everyone draw a picture of your family doing something together. Ask each person to share about their pictures. Ask: What do you think makes our family so great?

Read the passages. Discuss what it means to live together in harmony—cooperation, helping one another, and being friendly, warm and gentle. The Bible says to make every effort to live in peace with one another. Ask: What does "make every effort" mean? It means to do your best and to work very hard. Ask: Why is living in harmony and peace difficult to do? How can each person make living together as a family more peaceful?

Application

Ask each person to share what they think they need to change to help the family be more in harmony and more at peace with each other. Perhaps the children have been arguing or will not share with each other. Perhaps Mom and Dad need to stop arguing and to apologize for their sin. Perhaps someone has not been speaking gently at home, or no one has been helping to pick up toys and dirty clothes.

Discuss again how much fun the times shown in the photos were. Usually the most fun times are the most peaceful times. Talk about making every day at home together one of those "best times." It does not just have to be parties and outings that are fun. God wants our lives together to be fun and to be peaceful. If everyone works together and helps ones another, then every day can be the way God intended it to be.

Plans, Commitments or Follow-Up

Make a plan to help everyone remember to live in harmony. Perhaps you could sing part of the song "We Are Family" to each other if someone argues or does not talk nicely. You could quote the scripture memory verse to each other or give hugs. Have everyone rate the level of harmony at the end of the week. Follow these suggestions every week until the changes are obvious in your home!

Scripture Memory or Additional Study

Psalm 133:1

How good and pleasant it is
when brothers live together in unity!

4
Listening

—Tom and Mary Franz

Scripture: James 1:19–20

Objective

We want to teach our children that listening means hearing and understanding, and therefore obeying joyfully—the first time. Listening is also a way of showing respect. God gave us two ears and one mouth for a reason!

Activity

We begin this devotional with the song "Oh, Be Careful." We finish the second verse with "Be careful, little ears, *that* you hear."

We often start with a game of "telephone": whispering a "secret" into someone's ear, who in turn whispers it to the next person and so on until it reaches the last person in the circle. The last person says aloud what they heard, which bears little or no resemblance to the original message!

After having one of the children read the passage, we ask: "Why did God give us two ears and one mouth?" We talk about how crazy it would be if we each had two mouths that could talk at the same time!

Using simple puppets (dolls), we act out scenarios for the children. They love watching the puppets. We go through a few scenarios of how to listen, how to speak to be heard, how to properly interrupt and how to look into the person's eyes as we listen.

Application

Since our lives are busy and we often are on the phone or having guests over, we need to establish a proper way for our children to approach us. They need to know that we will listen to them shortly and that they need to be patient right then. For us, acting out scenarios like how to politely interrupt us when we are on the phone, in a study or in a conversation with an adult, has been very helpful. This has helped the children to feel secure because they know a way to communicate and to be patient. It gives us the ability to have a conversation with an adult that can be uninterrupted.

We also believe that this is part of a larger idea of teaching our children respect and self-confidence through looking at people's eyes when they are talking to them.I (Tom) bring Sammy to his nursery school. One of the teachers commented to me how Sammy looks her in the eyes when he greets her in the morning! Hey, it works!

Plans, Commitments or Follow-Up

Needs a follow up plan? Maybe some kind of positive reinforcement when the children interrupt appropriately throughout the week?

Scripture Memory or Additional Study

James 1:19

My dear brothers, take note of this: Everyone should be quick to listen, slow to speak and slow to become angry.

Fifty Songs for Family Devotionals

1. AMEN

A—men, A—men
A—men, A—men, A—men.

See the little baby, lying in the manger,
Early in the morning.

See Him in the temple, talking to the elders,
How they marveled at His wisdom.

See Him at the seaside,
preaching and healing,
To the blind and feeble.

See Him in the garden,
praying to the Father,
In deepest sorrow.

See Him there with Pilate,
Pilate gave a choice.
But they wanted Barabbas.

See Him bear His cross now,
up to Calvary.
Where they crucified my Lord.

See the empty tomb now, Christ has arisen.
And He lives with us today.

2. BUILDING UP THE KINGDOM

Building up the kingdom,
building up the kingdom,
building up the kingdom of the Lord.
Brother can you help me?
Sister can you help me?
Building up the kingdom of the Lord.
It's so high, you can't get over it.
So low, you can't get under it.
So wide, you can't get around it.
Gotta go through that door!
(repeat and speed up several times)

3. DEEP AND WIDE

Deep and wide, deep and wide,
There's a fountain flowing deep and wide.
Deep and wide, deep and wide,
There's a fountain flowing deep and wide.

4. DEEP DOWN IN MY HEART

I love the Lord Messiah...
deep down in my heart!
(repeat both lines)

CHORUS
I said deep deep, down down
deep down in my heart! (repeat both lines)

2. I love to sing to Jesus...
3. I love to share my faith...
4. I want to be a disciple...
5. I want to pray to God...

5. DO LORD

I've got a home in glory land that
out-shines the sun.
I've got a home in glory land that
out-shines the sun.
I've got a home in glory land that
out-shines the sun.
Look away beyond the blue.

CHORUS
Do, Lord, oh, do, Lord,
Oh, do remember me.
Do, Lord, oh, do, Lord, Oh,
do remember me.
Do, Lord, oh, do, Lord, Oh,
do remember me.
Look away, beyond the blue.

I took Jesus as my Savior;
You take Him too.
I took Jesus as my Savior;

You take Him too.
I took Jesus as my savior;
You take Him too.
Look away, beyond the blue.

I'm going to see my Jesus there
And you'll see Him too.

6. DON'T YOU WANT TO GO TO THAT LAND?
Don't you wanna go to that land?
(repeat twice)
Where I'm bound, where I'm bound?
Don't you want to go to that land?
(repeat twice)
Where I'm bound, where I'm bound?

2. Nothing but *love* in that land...
3. Nothing but *joy* in that land...
4. Nothing but *peace* in that land...
5. I've got a Savior in that land...

7. GIVE ME OIL IN MY LAMP
Give me oil in my lamp,
Keep me burning, burning, burning
Give me oil in my lamp I pray, (I pray)
Give me oil in my lamp
keep me burning, burning, burning
Keep me burning till the break of day.

CHORUS
Sing Hosanna, Sing Hosanna,
Sing Hosanna to the King of Kings
Sing Hosanna, Sing Hosanna,
Sing Hosanna to the King

2. Give me love in my heart,
   keep me loving, loving, loving
3. Give me joy in my heart,
   keep me singing, singing, singing

8. GOD IS SO GOOD
God is so good. God is so good.
God is so good. He's so good to me.

God loves me so. God loves me so.
God loves me so. He's so good to me.

God answers prayers. God answers prayers.
God answers prayers. He's so good to me.

9. HARD FIGHTIN' SOLDIER
CHORUS
Lord, I'm a hard fighting soldier
  on the battlefield.
(repeat twice)
And I'll be bringing souls to Jesus,
By the service that I yield.

2. I've got a helmet on my head and in my hand a sword and shield.
3. Jesus is my master, and he fights my battles still.
   He has never lost a battle and I know he never will.
   I've got the word for my sword and I've got faith for my sheild,
   And I'll be bringing souls to Jesus,
   By the service that I yield.
4. When I die, let me die in the service of my Lord.

10. HE'S GOT THE WHOLE WORLD
He's got the whole world in his hand (4x)

2. He's got you and me brother...
3. He's got you and me sister...
4. He's got _________ & ________...

11. I CAN'T KEEP IT TO MYSELF
I said I wasn't gonna talk about it
But I couldn't keep it to myself,
Couldn't keep it to myself,
Couldn't keep it to myself,

Said I wasn't gonna talk about it,
But I couldn't keep it to myself,
What the Lord has done for me, for me.

CHORUS
You oughta been there, (echo)
When He saved my soul, (saved my soul)
You oughta been there, (echo)
When He wrote my name on the roll;
I've been walkin', I've been talkin'
I've been singin', I've been shoutin'
What the Lord has done for me.

12. I HAVE DECIDED TO FOLLOW JESUS

I have decided to follow Jesus.
(repeat twice)
No turning back, no turning back.

2. Though none go with me, still
   I will follow.
3. The world behind me,
   the cross before me.
4. Will you decide now
   to follow Jesus?

13. I TRIED AND I TRIED

I tried and I tried, (Hallelujah),
I tried and I tried,
I tried and I tried, (Hallelujah),
until I found the Lord.

CHORUS
My soul...(just couldn't be contented)
My soul...(just couldn't be contented)
My soul...(just couldn't be content)
Until I found the Lord.

2. I searched and I searched...
3. I prayed and I prayed...
4. I found, yes I found...I finally found the
   Lord.

14. IF I DON'T GET TO HEAVEN

If I don't (echo) get to heaven (echo)
If I don't (echo) get to heaven (echo)
If I don't get to heaven, dear Lord.
It will be nobody, nobody,
no-no-no-nobody's
Nobody's fault but mine.

2. If I don't read my Bible...
3. If I don't share my faith...
4. If I don't pray every day...
5. If I don't make disciples...
6. If I don't get discipled...

15. IF YOU'RE HAPPY AND YOU KNOW IT

If you're happy and you know it,
clap your hands! (repeat)
If you're happy and you know it
then your life will surely show it
If you're happy and you know it,
clap your hands!

2. Stamp your feet
3. Shout "Amen!"
4. Do all three!

16. I'M GONNA VIEW THAT HOLY CITY

I'm gonna view that holy city,
I'm gonna view that holy city
one of these days.
I'm gonna view that holy city,
I'm gonna view that holy city
one of these days.

2. I'm gonna meet my loving Jesus...
3. I'm gonna sit at the welcome table...
4. I'm gonna feast on milk and honey...
5. I'm gonna sing and never get tired...
6. I'm gonna fly all over heaven...
7. I'm gonna high five holy Moses...
8. I'm gonna climb up Jacob's ladder...
9. I'm gonna worship God forever...

17. I'M HAPPY TODAY

I'm happy today, oh yes I'm happy today
in Jesus Christ, I'm happy today
because he's taken all my sins away
so that's why I'm happy today

2. I'm singing today
3. I'm praying today
4. I'm sharing my faith

I'm happy today, oh yes I'm singing today
in Jesus Christ, I'm praying today
because he's taken all my sins away
so that's why I'm sharing my faith

18. I'M IN THE LORD'S ARMY

I may never march in the infantry,
Ride in the calvary, shoot the artillery.
I may never zoom over the enemy, but
I'm in the Lord's army.
I'm in the Lord's army. YES SIR!!
I'm in the Lord's army. YES SIR!!
I may never march in the infantry,
Ride in the calvary, shoot the artillery.
I may never zoom over the enemy, but
I'm in the Lord's army. YES SIR!!

19. IN AND OUT

I'm in right (point in)
Out right (point out)
Up right (point up)
Down right (point down)
HAPPY ALL THE TIME
(repeat)

Since Jesus Christ came in (point in)
And took away my sin (stretch out)
I'm in right (point in)
Out right (point out)
Up right (point up)
Down right (point down)
HAPPY ALL THE TIME

20. IT ISN'T ANY TROUBLE

Oh, it isn't any trouble just to s–m–i–l–e.
(repeat)
If ever you're in trouble
it will vanish like a bubble (pop!)
if you only take the trouble just to
s–m–i–l–e!
2. P–R–A–Y
3. S–I–N–G
4. S–H–A–R–E
5. L–O–V–E

21. I'VE BEEN REDEEMED

I've been redeemed (echo)
By the blood of the lamb (echo)
I've been redeemed (echo)
By the blood of the Lamb
I've been redeemed
by the blood of the Lamb,
Filled with the Holy Ghost I am.
All my sins are washed away,
I've been redeemed.

Well, I went down (echo)
To the river to pray (echo)
Well, I went down (echo)
To the river to pray.
Well I went down to the river to pray,
Felt so good that I stayed all day.
All my sins are washed away

And that's not all (echo)
There's more besides (echo)
And that's not all (echo)
There's more besides.
And that's not all there's more besides,
I've been to the river and
I've been baptized.
All my sins are washed away,
I've been redeemed.

22. I'VE GOT THE JOY, JOY, JOY

I've got the joy, joy, joy, joy
down in my heart (where?)
down in my heart (where?)
down in my heart
I've got the joy, joy, joy, joy
down in my heart
down in my heart to stay.
CHORUS
And I'm so happy, so very happy
I've got the Love of Jesus in my heart
(Repeat Both Lines)

2. I've got the peace that passes understanding...
3. I've got the love of Jesus, love of Jesus...
4. I've got the wonderful love of my blessed redeemer...

23. JESUS

Je—sus, Je—sus,
Jesus in the morning.
Jesus at the noontime,
Je—sus, Je—sus,
Jesus when the sun goes down.

Love Him, love Him,
Love him in the morning,
Love Him at the noontime.
Love Him, love Him,
Love Him when the sun goes down.

3. Praise Him...
4. Serve Him...

24. JESUS CALLED THEM

Jesus called them one by one:
Peter, Andrew, James and John.
Next came Philip, Thomas too,
Matthew and Bartholomew.

CHORUS
Yes, Jesus called them.
Yes, Jesus called them.
Yes, Jesus called them.
And they all followed Him.

James the one they call the less.
Simon, also Thaddeus,
Twelve apostles Judas made.
Jesus was by him betrayed.

CHORUS

25. JESUS LOVES ME

Jesus loves me, this I know,
For the Bible tells me so.
Little ones to Him belong,
They are weak but he is strong.

CHORUS
Yes, Jesus loves me, (repeat twice)
The Bible tells me so.

Jesus loves me when I'm good.
When I do the things I should.
Jesus loves me when I'm bad,
But it makes Him very sad.

CHORUS

Jesus loves me, He who died,
Heaven's gates to open wide.
He will wash away my sins,
Let His little child come in.

26. JESUS LOVES THE LITTLE CHILDREN

Jesus loves the little children;
All the children of the world,
Red and yellow, black and white,
They are precious in his sight,
Jesus loves the little children
of the world.

2. Jesus died for all the children...

3. Jesus rose for all the children...
4. Jesus lives for all the children...

27. LORD GOD ALMIGHTY

Lord, God Almighty (echo)
Gonna sing, sing, sing for you (echo)
(repeat both lines)
Gonna work and pray
And sing every day for you
(repeat both lines)

2. Preach
3. Fight
4. Die

28. MY GOD IS SO BIG

My God is so big, so strong and so mighty,
There's nothing my God cannot do.
My God is so big, so strong and so mighty,
There's nothing my God cannot do.
The mountains are His, the valleys are His,
And the trees are His handiwork too.
My God is so big, so strong and so mighty,
There's nothing my God cannot do.

29. MY LORD, HE DONE DONE

CHORUS
My Lord (my Lord), He done, done,
(repeat twice)
He done, done what He said He'd do.

2. He done give us Jesus...
3. He done give us love...
4. He done give us joy...
5. He done give us hope...

30. OH BE CAREFUL

Oh be careful little eyes what you see!
Oh be careful little eyes what you see!
There's a Father up above
looking down with tender love, so
Be careful little eyes what you see.

2. Oh be careful little ears what you hear!
3. Oh be careful little mouth what you say!
4. Oh be careful little hands what you do!

31. OH, HOW I LOVE JESUS

Oh, (name), do you love Jesus?
(reply) Oh, yes I love Jesus
Are you sure you love Jesus?
(reply) Yes, I'm sure I love Jesus
Tell us why you love Jesus
(reply) This is why I love Jesus
Because he first loved me!

32. PEACE LIKE A RIVER

I've got peace like a river,
I've got peace like a river,
I've got peace like a river,
In my soul!—YAHOO!!
I've got peace like a river,
I've got peace like a river,
I've got peace like a river,
In my soul!—YAHOO!!

2. I've got love like an ocean,
3. I've got joy like a fountain,

I've got love like an ocean,
I've got joy like a fountain,
I've got peace like a river
In my soul!—YAHOO!!
(repeat)

33. PETER, JAMES AND JOHN

Peter James and John in a sailboat!
(repeat twice)
Out on the deep blue sea!
Cast their nets, but caught no fishes
(repeat twice)
Out on the deep blue sea.

Along came Jesus walking on the seashore
(repeat twice)
Out on the deep blue sea.

Cast your nets on the other side!
(Repeat twice)
Out on the deep blue sea

Caught their nets so full of fishes
(repeat twice)
Out of the deep blue sea!
Jesus said you'll fish for men.
(repeat twice)
so men will come to me.

34. ROLL THE GOSPEL CHARIOT
Roll the gospel chariot along.
(repeat twice)
And we won't tag along behind.
If our brother's in the way we will
stop and pick him up (repeat twice)
And we won't tag along behind.

If the Devil's in the way, we will
roll right over him (repeat twice)
And we won't tag along behind

35. SEA OF GALILEE
There's a sea of Galilee.
There's a sea of Galilee.
There's a sea, there's a sea.
There's a sea of Galilee.

There's a boat on the sea of Galilee.
There's a boat on the sea of Galilee.
There's a boat, there's a boat,
There's a boat on the sea of Galilee.

3. There are men in the boat
   on the sea of Galilee.
4. There are hands on the men
   in the boat on the sea of Galilee.
5. There are nets in the hands of the men
   in the boat on the sea of Galilee.
6. There are fish in the nets
   in the hands of the men
   in the boat on the sea of Galilee.
7. There are many, many fish
   in the nets in the hands of the men
   in the boat on the sea of Galilee.

36. SHOW ME THE WAY
The blind man sat by the road and he cried
(repeat twice)
he cried oh oh oh show me the way,
show me the way, show me the way,
the way to go home.

The woman sat by the well and she cried
(repeat twice)
she cried oh oh oh show me the way,
show me the way, show me the way,
the way to go home.

Jesus hung on the cross and he died
(repeat twice)
He cried oh, I am the way,
I am the way, I am the way,
the way to go home.

Jesus rose from the dead and He cried.
(repeat twice)
He cried oh oh oh show them the way,
show them the way, show them the way,
the way to go home. Jesus.

37. TAKE THE LORD WITH YOU
You've got to take the Lord with you, children, Everywhere you go. (Repeat twice)

CHORUS
In the street, in the home, on the job, all alone;
Highways, byways, highway, byway

2. Make disciples, daily... (Repeat twice)
3. Love your brothers, daily... (Repeat twice)

38. THANK YOU FOR MAKING ME ME!

If I were a butterfly,
I'd thank you Lord for giving me wings,
and if I were a bird in a tree,
I'd thank you Father for making me sing,
and if I were a fish in the sea,
I'd wiggle and I'd squiggle and I'd giggle with glee
but I just thank you Lord for making me, me.

CHORUS
Cuz you gave me a heart
and you gave me a smile
you gave me Jesus and you made me a child
and I just thank you Lord for making me, me.

If I were an elephant,
I'd thank you Lord for raising my trunk,
and if I were a kangaroo
I'd hop right up to you,
and if I were an octopus
I'd thank you Lord for my good looks!
but I just thank you Lord for making me, me.

CHORUS

39. THANK YOU, LORD

Thank you, Lord, for loving me.
And thank you, Lord, for blessing me,
Thank you, Lord, for making me whole
and saving my soul.

CHORUS
I want to thank you, Lord, for loving me.
Thank you, Lord, for saving my soul.

Let us all with one accord
Sing praises to Christ the Lord.
Let us all unite in song
to praise Him all day long.

CHORUS

Please reveal your will for me
So I can serve you for eternity.
Use my life in every way.
Take hold of it today.

CHORUS

40. THE CHRISTIAN JUBILEE

Sign me up, (echo)
for the Christian Jubilee.
Write my name (echo) on the roll.
I've been changed (echo)
since the Lord has lifted me.
Oh I want to be ready,
ready when Jesus comes

41. THE GOSPEL

Love, love, love, love,
The Gospel in one word is love.
Love your neighbor as your brother.
Love, love, love.

Peace, peace, peace, peace,
The Gospel in one word is peace.
Peace that passes all understanding.
Peace, peace, peace.

Joy, joy, joy, joy,
The Gospel in one word is joy.
Joy that fills to overflowing.
Joy, joy, joy.

42. THE LORD IS MY SHEPHERD

The Lord is my shepherd
I'll walk with Him always.
He leads through green pastures
I'll walk with Him always.
Always, always
I'll walk with Him always.
Always, always
I'll walk with Him always.

43. THE NEW TESTAMENT SONG
Matthew, Mark, Luke, John
Acts and the letter to the Romans
First and Second Corinthians
Galatians and Ephesians
Philippians, Colossians
First and Second Thessalonians
First and Second Timothy
Titus and Philemon
Hebrews, James
First and Second Peter
First and Second and Third John
Jude and Revelation.

44. THIS LITTLE LIGHT OF MINE
This little light of mine,
I'm gonna let it shine.
(repeat twice)
Let it shine, let it shine, let it shine oh yeah!

2. When I'm with my parents...
3. When I'm at the playground...
4. All around my neighborhood...
5. Let it shine till Jesus comes...
6. Hide it under a bushel, NO!...
7. Won't let Satan blow it out...

45. THIS IS THE DAY
This is the day, (echo)
That the Lord has made. (echo)
We will rejoice, (echo)
And be glad in it. (echo)
This is the day that the Lord has made,
We will rejoice and be glad in it.
This is the day, (echo)
That the Lord has made.

46. WE ARE SOLDIERS IN THE ARMY
CHORUS
We are soldiers. We're in the army,
We've gotta fight (unh–huh–huh)
We've gotta fight. (we've gotta hold)
We've gotta hold up
the blood stained banner;
We've gotta hold it up until we die.

You know ________(repeat),
he(she) was a soldier,
He put his hand to the gospel plow
(yes he did);
Well one day he got old, he couldn't fight anymore, He had to stand up and fight anyhow.

47. WE SHALL OVERCOME
We shall overcome, We shall overcome,
We shall overcome today;
O, deep in my heart, I do believe,
We shall overcome today.

The Lord will see us through,
The Lord will see us through,
The Lord will see us through today;
O, deep in my heart, I do believe,
The Lord will see us through today.

It's on to victory!
It's on to victory!
It's on to victory , today!
O, deep in my heart, I do believe,
It's on to victory today!

48. WHISPER A PRAYER
Whisper a prayer in the morning.
Whisper a prayer at noon.
Whisper a prayer in the evening
To keep your heart in tune.

God answers prayers in the morning.
God answers prayers at noon.
God answers in the evening
So keep your heart in tune.

Jesus may come in the morning.
Jesus may come at noon.

Jesus may come in the evening
So keep your heart in tune.

49. WHOSE SIDE ARE YOU LIVING ON?

Tell me whose side are you living on?
(all) I'm living on the Lord's side.
(repeat both lines)

CHORUS:
I'm livin', I'm livin', I'm livin', I'm livin',
I'm living on the Lord's side.
(repeat)

2. Singin'
3. Prayin'
4. Lovin'
5. Servin', etc...

50. WISE MAN

The wise man built his house upon the rock
(repeat twice)
and the rain came tumbling down. OH!

The rains came down
and the floods came up!
(repeat twice)
and the wise man's house stood firm!
BUT...

The foolish man built his house upon the sand (repeat twice)
and the rain came tumbling down. OH!

The rains came down
and the floods came up!
(repeat twice)
and the foolish man's house went SPLAT!!

SO...Build your house upon the Lord Jesus Christ (repeat twice)
and your house will stand firm!

Ten Helps for a Healthy Marriage

Suggested ways for couples to grow spiritually in their relationship

1. **Commendations and compliments**: Share what you really have appreciated in each other—and make it a great time of encouragement!
2. **Areas of need and/or problems**: Share things that have bothered you about your mate. However, mention only one or two things per session. We are talking about having a discipling time, not a gripe session! Be sure to listen carefully without becoming defensive. No one knows you as well as your life partner. Therefore, be anxious to get their perspective and learn from them. Humility is required and humility will be rewarded (maybe in some very exciting ways!).
3. **Plan your calendar and schedules for the week** (or next week, if your discipling time is near the weekend). Talk about areas of shared responsibility such as child care, use of the car, and other areas needing coordination between the two of you.
4. **Talk about your feelings**—your goals, desires, dreams, frustrations, fears and anything else that really brings out your heart and inner convictions. For those who find sharing at this level difficult (are you listening, men?), some specific exercises may help to strengthen your "feeling-expressing muscles." One such exercise is to talk back through your lives together a year at a time. Anything you remember from the early years of your life is most likely remembered because it was associated with an emotional experience, either positive or negative. Sharing these memories together will bond you and increase your understanding and appreciation of your partner. Another exercise is to share with each other something you have never shared before. The more difficult it may be to share it, the more it will help the sharer and the marriage bond. Bottom line, learn to share your hearts together. Real intimacy is much more a matter of heart-to-heart than body-to-body.
5. **Household management**: Talk about needs around the house (the Honey-do list)!
6. **Children**: Talk about how you each are feeling about how the children are doing. Make sure that you are unified about discipline and other parenting concerns. Your unity as a couple in this area is more important than almost anything else. Stay spiritually focused and stay unified in dealing with your children.
7. **Plan for family devotionals**: Talk about the needs in the family and what scriptures would best meet those needs. (See "Forty Scriptures to Build Character in Children" in this book.)
8. **Plan one-on-one times** with each of the children during the week.
9. **Finances**: Make sure that adequate communication on all financial issues takes place, and that each of you feels unified about the financial decisions that are reached.
10. **Prayer**: Don't neglect the most important thing!

Wyndham Shaw
Boston, Massachusetts

Five Keys to Making Disciples

1. **Pray.**
   Do not depend on your own resources. Depend on God. Jesus knew that he could do nothing on his own and we must understand the same thing (John 5:19).

2. **Make the most of every opportunity**.
   Whether you are out shopping, going to a game, eating in a restaurant, attending a neighborhood function, look for ways to build relationships and share your life (Colossians 4:2–6).

3. **Show hospitality.**
   Have people into your home, share a meal with them, serve them, show them that you are interested in their lives (Hebrews 13:2). Like Jesus, be a "friend of sinners" (Matthew 11:19).

4. **Study.**
   Devote yourself to learning the Scriptures so you can handle them correctly and help other people to see God's will for their lives (2 Timothy 2:15). Seriously commit yourselves to those training programs offered in your congregation. Get prepared to make disciples.

5. **Live with joy (Philippians 4:4).**
   As a child of God you are richly blessed. Enjoy your life. Enjoy your relationship with God. Let it show. People are attracted to those who have joy.

Twenty Ideas for Personal Growth and Greater Impact

1. Plan a Personal Retreat

Plan an eight-hour retreat to just be alone with God. Decide in advance how you will use each hour, but do not try to cram too much in. Leave plenty of room for God to move. Use the last half hour or hour to write down what you have learned, what you might want to do with a future time, and what you would advise others to do with a time like this.

2. Write Letters

Write one letter every week for the next ten weeks to people who have most profoundly influenced your life and taught you important things about character and leadership. List their names here:

1. ______________________________
2. ______________________________
3. ______________________________
4. ______________________________
5. ______________________________
6. ______________________________
7. ______________________________
8. ______________________________
9. ______________________________
10. ______________________________

3. Evaluate Your Fruit

If you are married, sit down with your spouse and read Galatians 5:22–23:

> *"But the fruit of the Spirit is love, joy, peace, patience, kindness, goodness, faithfulness, gentleness and self-control. Against such things there is no law."*

Ask your spouse to evaluate you at each point. Take notes. If you are not married, ask someone who is very close to you and sees you in a lot of different situations to do this for you. Plan a follow-up session in about a month to review your progress.

4. Become a Better Listener

Start by asking three people to evaluate you as a listener. Let one of those be your spouse, if you are married, or a close friend if you are not married. Tell them that you are working on becoming a better listener and want to get their honest feedback. Later, write them a note and let them know what you learned from their feedback.

5. Life-Changing Weekend

This one is just for married couples, but could probably be adapted for some who are single. Plan a month or two in advance to take another couple with the two of you away for an overnight. Especially pick a couple who would not expect you to ask them. Pick a couple who are weak or struggling with the their faith or their marriage. Save your money so you can pay all the expenses, especially if they would find it hard to pay. Go far enough away so that you have a good amount of time in the car. Plan some fun time and some time to have some good spiritual talks. Once back, write them a note that lets them know your vision for their relationship. It will be a weekend that will change their lives!

6. Personal Marriage Retreat

Go away with your spouse for a three-day, two-night retreat. Take along a copy of *Friends & Lovers* by Sam and Geri Laing. Find a really neat and memorable place to go. Plan ahead to take time to read the chapters and then discuss them. Do not turn on a TV. Do not read newspapers. Just drop out for a couple of days and focus on each other. Spend the last hour together talking about what you have learned and how you want to help other married couples enrich their intimacy and communication.

7. "Practice What You Preach" Exercise

Start by writing down ten things you strongly believe a servant of God should be doing. Next, evaluate how you think you are doing in each of these areas. Then go over what you have written down with a mentor (and your spouse if you are married) and get their feedback. Finally, write a letter to God describing the changes you want to make.

8. Learning from Problems

Write down five things in your life right now that are the most difficult for you to deal with. It might be your dating life, a problem in your marriage, a difficult relationship, some responsibility you don't feel well qualified for, or a number of other things. Next write down what you believe God is trying to teach you with each one of these, and spend some time being thankful that God is at work in all things for your good. Share your conclusions with someone close to you.

9. Appreciating and Showing Grace

Write down ten ways that God and others have shown grace to you. Then beside each, write down someone you need to show grace to in the same way.

10. New Territory

Write down ten things you have never done before, but things that could inspire others or help others to become Christians. Be reasonable, but still, let your mind go. Pick one of these and do it this week. Next week pick another and so on until you have finished the list. After the ten weeks, write down what God has done with your new adventures.

11. Plan a Third-World Week with Your Family

Obviously, this one is for first-world families. Unfortunately, third-world families cannot have a first-world week. You may want to discuss this fact. Unplug the television. Change your diet. Eat very simply. No convenience foods allowed. Have several times during the week when you cut the power off without warning. Combine this with reading about life in some impoverished countries.

12. Be Still!

Did your mother ever tell you that? Many of us tend to be doers. That is good and logical, but we still need time to be still and quiet (Psalm 37:7, 46:10; Isaiah 30:15, 32:17). For one week, set aside ten minutes a day to just be still and quiet. Do not read or plan or even pray during this time. Just be still. At the end of one week, write down what you have learned.

13. Memorize a favorite chapter from the Bible.

God's word is full of challenges to grow in knowledge. We are told to keep God's words in our hearts so that we will stay far from sin. Our people need a living example in this area. It is very easy to fall into laziness not only in evangelism, but with God and his word. This will keep us sharp and sharpen our swords in the spiritual battle out there.

14. Have a Deuteronomy 6 day with your children.

Take a one and a half hour block of time with each individual child, regardless of their ages. Take them somewhere special and communicate. Tell them why you love and are proud of them. Give them many examples. Also mention an area that they need to grow in. Ask how you can be a better parent. Discuss their views of God and get a feel for their hearts for his kingdom. After each child has had their individual times, close out the day with a family outing (movie, dinner, walk on the beach...).

15. When You Are Feeling Attacked or Defeated:

Write down a list of sins that were in your life when you decided to become a disciple. Show it to your spouse and others. Then write down how you felt when you repented and were baptized. Meditate on the cross. Write down 100 things you are grateful for. By the end of this time you will be neither depressed nor defeated. And you will be much easier to live with.

16. When You Feel Like Complaining:

Plan to serve. Put time in your schedule, for the week or the month, for one thing to do every day that will serve someone else that is either (1) Some way you have always wanted to serve, (2) Something that will surprise the person being served, (3) Something that will be anonymous service or (4) Any combination of these. Take your family to serve in a food kitchen, pantry, shelter, nursing home, etc. Make it one of your family nights every month.

17. When Your Trust For God is Weakening:

Write down a list of ten reasons why God should trust you. Write down a list of ten reasons why you should trust God. Write down the plans you had for your life that didn't work out. Compare them to the plans God had for your life to prosper you and not to harm you. Note the times your selfish ambition got you into trouble and the times your selfless service was rewarded by God. Write a short story on how your life would have worked out if you had not become a disciple. Share it with someone close and ask for comments.

18. When You Don't Know How to Express Your Feelings to God:

Study the Psalms. Note each of the emotions David felt and expressed about God. How did he resolve the negative emotions and how did he use the positive ones?

19. The Fall-Away Test

Write down a list of the hardest things you can imagine that could happen to you.

Circle the ones that could make you fall away from God. That is where the cracks in your faith are.

Read Romans 8.

20. Stretch Yourself

Share your faith in a way that is uncomfortable and/or unfamiliar to you. Study with a person who intimidates you. Take your children out for a treat and ask them how you could be a better father or mother. Or you come up with something that stretches you, and go do it.

Contributors: Jimmy Allen, Tom Jones,
Roger Lamb, Wyndham Shaw

A Dozen Passages to Help in Your Ministry

1. **When you are discouraged by the lack of responses...**
   2 Corinthians 4:1: Therefore, since through God's mercy we have this ministry, we do not lose heart.
   And...
   Galatians 6:9: Let us not become weary in doing good, for at the proper time we will reap a harvest if we do not give up.

2. **When you are frustrated and impatient with someone...**
   1 Timothy 1:16: But for that very reason I was shown mercy so that in me, the worst of sinners, Christ Jesus might display his unlimited patience as an example for those who would believe on him and receive eternal life.

3. **When you are lacking motivation and desire...**
   2 Corinthians 5:14–15: For Christ's love compels us, because we are convinced that one died for all, and therefore all died. And he died for all, that those who live should no longer live for themselves but for him who died for them and was raised again.

4. **When you find it hard to have vision for someone...**
   1 Corinthians 1:26–29: Brothers, think of what you were when you were called. Not many of you were wise by human standards; not many were influential; not many were of noble birth. But God chose the foolish things of the world to shame the wise; God chose the weak things of the world to shame the strong. He chose the lowly things of this world and the despised things—and the things that are not—to nullify the things that are, so that no one may boast before him.

5. **When you are opposed or slandered...**
   Matthew 5:11–13: "Blessed are you when people insult you, persecute you and falsely say all kinds of evil against you because of me. Rejoice and be glad, because great is your reward in heaven, for in the same way they persecuted the prophets who were before you.
   "You are the salt of the earth. But if the salt loses its saltiness, how can it be made salty again?

6. **When you meet resistance and pride...**
   2 Timothy 2:24–25: And the Lord's servant must not quarrel; instead, he must be kind to everyone, able to teach, not resentful. Those who oppose him he must gently instruct, in the hope that God will grant them repentance leading them to a knowledge of the truth.

7. **When you have done everything you know to do for someone...**
   Colossians 4:12: Epaphras, who is one of you and a servant of Christ Jesus, sends greetings. He is always wrestling in prayer for you, that you may stand firm in all the will of God, mature and fully assured.

8. **When you feel you need more love for someone...**
   Ephesians 5:1–2: Be imitators of God, therefore, as dearly loved children and live a life of love, just as Christ loved us and gave himself up for us as a fragrant offering and sacrifice to God.

9. When a younger disciple has blown it…

2 Corinthians 2:7–8: Now instead, you ought to forgive and comfort him, so that he will not be overwhelmed by excessive sorrow. I urge you, therefore, to reaffirm your love for him.

10. When you have blown it…

1 John 1:7–9: But if we walk in the light, as he is in the light, we have fellowship with one another, and the blood of Jesus, his Son, purifies us from all sin.

If we claim to be without sin, we deceive ourselves and the truth is not in us. If we confess our sins, he is faithful and just and will forgive us our sins and purify us from all unrighteousness.

11. When you feel fearful and timid…

Acts 18:9: One night the Lord spoke to Paul in a vision: "Do not be afraid; keep on speaking, do not be silent."

And…

Hebrews 2:11: Both the one who makes men holy and those who are made holy are of the same family. So Jesus is not ashamed to call them brothers.

12. When you are tempted to be less than honest and forthright...

2 Corinthians 4:2: Rather, we have renounced secret and shameful ways; we do not use deception, nor do we distort the word of God. On the contrary, by setting forth the truth plainly we commend ourselves to every man's conscience in the sight of God.

Forty Scriptures to Build Character in Children

Deuteronomy 6:5
Luke 6:45b
Luke 12:48b
Luke 14:11
John 14:15
Romans 8:28
Romans 12:17a
1 Corinthians 10:13
1 Corinthians 10:24
1 Corinthians 13:4–8a
2 Corinthians 10:5
Galatians 5:22–23a
Galatians 6:9
Ephesians 4:32
Philippians 2:3
Philippians 2:14
Philippians 4:4a
Philippians 4:13
Colossians 3:20
1 Thessalonians 5:16–18
1 Timothy 4:12
Hebrews 3:13
Hebrews 12:11
James 1:19
James 1:22
1 Peter 5:5
1 John 4:11
Joshua 1:7
1 Samuel 16:7b
Psalm 119:9
Psalm 139:23–24
Proverbs 3:7
Proverbs 6:16–19
Proverbs 11:25
Proverbs 12:15
Proverbs 13:24
Proverbs 17:22
Proverbs 18:17
Proverbs 21:3
Ecclesiastes 7:14

Twelve Ways to Keep the Holidays Spiritual and Joyful

1. **Matthew 6:33**—Seek the kingdom of God and his righteousness first. Decide you will not let anything distract you from great time with God every day. It is a challenging time of the year. You will need this more than ever. Every day you need to hear spiritual wisdom. Every day you need a close walk with God. Make plans and follow through.

2. **Psalm 119:97, 99**—Meditate on great passages that deal with situations you are going to be in, challenges you will face. Keep them ever before you. (Example: James 3:17–18).

3. **Hebrews 3:12**—Encourage one another daily. Don't think for a minute that you will not need this during the holidays. (Don't think for a minute the enemy takes two weeks off and goes to visit his nephew Wormwood.) Talk things over with a Christian friend and get a plan. Discuss the kind of encouragement that will be needed and how to make it happen.

4. **Matthew 5:14–16**—Let your light shine! Be different. Preach a sermon with your life. Show love, say "I love you," be a servant, be thankful, be kind, be unselfish.

5. **Colossians 3:13**—Resolve conflicts, ask for forgiveness, practice forgiveness. There will be bumps. Some will hurt. But confess or forgive and get back on track. *Romans 12:18: "If it is possible, as far as it depends on you, live at peace with everyone."*

6. **Proverbs 19:20**—Get advice about difficult situations, long standing problems. If you are leaving town, get advice about how long to be gone, about how to get with disciples in other cities. If you have never opened up your various family dynamics and received input, make this a priority.

7. **Colossians 4:5**—Be wise in the way you act toward outsiders; make the most of every opportunity. Realize with family, it usually takes time. Plant and water seeds, but don't try to force them to grow overnight. Watch out that you don't come across as self-righteous or spiritually arrogant.

8. **Romans 12:1–2**—Be alert to how the world will try to squeeze you into its mold (with family, office parties, or just in buying what everybody else is buying.)

9. **Ephesians 4:22**—Watch out for the reappearance of your old self. Often when we go back into situations with family we revert to old ways that we thought we had put off. Think about these things in advance. Write them down. Pray about them. Ask others to pray about them. Be pro-active. Out-smart Satan.

10. **Ephesians 6:4**—Parents, have great time with your own family. Don't exasperate. Build memories. Teach them with words and with your life. Deal with discipline issues firmly, but don't let it cause you to lose your joy. Note: Think through your holiday schedule in advance. Balance the time between various needs. Give to others, but make sure you get time with your immediate family. Communicate in advance so expectations will be clear.

11. **2 Corinthians 6:13**—"Open wide your hearts." If the holidays bring up painful issues for you (and they do for many), open your heart up to someone. Talk it through. Get perspective. Get help from the Scriptures. Some will not be able to be with their families. You may feel down about that. That's normal. But work it through. God's plan is for you to be a light this season, and he will be with you.

12. **Psalm 68:6, Proverbs 14:31**—Don't forget the lonely and the poor. Reach out and share with those in need.

Reaching Out to the Poor and Needy

Mohan and Helen Nanjundan, *London, England*

It was a warm summer morning in the southern Indian city of Hyderabad, home to five-million people. We had arrived in the city a few hours earlier and were excited to get a firsthand view of the work for the poor being done by the HOPE *worldwide* staff there. Hyderabad is a city with a thriving construction industry. The building boom has attracted the rural poor into this metropolis in droves, including many from India's colorful Banjara (itinerant gypsy) community.

For the poor these opportunities to work are a mixed blessing. There are jobs on the building sites, but most are only temporary. Workers are migratory and have to frequently move from site to site, families in tow. The conditions on the sites are often dangerous and the risk of accidents is ever-present, as well as obvious health hazards associated with dust and pollution. The children of the workers are malnourished, illiterate and constantly uprooted. Food is abundant, but expensive, in the city. Dreams here die fast for the poor.

Daily Grind

We visited two work sites: one is in a remote area, the other downtown. HOPE *worldwide* workers serve at four construction sites in the city, educating the children and helping with basic medical needs, especially malnutrition. The children were always smiling, chattering and full of life. There was something these children understood that often escapes us grown-ups—that joy is not equal to the sum total of your possessions!

Fathers and mothers both work at the construction sites. Poor women frequently do very heavy labor. A few grandmothers were present and were delighted to meet us. We looked around at their homes—dwellings made of sticks, rags and torn plastic sheeting. Inside nothing but a few cooking utensils, no toys, no sign of anything but the most basic of basics. We have seen homes like this many times in our work, yet we still choke on our tears.

The realness of the people we met that morning remains indelibly etched on our hearts and minds. We felt one with them. What struck us the most was that there was no real difference between us and them. Only by the grace of God, were we so fortunate in life, while these families faced such terrible hardship. We felt very undeserving and so very blessed. It was a wake-up call to gratefulness!

A Jesus Wake-up Call

Experiences like this inevitably result in different responses. Either you can harden your heart to the needs of others, allowing selfishness to scar your very soul or you can wake up to the call of discipleship, seek Jesus and ask yourself the question: What must I do?

In Mark 10:17–22 when the rich young ruler asked "What must I do?", Jesus' response is direct, instructive, challenging and absolute. Jesus knew this man's heart and was willing to make sacrifice and giving to the poor the acid test for this man's eternal destiny. Knowing our hearts, would Jesus ask us the same? What would our response be? Would we pass the test? Would we be willing to give up everything for the sake of the poor? As his followers we *must* love the poor to inherit eternal life. It's not an option. It's a command of Jesus, and we *must* obey everything he has commanded us (Matthew 28:19-20).

Our experience and conviction is that personal motivation begins with personal involvement. Get to know someone who is poor and needy. Jesus surrounded himself with the poor and needy. People in need must become real people to us. They need to become faces with names. They need to become our friends. On that warm summer day in Hyderabad our motivation to help the poor was rekindled because we touched and were touched by real people. And the heart of the matter is that we needed to be with them as much as they needed us to help them.

A homeless person, a child in an orphanage, a lonely senior citizen in a nursing home, a sickly person in a hospital—there are many opportunities to get to know people in need. Fix a time when you will go to visit your "friend" in need. Go on your own, or go with someone else, or even go as a group, but *go*. Cook a meal for them, celebrate their birthday or just "hang out" with them and listen. Get personally involved! We guarantee, it will change your heart, not to mention how it will change their lives! Very often they need friends more than they need money. As you spend time with the poor and needy, think about what it would be like to be in their situation. It will change your perspective for eternity.

Ten Reasons Disciples Should Take Care of Themselves Physically

Don't you know that you yourselves are God's temple and that God's Spirit dwells in your midst? If anyone destroys God's temple, God will destroy that person; for God's temple is sacred, and you together are that temple. —1 Corinthians 3:16-17

Do you not know that your bodies are temples of the Holy Spirit, who is in you, whom you have received from God? You are not your own. —1 Corinthians 6:19

The majority of western society's health challenges are brought on by excess. Too much food, too much drink and way too much of a sedentary lifestyle. These are the scourges of first world economies. We can't do anything because of health challenges that are beyond our control and should never feel guilty, or think we are cursed by God because of it (John 9:3). In fact all of the admonitions below are centered on health challenges we have some control over.

1. **We are created in God's image.** The first book of the Bible makes it clear—we are created in the image of God (Genesis 1:27). That image was marred in the fall of Adam and Eve, but not destroyed. That truth alone should supply more than enough impetus to take care of ourselves. Our mortal bodies are given to us to reveal the life of Jesus (2 Corinthians 4:11).
2. **Physically—there is no do-over.** This point might sound silly, but sometimes we live as if we have bodies to spare, or that we will be exempt from the ravages of nature. No matter how much medicine advances, when this body wears out, we don't have a replacement until the day of resurrection (Hebrews 9:27).
3. **Poor discipline is a bad witness.** It's hard to tell people to be disciplined in their Bible study, prayer life, giving, etc., when they can look at us and see we are undisciplined in exercise and nutrition. A lack of effort in one area of life is often indicative of problems in other areas. The scriptures call us to a life of self-control and discipline (Titus 1:8).
4. **Poor health is a big expense.** Eventually, the costs of neglect of health add up. Medical bills pile up. Health, Life and Disability insurance costs increase. Moreover, bad health makes us less productive at work. Others are forced then to carry some of our load. We lose self-respect and esteem when we let ourselves go physically (Proverbs 15:32).
5. **Our families deserve better.** Frankly, it's unloving not to take care of ourselves (Ephesians 5:29). Our families worry about us when we struggle to climb steps, find clothes to fit, or tire-out from doing simple household chores. Our love for them ought to motivate us to stay as healthy as possible. If we work to not indulge the flesh, there will be more opportunities to serve our families and the kingdom of God (Galatians 5:13).
6. **Being out of shape might indicate idolatry.** Those words might be difficult to hear, but they're necessary ones. If we cannot push away from food, or find time to exercise in order to take care of our bodies, we must ask if something other than God has become our god (1 Timothy 4:8).
7. **Better health means more energy to do God's work.** God's work is not easy. Those who strive to advance the cause of Christ know that the burdens are sometimes heavy. When you include the time for our regular occupations, family and household obligations, and the time to

reach out to people with the good news—the hours are often long. Being out of shape makes the work only that much more difficult. The apostle John prayed for the disciples that he wrote too, that they would enjoy good health and their souls would prosper—in other words, good health gives us more opportunities to grow spiritually (3 John 2).

8. **Proper care requires rest—and it's godly to rest.** Our creator expects us to take time off, focus on him, and enjoy his blessings. One of the ten commandments was to take a whole day off (Sabbath)—to rest body and mind (Exodus 20:9-11). In fact, not taking time to rest can be self-centered—that is, we think we must be doing everything, or it all depends on us (Psalms 127:2).

9. **We might be called to a mission field far from home.** Many mission team leaders or organizations will not consider taking someone who is out of shape or in bad health. Mission work and serving in needy communities around the world is often hazardous, rigorous, and the stresses of cross-cultural living are only compounded by poor health and lack of discipline (Proverbs 5:23). Western culture, and comfort in general has made us soft. We forget most third-world countries do not have air condition, abundant food, clean water supplies, and top medical care. Thus, being fit, with robust health is a big help for those who want to serve in the poorest regions of the world.

10. **Our body is the temple of the Holy Spirit.** This is a truth that is hard to fathom, but God really does live within us (1 Corinthians 6:19). The God who created us and indwells us expects us to be wise stewards of the body he gave us. God calls us to a high standard and obligation when it comes to taking care of our bodies and we will be held accountable for the way we managed our health.

In the book of 1 Samuel, the prophet Samuel is sent by God to anoint the next king of Israel. When David (who was out tending the sheep) is brought before Samuel, it says of David, *"He was glowing with health and had a fine appearance and handsome features. Then the Lord said, 'Rise and anoint him; this is the one'"* (1 Samuel 16:12). David would certainly need to be healthy as he spent the next several years running for his life from King Saul. Unlike David, we may not all be blessed with handsome features, but with discipline and self-control, we can all work to maintain as good as health as we can, to enable us to do the most good, for the most people, for as long as possible, to advance the cause of Christ in our generation.

—Toney Mulhollan
Spring, Texas

If you want to read more about biblical attitudes of discipline and training read *The Heart of a Champion*. Available at www.ipibooks.com.

40 Ways to Help Those in Need

1. Donate food to your church food pantry, or if they don't have one, donate to your local food pantry.
2. Choose a day to serve at a local food pantry. Check their website; most contain requirements for service.
3. Respect people who are poor or homeless. Give them the same courtesy and goodwill that you would accord your friends, your family, or your employer. Treat them as you would wish to be treated if you needed assistance.
4. Respond with kindness to all those in need. We can make quite a difference in the lives of people when we love them rather than ignore or dismiss them. Try a kind word and a smile. Don't assume they are in this predicament because of bad choices.
5. Get freezer-size zipper-lock plastic bags and create "care packages" with bottled water or an electrolyte drink, a nutritious snack, and a church invite. Keep four or five in your car and distribute them as the opportunity arises.
6. Purchase $5 gift certificates from fast food restaurants to give away as needed.
7. Volunteer at a nursing or senior adult center. Mother's or Father's Day are great days to visit. Ask the director of the facility which patients most need encouragement or get few visits from relatives.
8. Contact your Texas Department of Social Services and get certified to be a foster parent. The majority of states are greatly in need of foster parents.
9. Adopt a child. In Texas, children can be adopted at no cost through the Department of Social Services. Adopting children in need helps break the cycle of poverty.
10. Donate money to help families who are in the process of adopting.
11. Downgrade your cell phone or cable plan and donate the money to HOPE *worldwide* or some favorite charity.
12. Drop off toys or handheld video games at your local children's hospital most hospitals' websites will list needed items.
13. Carefully go through your closet and donate all clothes and shoes that you no longer use. Perhaps even downsize your wardrobe and donate the excess to Goodwill or the Salvation Army.
14. Downsize your electronics collection (televisions, iPads, Kindles, etc.) and give to church friends in need or to the poor in your community.
15. If you have spare bedrooms, open your home to host people at no cost who have medical treatment or have other needs.
16. Sponsor a child through Compassion International or Food for the Hungry.
17. Sign up to coach a youth sport in a poor community in your city. Use the opportunity to tell kids they're smart, needed, and important.
18. Donate time and money for Meals on Wheels or other organizations that serve the elderly who are homebound or disabled.
19. Sign up to drive cancer patients or others in need of medical service to their appointments.
20. Start a group in your church that is dedicated to home repairs to help single moms and other needy individuals.
21. Find a widow or widower in your neighborhood and invite them to your home for a meal.
22. Research and compile a list of soup kitchens, homeless shelters, and free medical clinics to print out and give out to the homeless and needy.
23. Find out the items most needed by your local homeless shelter (e.g., towels, blankets, socks) and donate them.
24. Mentor disciples who are unemployed or

underemployed on how to improve their job skills or how to work harder to improve their value to employers.

25. For those who are perpetually unemployed, help them to develop skills that are required by the marketplace. Spend some weekly time helping them research jobs that may be suitable to their skills.
26. Build a relationship with someone who is indigent. Offer to be their friend and personal coach, monitoring their weekly progress until they become independent and productive.
27. Set up a donation drop box and invite the community to donate items that will help the needy.
28. Buy an MP3 player (you can find many inexpensive models now) and fill it with uplifting songs, some sermons, and an audible version of the New Testament. Give it to a homeless or needy person.
29. Instead of having a garage sale, take all those items and donate them to an organization that helps the poor.
30. Volunteer your professional services. You can help people who are homeless with your job talent and skills. Doctors, psychiatrists, counselors, and dentists can treat the homeless in free medical clinics. Lawyers can help with legal concerns.
31. Volunteer for follow-up programs. Some people who are indigent need help and training with fundamental tasks such as paying bills, balancing a household budget, or cleaning.
32. Tutor homeless children. A tutor can make all the difference. Just having extra attention can motivate a child to do their best. Many programs exist in shelters, transitional housing programs, and schools that need interested volunteers.
33. Help tutor the poor, or recent immigrants, especially teaching them English. Education is one of the greatest tools in moving someone toward self-sufficiency.
34. Volunteer at shelters that serve battered women. Most women who are battered are involved in abusive relationships. Lacking resources and afraid of being found by their abusers, many have no recourse other than a shelter or life on the streets.
35. Educate your children and get them involved. Volunteer as a family at a shelter or housing program. Suggest that your children sort through their toys, books, and clothes and donate some to organizations that help the poor and needy.
36. Donate a weekend to serve with Habitat for Humanity. This housing ministry builds homes for families who are in great need or who are in danger of becoming homeless.
37. Donate blood in your community. Donate plasma and give the funds to indigent medical care.
38. Fast at least one day a week on behalf of the poor and donate the money saved to a worthy cause.
39. Plan a trip to serve the needy in a third-world country (check HOPE *worldwide* for future opportunities).
40. Sign up to be an organ donor. It's a great way to serve those who are in medical crisis, and you won't need that body anyway!

For an indepth analysis of how Jesus helped the poor read the book by G. Steve Kinnard, *Jesus and the Poor*. www.ipibooks.com.

Revive Us Again—Exposition of Nehemiah 8-9

When we've been disciples for an extended period of time, it can be a great temptation to become complacent in our faith and in our walk with God. This is always a temptation. After the Israelites went into the promised land, God gave them a powerful warning:

"When you have eaten and are satisfied, praise the LORD your God for the good land he has given you. Be careful that you do not forget the LORD your God, failing to observe his commands, his laws and his decrees that I am giving you this day. Otherwise, when you eat and are satisfied, when you build fine houses and settle down, and when your herds and flocks grow large and your silver and gold increase and all you have is multiplied, then your heart will become proud and you will forget the LORD your God, who brought you out of Egypt, out of the land of slavery (Deuteronomy 8: 10-14).

We must be continually reminded to return to our original love, commitment and exuberance for God. The children of Israel had several feasts and a day of atonement to annually remind them of where God had brought them from. Nehemiah is a powerful book that gives us examples, direction and practical insight into reviving our hearts. After the wall of the city had been rebuilt, the Israelites "settled in their towns" (Nehemiah 8:1). We too, can settle. So let us study Nehemiah 8-9 and see how God moved in the hearts of his people to restore their commitment (Read Nehemiah 8:1-9:4).

1. Everyone was Eager and Attentive

A. They were united. "All the people assembled as one man" (Nehemiah 8:1). An important part of being assembled as "one man" is to be on time. Its difficult to be united if we are coming into services or classes as late as 15, 20 or even 30 minutes. In fact it demonstrates as lack of concern for others and can certainly distract people who are trying to listen, learn and participate.

B. The Law (the Word of God) was brought before the people and before all who could understand (Nehemiah 8:2). An important part of all our services, whether it be Sunday, midweeks or special events, is to open God's Word and let it speak to us.

C. The people "listened" from daybreak until noon (Nehemiah 8:3). It is clear that the believers didn't struggle with the length of services and neither should we. Hearing God's word must be a priority.

D. The people had a reverance for the Word. When he opened it, " the people all stood up" (Nehemiah 8:5).

E. The people "listened attentively" (Nehemiah 8:3, 13). What is our attitude when we hear the Word read? Are we listening, searching out and confirming what we hear taught?

F. They were reminded about what happend to those who refused to listen or pay attention to the Word of God (Nehemiah 9:17, 26, 34). As disciples we must obey the Word and help others to obey also.

Doesn't this show the importance of time with God's people, Bible Study times, fellowship, Sunday services, Bible Talks, devotionals, and Family Group meetings. We can allow "thorns" of any kind to take us away from Bible study or the meetings of the church.

2. They were Earnest and Expressive

A. There was a physical and yes dynamic participation and posture in their worship.

1. They stood up (Nehemiah 8:5). Are we laidbacked or are we participating with heart and soul?

2. The people lifted their hands (Nehemiah 8:6). This was also a practice in the early church as Paul said that he wanted men everywhere lifting up holy hands in prayer to God (1 Timothy 2:8).

B. There was vocal participation.

1. The people responded, "Amen! Amen!" (Nehemiah 8:6). Amen is making a solemn and binding agreement! Again, in the New Testament Paul assumed people who be enjoining the service and expressing their agreement with "Amens" (1 Corinthians 14:16).

2. They humbled themselves as "they bowed down and worshiped the Lord with their faces to the ground" (Nehemiah 8:6). There was a sincere humility that flowed from their devotion to God.

C. There was an emotional participation.

1. For all the people "had been weeping" as the listened to the word of God read.

2. They had joy and expressed it (Nehemiah 8:10, 17).

3. The Word was Clearly Explained

A. God's Word was read and the leaders "made it clear...giving the meaning so that the people could understand" (Nehemiah 8:8).

1. Does God's Word play a major role in your family? Is is read, discussed and put into practice? Is is quoted in your home? Is it memorized and shared?

2. When they discovered the truth in God's Word they put it into practice (Nehemiah 8:14-15).

B. When the Word was truly explained and understood there was radical repentance.

1. They fasted, prayed and even wore sackcloth expressing their humility (Nehemiah 9:1).

2. They separated themselves from worldliness that had affected their lives (Nehemiah 9:2).

3. They publicly confessed their sins and their wickedness (Nehemiah 9:2).

4. They recommited their lives to the Word, confession and worshiping God (Nehemiah 9:3).

4. There was Exultation and Worship

A. They had a celebration and feast (Nehemiah 8:9-12, 8:16-17).

1. The leaders called everyone to celebrete, express their joy.

a. Joy and Unity go together. Joy and the Word go together. Joy and Worship go together!

Nehemiah 8 and 9 is a powerful and practical example of how to repent and revive our commitment to God. Lets stay in the Word of God and let it move us ever closer to the kind of people that God will use to impact and change our city, region and world.

—Toney Mulhollan
Spring, Texas

If you want to read a comprehensive work on repentance, read Edward Anton's *Repentance—A Cosmic Shift of Mind & Heart*. Available at www.ipibooks.com.

Spiritual Thinking vs. Negative Thinking

"But the men who had gone up with him, said, "We can't attack these people; they are stronger than we are." And they spread among the Israelites a bad report about the land they had explored. They said, "The land we explored devours those living in it. All the people we saw are of great size. We saw the Nephilim there (the descendants of Anak come from the Nephilim). We seemed like grasshoppers in our own eyes, and we looked the same to them." —Numbers 13:31-33

If there is power in positive thinking (especially *spiritual* positive thinking!), there is also power in the opposite. Of course, this power is satanic in nature, and using it will accomplish his ends rather than God's. But without question, we are trained by our families and by our cultures to be negative in our evaluations of ourselves, others and circumstances. The most cursory glance at any newspaper will provide plenty of proof for this. Years ago, I vividly remember hearing a radio report of a study that was conducted to evaluate the results of those who characteristically thought negatively and those who thought positively. The findings of the study indicated that the negative thinkers were much more accurate in their assessments of situations, but the positive thinkers were able to produce positive results in negative situations. Even those without true spiritual perspectives have figured out that negative thinking produces negative results.

One of the most graphic Biblical accounts showing the power of negative thinking is Numbers 13, the record of the twelve spies sent to spy out Canaan. In reading this account, several obvious lessons show us paths to avoid at all costs. One lesson is that the negative often excites stronger emotions than does the positive. In spite of the faith-filled pleas of Joshua and Caleb, the two spies with a good report, the nation was easily and strongly swayed by the negative report. They quickly forgot God's amazing miracles and victories and were absolutely filled with "grasshopper thinking."

As humans, we are so prone to assume the worst and believe the worst. We focus on what is wrong or on what we are afraid is wrong. Negative thinking is a pervasive tendency. It must be seen as what it is—an unloving, unfaithful response to God's promises. In terms of Paul's definition of love in 1 Corinthians 13, spiritual thinking which is loving means that we do not delight in evil but rejoice with the truth—always protecting, always trusting, always hoping, always persevering (vv 6-7).

A second lesson gleaned from Numbers 13 is that a majority of people inevitably practice negative thinking. In this case, the ratio was ten to two among the spies and presumably a million to one in the multitude. We would much rather curse the darkness than light a candle. Those who do not jump to negative conclusions and think the worst are thought to be strange. No wonder so many people reacted negatively to Jesus. He was completely realistic about man's sinful condition, but he was full of faith and confident that men could be changed by God's power. The leaders of his time thought that he was demon-possessed. The narrow road of Matthew 7:13-14 is the path of a small minority. Only eight people in Noah's day were able to rise above the crowd and trust in the promises of God (1 Peter 3:20). In Elijah's day, thankfully there were 7,000 who had refused to bow the knee to Baal (1 Kings 19:18), but that was a small minority in Israel. In the aftermath of the crucifixion, how many were confident that resurrection would follow? Next to nil. If we are to follow Jesus, we had better get comfortable with always being in the minority and with being thought of as weird by the majority. I've got to love the church—it's the only place where I am really accepted as somewhat normal.

A third lesson from Numbers 13 is that negativism is deceptive to observers. It seems so, well, normal. Since Satan is the great deceiver, this should not come as any surprise. What does come as a surprise is how completely we can all be deceived by sin at times.

We can feel that we are doing right with a perfectly clear conscience, only to discover later that we were clearly wrong in the matter. The problem is that the negative view was quite a lot of reality to commend it, and it's often mixed with some positives.

For example, in Numbers 13:27-28, we read this report of the spies: *"They gave Moses this account: 'We went into the land to which you sent us, and it does flow with milk and honey! Here is its fruit. But the people who live there are powerful, and the cities are fortified and very large. We even saw descendants of Anak there'"* (Numbers 13:27-28). Although the negative was prefaced with the positive, the negative carried the day. In our conversation, the content following the conjunction "but" shows convincingly whether we are focused on the positives or not. If we end with the negative, it will lodge in our hearts and the hearts of others. Being realistic with the facts is good. but with faith is better—it's essential. Note the difference in the two reports given to the Israelites: *"Then Caleb silenced the people before Moses and said, 'We should go up and take possession of the land, for we can certainly do it.' But the men who had gone up with him said, 'We can't attack those people; they are stronger than we are'" (Numbers 13:30-31).*

How are you at being focused on the positives about situations and other people? Do you justify negativity by claiming that you must deal honestly with reality? In Romans 4:19, we find that Abraham faced the facts of his situation, but then he "faithed" them. The facts are the facts are the facts, but God is greater than any reality that blocks what he wants done in our lives. It is not, "God is powerful and good, but look at these worrisome facts." It must rather be, "the worrisome facts are present, but God is bigger and stronger than any combination of them."

Faith looks beyond humanistic realities to divine possibilities. The physical components and characteristics of water are such that man cannot walk on it, but try convincing Peter of that one! God is God, and we cannot be deceived into allowing our faith to be destroyed in any situation, however challenging it may seem from a human viewpoint!

A fourth lesson from Kadesh Barnea (where the spies were sent out from) should be quite obvious: Leaders have the most responsibility for determining the thinking of the group they lead. However, the followers who are influenced by them are absolutely responsible for their choices. The nation was punished for their lack of faith, not just the leaders. What a tragedy! Just think of what might have been. After leaving Egypt, the Israelites could have gone quickly into the Land of Promise. Forty years of attending funerals could have been averted (all of those twenty years old or older would die before the nation could enter Canaan). Negative thinking shows up first in leadership. Only if leaders are positive do you find out who the negative thinkers are back in the pack (and some are always there).

Leaders have the God-given responsibility to lead, but followers have the responsibility to follow. Hebrews 13:17 says: *"Obey your leaders and submit to their authority. They keep watch over you as men who must give an account. Obey them so that their work will be a joy, not a burden, for that would be of no advantage to you"* (Hebrews 13:17). The Greek term translated "to submit to their authority" means literally to "be persuaded." True, leaders must be willing to reason and persuade, but the passage is addressed to followers. They must have a mind to be persuaded, to be open to changing their mnds.

This event is a chilling reminder of thinking negatively and unfaithfully. We must see the power of negativity and avoid it like the plague it is. When you begin to lack faith about anything, rest assured that Satan is near. True, we need to recognize when something is wrong, but then we must look for godly solutions. Entertaining negative thoughts with no plan to change the situation is dangerous to our spiritual health and to all the things that God wants us to accomplish in his Kingdom.

—Gordon Ferguson
McKinney, Texas

The Curse of Consumerism

In case you were wondering, the spirit of the West—the wild, wild West—has nothing to do with cowboys, sagebrush, tumbleweed and rodeos. We're using the word in its sociopolitical sense to refer to affluent Northern and Western Europe and North America. The spirit of the West is the spirit of materialism and of the society that lives to consume, and consumes to live: a vicious cycle of emptiness (1 Peter 1:18) that leaves us with a deep sense of meaninglessness (as in Ecclesiastes). Every nation of the world breathes this spirit, whether its citizens fall into the category of "have's" or "have-not's."

Neither Poverty nor Riches

The challenge of the Spirit is not to win the lottery and give it all away. It is to love those less fortunate than us, to live more simply and to keep ourselves from being "polluted by the world," as James put it. The spirit of materialism (a.k.a. Mammon) is everywhere, and it can be difficult even for disciples of Jesus Christ to navigate between the treacherous rocks of indulgence and indigence. The Scriptures urge modesty in our use and possession of material goods in Proverbs 30:7-9.

Materialistic Christians?

We as Christians claim to value the spiritual over the material, but do our lifestyles back up our claim? If we do not have a passion to help the poor (Galatians 2:10), it is unlikely we have escaped the virus of materialism unscathed. The Bible is full of warnings against materialism (1 John 2:15-17, Revelation 3:14-20, Ecclesiastes 4:4). Sometimes it takes a visit to the Third World to appreciate the plight of the poor.

Don't just assume that, because you have repented, been baptized and attend church you are free of materialism. The spending habits of many Christians vary little from those of their unbelieving friends. When I read Richard Horsley's *The Liberation of Christmas*, I was astounded by its opening exposé of the rampant materialism of our country, where twenty-eight percent of the world's resources are consumed in the month between Thanksgiving and Christmas! Isn't there inequality here—some gross distortion?

The Incubator

The virus of materialism is inculcated through parental upbringing and our educational institutions. The lack of spirituality in modern culture has seriously weakened our immune system: We succumb easily to the spirit of materialism.

If the virus enters through the values we have inherited, surely it is fed through the message we read, hear and see enfleshed in those around us every day. The message: Money is the bottom line. Your "net worth" is defined solely as your monetary worth. If you are not affluent, you are worth little. If you are rich, you are valuable. If you are living in poverty, you do not exist. This is clearly at odds with everything God tells us in his word. Instead of loving people and using things, we have been discipled to love things and use people. How does this pernicious virus incubate in our hearts? *Television* is the incubator, and it breeds *materialism* quite effectively, and in particular consumerism—where we buy far more than we truly need, and find value in material things rather than in the things of the Spirit. TV has also effectively inoculated us against caring for the poor. A few shots of poverty now and again keep its grinding reality mentally at bay. Images of the needy and of war numb our consciences. But how does Jesus Christ feel about it?

Television and Consumerism

Yes, TV is the primary medium through which consumerism, violence, immorality and secularization are brought into our lives. Nearly every American household owns at least one television set. (When I was little, our home had one black and white model; by the time I left for college, the number had swelled to five.) What are the results of our television and internet driven consumerism? Consider the social erosion facilitated by the greed of big business and its slick advertisers:

- *Financial shipwreck.* Impulse spending, unprincipled and unbudgeted personal finances, credit card "slavery" and staggering personal (and national) debt plague most of us. Such recklessness is powerfully promoted by the corporations and their cronies. Money is one of the most common subjects of marital disputes. To make things worse, we deprive our children of the opportunity to learn from our mistakes by keeping the subject of money "hushed."
- *Disintegration of relationships.* The basic social unit is being reduced to the individual alone, as we are tempted to sit at home in front of the TV set. Alienation results when social erosion affects the familial level.
- *Disintegration of health.* Television has wrought great harm in its contribution towards nicotine addiction, alcoholism, etc. Laziness is condoned in principle as the lives of the "rich and shameless" are paraded on screen. We as a nation are grossly out of shape.
- *Ruin of family values.* TV eats up precious family time. A 1996 USA Today poll found the average male watches twenty-eight hours of TV a week; some children, to their detriment, watch even more. In TV-land marital infidelity is depicted as "natural," family dysfunction as normal. "Family," thanks to some of the media, is gaining negative overtones.
- *Pathetic role models.* When convicted felons are kids' role models, we are in trouble!
- *Erosion of morality.* Violence, promiscuity and materialism are glorified in the media and are prime agents in our moral decline. This clearly translates into injustice, crime and hedonism.
- *Secularization.* These days, money is the bottom line. When worth is defined as financial worth, humanity is emptied of that which is truly valuable. Jesus noted that the Pharisees loved money, yet he assures us that what is highly valued by men is detestable in the sight of God (Luke 16:15).

Yes, TV is, for better or worse, the most influential "educational institution" of the world today. How much are you watching? Perhaps more important, how much do you allow your children to view "the tube"? Stating there is a direct connection between television viewing and materialism is like saying there is a correlation between warfare and bloodshed. As the younger generation is fond of saying, "Duh"! Consumerism is a form of slavery at best and the suicide of the family at worst. Truly it is the curse of Western culture.

The Spirit Says...

If we claim to be led by the Spirit, surely we cannot afford to ignore the words of the Spirit, which delights in helping the needy and in living simply. Let me suggest here that you take your Bible and read carefully Isaiah 58:1-10, and meditate on the kind of religion God accepts.

The Spirit says here (and throughout the inspired word of God) that our inwardly directed spirituality as the people of God (fellowship, worship, meditation) must be balanced by an outward focus (letting our light shine, evangelism, care for the needy). But should we be surprised? Consider Jesus: *"Though he was rich, yet for your sakes he became poor, so that you through his poverty might become rich"* (2 Corinthians 8:9). Since Christ identifies with the poor, and not just with the rich, does he not expect us to follow in his footsteps? Remember the powerful words of Jesus as he addresses the plight of the poor, hungry and needy and our call to serve them: *"I tell you the truth, whatever you did for one of the least of these brothers of mine, you did for me"* (Matthew 25:40).

—Douglas Jacoby
Marietta, Georgia

Keep Building Your Faith

"However, when the Son of Man comes, will he find faith on the earth?" —Luke 18:8

Genuine faith is so radical, and at times so rare that Jesus wondered aloud if it would even exist when he returned. Jesus addressed faith more than any other topic. When he came across amazing faith, he always pointed it out. Faith is the essential ingredient in our Christian walk.

The Bible records, *"The Spirit clearly says that in later times some will abandon the faith and follow deceiving spirits..."* (1 Timothy 4:1). It also says that *"Some people, eager for money, have wandered from the faith and pierced themselves with many griefs."* (1 Timothy 6:10). Others have become involved in godless chatter and have adopted unbiblical teaching which causes them to wander from the faith (1 Timothy 6:20-21).

Lack of devotion to the fellowship and to God's Word is a reflection of weak faith. Many are choosing to ignore the dire consequences of a loss of faith. If we do, Jesus' sobering words will be fulfilled.The world would like nothing better than to destroy our faith. We must realize Satan's schemes and fight for our faith. Here are some principles and actions that will help us renew our faith.

1. Begin with Self-Evaluation. Listen to the words of Paul as he addresses disciples in Corinth who had struggles with their faith. Paul says, *"Examine yourselves to see whether you are in the faith; test yourselves. Do you realize that Christ is in you–unless of course you fail the test"* (2 Corinthians 13:5-6). No one knows better the condition of our faith than ourselves. For many, in their heart of hearts, when they are alone with God, have felt the loss of faith, loss of vision for the future, and a loss of belief that God will use them to advance his kingdom in the world.

Some have questioned the wisdom of examining our faith. Paul did not. He wrote to the disciples in Thessalonica (a congregation that he himself had planted) and said, *"For this reason, when I could stand it no longer, I sent to find out about your faith. I was afraid that in some way the tempter might have tempted you and our efforts might have been useless"* (1 Thessalonians 3:15). Indeed the faith of the Thessalonian church was being challenged, and Paul said, *"Night and day we pray most earnestly that we may see you again and supply what is lacking in your faith"* (1 Thessalonians 3:10). The values of our world will be a continual assault on our faith and we must be vigilant in assessing and building on our faith.

2. Build your Faith on God's Word. Faith built on anything other than the Word of God will crumble. Some have built erringly on men, or a dream, and have seen it fail before their very eyes. Paul reminded the Roman Christians, *"Consequently, faith comes through hearing the message, and the message is heard through the word of Christ"* (Romans 10:17). Jesus said in the Parable of the Sower, concerning the Word of God, *"But the seed* (his Word) *stands for those with a noble and good heart, who hear the word, retain it, and by persevering produce a crop"* (Luke 8:15). Most importantly, it will be God's words that will judge us on the last day (John 12:48).

3. Access Grace though Faith. Forgiveness and freedom are found through faith. No amount of good works can ever earn forgiveness. Good works will never out-weigh the burden of guilt. Paul reminded the Ephesians, *"For it is by grace you have been saved,* ***through faith****—and this not from yourselves, it is the gift of God—not by works, so that no one can boast. For we are God's workmanship, created in Christ Jesus to do good works..."* (Ephesians 2:8-9). Faith opens the door to grace. It begins at baptism, but is present throughout our Christian lives *"if we walk in the light as he is in the light"* (1 John 1:7).

4. Make every Effort to add to your Faith. Faith does not grow in a vacuum. It radiates, grows, impacts, and changes our lives and our world when it is built on. Peter tells us that to escape the corruption of the world and its evil desires we must *"Make every effort to* *add to your faith, goodness; and to goodness, knowledge; and to knowledge, self-control; and to self-control, perseverance; and to perseverance, godliness.... For if you possess these qualities in increasing measure, they will keep you from being ineffective and unproductive...*" (2 Peter 1:5-8). There is nothing more amazing than making every effort and it is the only way to be productive. Making every effort stands in stark contrast to actions that are half-hearted, reluctant and indifferent.

5. Let Deeds flow from your Faith. How could James make it any clearer? He asks, *"What good is it, my brothers, if a man claims to have faith, but has no deeds? Can such faith save him?"* James then says bluntly, *"Faith by itself, if it is not accompanied by action, is dead."* (James 2:14-17), He again reinforces the point by saying, *"Show me your faith without deeds, and I will show you my faith by what I do!"* (James 2:18).

James' admonition here is a reflection of what Jesus promised that faith in him would produce. He told his followers, *"I tell you the truth, anyone who has faith in me will do what I have been doing. He will do even greater things than these, because I am going to the Father"* (John 14:12). Is our faith reflecting this promise of Jesus?

The call of the hour is to make decisions to increase our faith. Faith is an individual decision. The choice for faith has eternal consequences and God wants each of us to have that faith. The fruit of our faith will be seen in our lives and in the life of our church.

"So the churches were strengthened in the faith and grew daily in numbers" —(Acts 16:5).

—Toney Mulhollan
Spring, Texas

For practical steps on continuing to build a deep relationship with God read *Be Still My Soul,* by Sam Laing. Available at www.ipibooks.com.

Part Four

Planning and Evaluation

Your Ten Deepest Convictions

(Those things you believe most deeply.
Those convictions that most impact your life)

1. ______________________________
____

2. ______________________________
____

3. ______________________________
____

4. ______________________________
____

5. ______________________________
____

6. ______________________________
____

7. ______________________________
____

8. ______________________________
____

9. ______________________________
____

10. ______________________________
____

Personal Mission Statement

Fifty Things You Want to Do Before You Die
(from the mundane to the sublime)

1. ____
2. ____
3. ____
4. ____
5. ____
6. ____
7. ____
8. ____
9. ____
10. ____
11. ____
12. ____
13. ____
14. ____
15. ____
16. ____
17. ____
18. ____
19. ____
20. ____
21. ____
22. ____
23. ____
24. ____

25. ______________________________
26. ______________________________
27. ______________________________
28. ______________________________
29. ______________________________
30. ______________________________
31. ______________________________
32. ______________________________
33. ______________________________
34. ______________________________
35. ______________________________
36. ______________________________
37. ______________________________
38. ______________________________
39. ______________________________
40. ______________________________
41. ______________________________
42. ______________________________
43. ______________________________
44. ______________________________
45. ______________________________
46. ______________________________
47. ______________________________
48. ______________________________
49. ______________________________
50. ______________________________

Chapters in Your Autobiography

(If you were to write an autobiography
what would be ten chapter titles?)

1. ____________________
2. ____________________
3. ____________________
4. ____________________
5. ____________________
6. ____________________
7. ____________________
8. ____________________
9. ____________________
10. ____________________

Ten Sins God Has Forgiven in Your Life

(Sure, the list could be much longer!)

1. ____________________
2. ____________________
3. ____________________
4. ____________________
5. ____________________
6. ____________________
7. ____________________
8. ____________________
9. ____________________
10. ____________________

Ten Things You Most Appreciate About God

1. ______________________________
2. ______________________________
3. ______________________________
4. ______________________________
5. ______________________________
6. ______________________________
7. ______________________________
8. ______________________________
9. ______________________________
10. ______________________________

Ten Things You Most Appreciate About Your Spouse

1. ______________________________
2. ______________________________
3. ______________________________
4. ______________________________
5. ______________________________
6. ______________________________
7. ______________________________
8. ______________________________
9. ______________________________
10. ______________________________

Ten Reasons You Have to Be Joyful and Thankful in *All* Circumstances

1. ____________________
2. ____________________
3. ____________________
4. ____________________
5. ____________________
6. ____________________
7. ____________________
8. ____________________
9. ____________________
10. ____________________

Ten People Who Are Great Examples in Your Life

1. Of faith ____________________
2. Of love ____________________
3. Of perseverance ____________________
4. Of joy ____________________
5. Of boldness ____________________
6. Of integrity ____________________
7. Of kindness ____________________
8. Of patience ____________________
9. Of openness ____________________
10. Of humility ____________________

Ten People You Want to Bring to Christ

1. ______________________________
2. ______________________________
3. ______________________________
4. ______________________________
5. ______________________________
6. ______________________________
7. ______________________________
8. ______________________________
9. ______________________________
10. ______________________________

Ten People Who Have Left God but Can Be Brought Back

1. ______________________________
2. ______________________________
3. ______________________________
4. ______________________________
5. ______________________________
6. ______________________________
7. ______________________________
8. ______________________________
9. ______________________________
10. ______________________________

Ten Old Friends You Need to Call

1. ______
2. ______
3. ______
4. ______
5. ______
6. ______
7. ______
8. ______
9. ______
10. ______

Ten Books You Want to Read

1. ______
2. ______
3. ______
4. ______
5. ______
6. ______
7. ______
8. ______
9. ______
10. ______

Ten Things You Want Said About You When You Die

1. ______________________________
2. ______________________________
3. ______________________________
4. ______________________________
5. ______________________________
6. ______________________________
7. ______________________________
8. ______________________________
9. ______________________________
10. ______________________________

To read more about Heaven and Hell read Douglas Jacoby's book above. Available at www.ipibooks.com.

To learn more about the afterlife read *What Happens After We Die?* Available at www.ipibooks.com.

SPEAKING OF GOD DR. JOHN M. OAKES
Spiritual Transformation Cresenda Jones
MESSIANIC JUDAISM DOUGLAS JACOBY
Go in the Strength You Have Rayola Osanya
A HOUSE OF PRAYER C. SCOTT DAVIS
LOVE, LAUGHTER, AND LAW
Jesus and Mental Health Marvin K. Lucas
WHAT NOW, GOD? JEANIE SHAW
SINGLES MINISTRY CAN CHANGE THE WORLD FERNANDO ALEJANDRO
Mindpowered Singles CRESENDA JONES
Journey of the SOUL
THE UPWARD CALL PAT GEMPEL, EDITOR
CALLING OUT THE PEOPLE OF GOD DOUGLAS JACOBY
R.K. McKEAN
The Sacred Journey
WILDFIRE DAREN OVERSTREET
The Recovery Journey TIMOTHY SUMERLIN, PH.D.
This Doesn't Feel Like Love Either LAMBS

Made in the USA
Coppell, TX
09 June 2026

80048164R00107